Changing Your Mind

Changing

Your Mind

The Law of
Regretted
Decisions

E. Allan Farnsworth

YALE UNIVERSITY PRESS   NEW HAVEN & LONDON

Designed by James J. Johnson and set in Melior Roman and Syntax types by Tseng Information Systems. Printed in the United States of America.

Library of Congress Cataloging-in-Publication Data

Farnsworth, E. Allan (Edward Allan), 1928–
    Changing your mind : the law of regretted decisions / E. Allan Farnsworth.
    p.   cm.
    Includes bibliographical references and index.
    ISBN 0-300-07305-4 (cloth : alk. paper)

    1. Contracts.   2. Promise (Law)
3. Regret.   I. Title.
K840.F37   1998
346.02—dc21   97-52196

A catalogue record for this book is available from the British Library.

The paper in this book meets the guidelines for permanence and durability of the Committee on Production Guidelines for Book Longevity of the Council on Library Resources.

10 9 8 7 6 5 4 3 2 1

To the friends and colleagues who have made this a better book

Contents

Part II. Relinquishments and Preclusions

Preface

In this book I survey some of the general principles underlying the legal rules that apply when you change your mind and reverse a decision. To the lawyer's mind, these rules are scattered throughout separate fields: contracts, torts, property, trusts, wills, agency, and even family law and procedure. Because lawyers are not wont to perceive analogies among these fields, the mere fact that one rule is a rule of contract law and another is a rule of property law often suffices to distinguish the two. In writing this book I have tried to suppress the tendency to fall back on such distinctions and sought to identify principles that are not confined to a single field of law and to follow them from one field to another. Mainly I have found harmony rather than discord. But anomalies remain, reflecting the law's compartmentalization, and from these I draw conclusions that will, I hope, further the rationalization of legal concepts and the identification and eventual correction of their deficiencies.

While working on this book I was asked whether I was "writing *another* book about contracts." (It had not occurred to me that "another" might serve as a pejorative.) This is surely *not* another book *just* about contracts, because it

ranges over many other fields of law. But to some extent it
is another book about contracts, since some of the principles
discussed are rooted in contract law. I regard contract law as
an important source of such principles for situations that do
not involve what we commonly think of as contracts in the
strict sense—situations at the margins of contract law. But
rather than view these as merely principles of contract law
that might be applied in other fields, I see them as more universal. Contract law is of interest not for its own sake but as
a fountainhead of such principles.

My emphasis on contract law is redolent of the late
nineteenth and early twentieth centuries, when scholars of
contract law aspired, as Samuel Williston put it in the pref-
ace to his 1920 treatise, *The Law of Contracts,* "to treat the
subject of contracts as a whole, and to show the wide range
of application of its principles." Over the ensuing decades,
however, some academics came to find Williston's imperial-
istic view of contract law unfashionable: the field was being
diminished either through erosion by such specialized fields
as consumer protection or through gradual absorption by the
field of torts.

Nonetheless, the continued vigor of the institution of
contract and of the law that has grown up around it continues to infect scholars in other fields. While specialists
quarrel over how far corporations should be free to contract out of the rules of corporate law, philosophers struggle
to define social justice in terms of the contracts that would
be made in hypothetical circumstances. And all the while,
courts oblivious to academic denigrations defer to general
principles of contract law in situations ranging from military
enlistments to interstate compacts, all far removed from the
commercial setting in which those principles were typically
spawned. I believe that the study of these principles and
their relevance will enhance the ability of courts to reach
just solutions in many situations not entailing contract law.

Because this book is not *just* about contracts but ranges over a variety of fields of law, I am indebted to my many colleagues expert in those fields, both in this country and abroad, who have shared their insights and corrected my misconceptions. And because I have aspired to explore these principles in a way that might be followed by a reader having at most a passing familiarity with the law, I am equally indebted to my many friends expert in none of those fields who have helped me eliminate the jargon of my profession, simplify my presentation, find references from outside the law, and prevent this from being a larger book. For indispensable aid in putting the manuscript in final form I owe much to my research assistant, Dmitry Selipanov.

Changing Your Mind

Prologue

This book is about regret and the law. "Every day," shrills a movie advertisement, "you make a million decisions."[1] How free are you to disregard one of them if you change your mind?

We prize the freedom to change our minds. Two centuries ago the French philosopher Jean-Jacques Rousseau asserted, "It is absurd that the will should put itself in chains for the future."[2] You should be free to change your mind and disregard your decision as long as you have done nothing more than make up your mind. Although you begin the day by deciding to get out of bed, you are free to change your mind and sleep in if you have no appointments. In forming an intention to get out of bed you have taken only the first step—deciding to do so—and can just as well form a contrary intention.

But the law imposes limits to this freedom to change our minds. Suppose that you *resolve* to stop smoking, *promise* to sell your farm to a purchaser, *will* an heirloom to a relative, *start* to rescue a drowning person, *give* a collection of manuscripts to a university, *declare* that you hold a painting in trust for a friend, *cancel* a debtor's $10,000 note, *ratify* a contract made as a teenager, *represent* that a companion is

1

the owner of your emerald ring, or *refrain* from protesting a neighbor's use of your land. Now you have done something more than make a decision. By resolving, promising, willing, starting, giving, declaring, canceling, ratifying, representing, or refraining, you have taken a second step. Should the law restrain you if you change your mind and regret having taken that step? Should the law impose sanctions if you disregard that step? In the twenty chapters that follow I consider the general principles that bear on the answer to this question. One challenge for the law is to devise bright-line rules that reflect these principles.

Consider the case of Enricho Navarroli, charged by the state of Illinois with dealing in drugs. The state, through its attorney, decided to go easy on Enricho if he would help to dismantle the drug ring. So the state took a second step and promised Enricho that it would reduce the charges and agree to probation if he would in return promise to cooperate as an undercover agent and plead guilty. Enricho not only gave his return promise but also carried out part of his side of the deal by serving as an undercover agent at considerable risk to himself and his family. Before he pled guilty, however, the state changed its mind and refused to go easy on him, contending that it was not bound to carry out its decision.

But the state had done more than reach a decision. It had taken a second step by making a promise, and Enricho had not only given his own promise in return but had partly performed it. Should the state have been free to change its mind and renege on its promise? The trial judge thought not. He concluded that the promise was binding and ordered the state to perform its promise.

In reaching this decision the judge applied one of the most compelling general principles of contract law. Nearly two millennia ago the Roman jurist Papinian stated that principle: "No one can change his mind to someone else's disadvantage." [3] Lawyers know this as the *reliance* principle, under which a promisee's reliance on a promise results in commitment on the part of the promisor. The state of Illinois had changed its mind to Enricho's disadvantage after he had relied on the state's promise. If such promises were not enforceable, as a judge on the Supreme Court of Illinois later put it, "a prosecutor could persuade a defendant to swim the English Channel . . . and then, for no reason at all, break the bargain and force the defendant to go to trial. . . . [J]ust as we enforce commercial contracts so as to better serve the public interest in the free flow of commercial exchange, so enforcement of executed or partially executed plea bargains serves the public interest in the efficient administration of justice."[4] The outcome of this case is discussed in the Epilogue.

In the twenty chapters that follow I examine the reliance principle and other general principles that apply in a variety of fields of law when you change your mind and feel regret. Part I covers what I call commitments, and Part II covers what I call relinquishments and preclusions. By "commitment" I mean a voluntary undertaking to do something in the *future,* an undertaking that the law recognizes as irrevocable in some way. Resolving, promising, willing, and starting fall into Part I. I use "relinquishment" and "preclusion" to refer to two kinds of voluntary surrender of something in the *present,* a surrender that the law recognizes as irreversible in some way. Giving, declaring, canceling, ratifying, representing, and refraining fall into Part II.

I identify and discuss a half-dozen principles that underlie the legal rules governing the irrevocability of a commitment and the irreversibility of a relinquishment or preclusion. In addition to the reliance principle—and its corollary, the assent rule—are the intention principle, the dependence principle, the public interest principle, the anti-speculation principle, and the repose principle. I conclude that the remarkable preoccupation with the reliance principle, first among scholars and later among courts, has contributed to a neglect—almost a disregard—of the other principles and encouraged a strain of latent paternalism.[5] Why, for example, should the law deny you the power to commit yourself even if changing your mind does not work "to someone else's disadvantage"?

I begin with commitments for three reasons. The first is that the analysis of commitments is familiar ground, because promises have historically occupied center stage in discussions of changing your mind. The second reason is that it is easiest to observe and justify paternalism where commitments are involved. And the third reason is that common law judges have shown a propensity for finding a promise where what is involved is a relinquishment, with the result that the paternalistic rules crafted for commitments have exercised a pervasive and perverse influence beyond their proper bounds.

In the first two chapters, I ask why one might want to be committed (Chapter 1) and why one might want not to be committed (Chapter 2). Because most commitments are promissory, I then explain how a promise expresses commitment (Chapter 3). The three chapters that follow consider *why* a promise should result in commitment (Chapter 4), *when* under legal rules a promise does result in commitment (Chapter 5), and *how* these legal rules can be explained (Chapter 6). In these chapters I return to Enricho's case and ask whether the state should have been committed if Enricho had given his return promise but had done nothing in reliance on the state's promise. Next comes a discussion of when promises to make gifts should result in commitment (Chapters 7 and 8). Since not all commitments are based on promises, I then ask when a commitment may arise without a promise (Chapter 9). Part I concludes with a discussion of how courts limit commitments by confining their scope (Chapter 10) and how courts soften commitments in granting remedies (Chapter 11).

It is not difficult to think of reasons why you might want

not to be committed to carry out a decision if you changed your mind. What reasons, then, might you have for wanting to be able to commit yourself to carry out a decision *despite* a change of mind? Why might you *want* the law to restrain you?

PART I

Commitments

CHAPTER ONE

Wanting to Make a Commitment

How Odysseus was bound to carry out his decision to stay his course. Some reasons why you might want to be bound to carry out your decisions and how you might take a second step, by making a promise or a resolution, to achieve this. Why courts do not enforce resolutions and how promises differ. Why you might want to be able to commit yourself by a promise in order to enhance your worth in the eyes of others and in your own eyes as well.

Why would you want to make a commitment—to put your future in chains? Literature offers no more graphic answer than the legend of Odysseus, who sought to be fixed in his decision to stay his course and avoid shipwreck on the rocks though tempted by the Sirens' song. So he took a second step. Having stopped the ears of his crew with wax to make them deaf to the music, he followed the advice of the sorceress Circe to have his men

> tie you hand and foot . . . lashed by ropes to the mast
> so you can hear the Sirens' song to your heart's content.
> But if you plead, commanding your men to set you free,
> Then they must lash you faster, rope on rope.

So when the Sirens

> sent their ravishing voices out across the air . . .
> I signalled the crew with frowns to set me free—
> they flung themselves at the oars and rowed on harder,
>   Pirimedes and
> Eurylochus springing up at once
> to bind me faster with rope on chafing rope.[1]

On the strength of his second step, Odysseus carried out his decision to stay his course.

Although you might long for a world in which you were free to follow your every whim or caprice, that world might turn out to be less than ideal. The tale of Odysseus and the Sirens suggests one reason for this—though not, as we shall see, the most important reason. Like Odysseus, you might suspect that you lack self-control and want to be sure to stay your course despite a change of mind.

At times we all have wished for help in making a decision irrevocable, immune from a foreseeable weakness of will when tempted by our Sirens. Our concern is usually less dramatic than fear of shipwreck. We may merely want to avoid the inconvenience and inefficiency involved in reconsidering a decision. Making up one's mind in the first place consumes time and energy, and reconsidering a decision consumes more, whether it leads to a change of mind or not. Nobel Prize–winning physicist Richard Feynman points out that sometimes it is "much easier to just plain *decide*. Never mind—*nothing* is going to change your mind." He recalled how as a student he "got sick and tired of having to decide" what kind of dessert to order at restaurants and so "decided it would *always* be chocolate ice cream, and never worried about it again." [2] Often it is best to lay a decision to rest—to go on to other things without the temptation to reconsider.

Various strategies may help you stay your course. You might, like the mythic Odysseus, try tying yourself to the mast. Legislatures that want to avoid reconsidering their initial decisions sometimes do this by adopting standing rules that foreclose reversal of those decisions. A notable example is the British Parliament's strict rule against reconsidering during the same session a vote once taken. [3] If you want to avoid reconsidering your decision to give up eating sweets you might throw away your chocolates or give them to a less abstemious friend. [4] (The irreversibility of your gift is a matter involving a relinquishment that is left to Part II.) The actress Shirley MacLaine is said to have acknowledged that she remained married to Steve Parker for nearly thirty years in part to keep herself from marrying again.[5]

More popular is the less draconian strategy of reinforcing your initial decision by taking a second step—embodying it in a *resolution* or in a *promise.* By a resolution you manifest your intention to carry out your initial decision. (Telling yourself "I resolve . . ." instead of merely "I decide . . ." may discourage backsliding by magnifying your resulting loss of self-esteem.) As far as the law goes, however, your resolutions are your own business. They do not commit you to carry out your decisions. Had Odysseus resolved to stay his course, his resolution would not have tied him to the mast if the Sirens had changed his mind. Perhaps this is just as well, for life might be too difficult if we had to keep all or even most of our resolutions. For better or for worse, the law does not enforce resolutions.

The reason is a practical one. Because legal rules are commonly applied in an adversary procedure, courts show no concern with backsliding unless someone is in a position to complain about it. There is an analogy in the law of trusts. Usually a trust can be enforced through an action brought by the beneficiary of the trust against the trustee. Sometimes, however, there is no beneficiary who can bring an action to enforce the trust. If the trust is charitable—for instance, for the benefit of the poor—a court will allow the attorney general to bring an action to enforce the trust. But the attorney general has no standing if the trust is not charitable, as in the case of a trust to erect a tombstone or to care for a favorite cat. The trust is unenforceable because there is no one to enforce it—no one in a position to complain if it is not carried out.[6]

Under the same reasoning, your resolutions are unenforceable because there is no one to complain if they are not carried out. A resolution by Odysseus to stay his course would not have spoken to his crew, and, though carrying out his resolution might have benefited them, they could not have complained had he succumbed to the Sirens. No court will intervene if your whims and caprices cause you to back-slide on such a resolution.

In this the law accords with common perception. If you announce to your bridge club your resolution to give up sweets, no one is likely to perceive that announcement as having created a commitment to other members entitling them to complain if you wolf down a box of chocolates. You may be ridiculed, but you are not likely to be accused of "re-neging," as you would be if you tried to go back on a bid of four spades.[7] (One might ask whether there are *no* cir-cumstances in which a person who benefits from another's resolution could enforce that resolution, a question that will be put off until Chapter 9.)

If you make your will, it is taken, like the resolution announced to your bridge club, as speaking to the world in general and therefore to no one in particular ("I declare this to be my last will . . ."). Because it is understood that, in a sixteenth-century writer's words, "a man may as oft as hee will make a newe testament, even untill the last breath," you can revoke your will as long as you have life to do so.[8]

It would be a mistake, however, to assume that the law has an innate hostility toward your resolutions or seeks out of paternalism to protect you from them for your own good. You could deliver, say, $1,000 to a friend as a gift on the con-dition that it would revert to you at the end of a year if you kept your resolution to give up sweets, agreeing in effect to forfeit $1,000 if you did not keep your resolution.[9] You could then present a dispute to a court in an adversary proceed-ing if at the end of a year you claimed the right to reclaim the $1,000 from a recalcitrant friend. Since there is no rea-son why a court would not entertain such a dispute (Chapter 13), the reason for the unenforceability of resolutions must be the purely practical one suggested.

But it will do no good to doctor your resolution in an attempt to make it enforceable. It will not help to say "I swear" to the Almighty, "I vow" to some revered figure, or "I pledge" to some abstract authority, for there is still nobody—

not even an attorney general—to complain. You cannot make your will irrevocable by declaring to the world that you will not revoke it. As an English court said some three centuries ago, even "if I make my testament and last will irrevocable, yet I may revoke it, for my act or my words cannot alter the judgment of the law to make that irrevocable, which is of its own nature revocable."[10] Nor will it help to say, "I promise myself," for nobody can complain if you renege on such a phony promise.

Decisions embodied in promises are, as a matter of law, vastly different matter from those embodied in resolutions.[11] While promising resembles resolving in that it too involves a second step to aid one in carrying out an initial decision, it differs in that it involves two persons. A promise requires not only a promisor but also a promisee—someone to whom the promisor expresses commitment and who can complain if the promise is not performed (see Chapter 3). In the words of the Roman philosopher Seneca, "The word 'owe' has no place unless two persons are involved."[12] On like reasoning, a California appeals court held that a losing political candidate could not enforce the winner's signed pledge to abide by a Code of Fair Campaign Practices. The pledge did not commit the winner because two persons were not involved. The pledge had "no promisee."[13] Had a determined Odysseus promised his crew that he would stay his course, that would have been no mere resolution.

Since you rarely make promises in order to tie yourself to the mast, the function of promising is usually very different from the function of resolving. While you make a resolution with a view to self-control, you most often make a promise with a view to self-interest. You make it in order to get what you want from someone else whose self-interest is in having your commitment in return. You make it as part of an exchange in which you swap your commitment for something that you want.[14] And having the power to give such a commitment is a second and far more important reason why you might not want a world where you were free to follow your every whim or caprice—why it is important to you to have the power to bind yourself. It is indeed so important a reason that, as we shall see, it has become the central—virtually the exclusive—focus of contract law (Chapter 7).

Thus a borrower gives a promise of repayment in exchange for a loan from a bank, which in turn wants the borrower's commitment to repay the loan. Like the borrower, we exchange our promises for other things—often other promises—that we want, just as the state of Illinois exchanged its promise to go easy on Enricho for his promise to cooperate and plead guilty. (Not all significant promises are made as parts of exchanges. See Chapters 7 and 8.)

Complete freedom to renege on your promises would make it difficult for you to deal with others by lowering your worth in their eyes. Keeping your resolutions may be of little concern to others, but keeping your promises is an altogether different matter. Who would swap for your promises if you were free to renege on them? How would you borrow money or buy on credit? As the American legal philosopher Karl Llewellyn put it, "Remove the legal sanction and men will give credit with more care."[15] And as one of the judges who heard Enricho's case on appeal argued, "Few informed defendants will aid the prosecution in return for a promise when they know it is not enforceable by a trial court."[16]

Would you have to get someone to guarantee your performance, as a teenager may have to get an adult? Would you have to pay in advance to have a leaking roof fixed? Would it be enough if you developed a reputation for performing your promises? The value of your promises to yourself depends on the assurance of ultimate performance that your promises give to others. Promises that you could freely disregard would be as worthless to you as to others. As a federal Court of Appeals judge put it, "Having the power to bind ourselves in exchange for similar concessions from others gives us a significant measure of control over our lives."[17]

This means not only making decisions but also being able to make commitments to carry out those decisions. (Because a promisor's death revokes the promise, your ability to commit your estate also hangs in the balance.) Even the federal government was forced, over the latter half of the nineteenth century, gradually to abandon the sovereign immunity that had left aggrieved parties to government contracts with no recourse other than the introduction of a private bill in Congress.[18] All this suggests a focus on the promis*ee*—the person who is in a position to complain if you renege.

But this is not all. Freedom to renege on your promises would lower your worth in your own eyes. To be sure, our freedom to ignore resolutions may also affect our self-respect. (Our need for psychiatric help is said to increase early in the New Year.) But because our promises involve others, we see them as having a dimension that our resolutions lack. In a society in which most people can swap binding promises with others, surely it would lower your worth in your own eyes if you could not do the same.

How would a modern woman see herself were she to return to fifteenth-century Florence, where by statute a woman could not commit herself without a man's approval since, as a jurist of the time explained, the "laws have less confidence in a woman."[19] Or to nineteenth-century America, where a leading commentator could write that a married woman, being "under the power of her husband, . . . can have no will of her own, and by reason of this lack of freedom of will she cannot contract"?[20] We do not long for a paternalistic legal system that in our "own best interests" denies us the power to commit ourselves. These arguments focus on the promisor.

The advantages of being able to make commitments come only at some cost in freedom to renege on promises. In later chapters we shall see that the legal rules governing the enforceability of promises tend to be justified largely in light of the significance that your commitments may have to *others*. And I shall suggest that it is wrong to let this tendency obscure the significance that your commitments may have to *you*.

The chapters that follow focus on the restraints that the law imposes on your freedom to renege on your promises. To be sure, even if the law imposed no restraints you might honor your promises because of extralegal restraints. Some of these are external: you might fear diminished standing among peers, harm to reputation, impairment of relationships, or loss of future opportunities. Who is insensitive to shame, ridicule, or mistrust? As the Supreme Court of Minnesota remarked in discussing the importance of a newspaper's observance of a confidentiality agreement between its reporter and its news source, "the keeping of promises is professionally important" because "if it is known that promises will not be kept, sources may dry up." Other restraints are internal: you might be moved by a sense of integrity, acquired by upbringing, education, or introspection. Why else do we use the word "honor" in this connection? As the Supreme Court of Minnesota went on to say, "to break a promise of confidentiality which has induced a source to give information is dishonorable."[21]

Because this is a book about regret and the law, its concern is mainly with legal restraints—a concern shared by Faust in bargaining with Mephistopheles.

> So even hell has laws. Good; in that case
> One might conclude a pact with you
> Gentlemen, and a guaranteed one too?[22]

For the law, the question is not *why* do you honor your promises but *when* should you be restrained from reneging on your promises. Since extralegal restraints cause some promisors to honor their promises quite without regard to what the law requires, the law has an impact in restraining promisors only to the extent that they would otherwise renege. And a rule of law may be influenced by the likelihood that extralegal restraints will deter a promisor from reneging. I will not, however, focus on such restraints.

Having seen some reasons why you might want the law to restrain you from reneging, let us look at the other side of the coin. What are some of the reasons you might want not to be bound by your promises?

CHAPTER TWO

Regretting Being Committed

Why you might regret being committed and want to be free to re-nege on a promise. How regret goes to the decision to take the second step of making a promise, and how the law's tolerance of regret reflects paternalism. Reasons for regretting such a step when taken: decisions that are unfairly influenced, uninformed, or ill considered. Tolerance of reasons for regretting such a step only after the passage of time: decisions that are improvident or obsolete.

Even though you wanted to be committed at the time you made your promise, you may in hindsight wish that you were not. Rare is the promisor who has never felt regret—the sensation of distress that comes from such hindsight. As Faust observed,

> A pledge that binds
> Is a thing rooted in our minds,
> And we accept this. Happy is the man
> Of pure and constant heart, who can
> Regret no choice, no loss![1]

Regret may not only sully your past but, as *The Rubaiyat* suggests, may also induce fear as to your future.

> Ah, my Beloved, fill the Cup that clears
> Today of past Regrets and future Fears.[2]

Two-faced Prudence looks forward as well as backward, aware not only of the past but of possible consequences for the future,[3] and your fear of future regret often shapes your present actions. Your willingness to take a step, beyond merely making up your mind, will depend on your freedom to disregard that step once it has been taken, and the apprehension of regret may discourage you from taking it at all, or at least induce you to hedge it to avoid regret.

Sometimes you want to make a promise but fear regret if you are committed. If, in the middle of negotiations, you want to record your tentative agreements without committing yourself, remaining free to renege at any whim, you could make a "gentlemen's agreement" by stating that you do not want to be legally bound by your promises. And even if you do not want to be completely free to renege you may resist being as firmly bound as the mythic Odysseus and want to be excused if things have changed when the time comes to carry out your promise. If you have sometimes had "past Regrets" because of unexpected difficulties in performing, you could allay your "future Fears" by including in your agreement a force majeure clause, excusing you from performing should such difficulties arise.

But you cannot always count on foresight in making your promises, so even if you do not long for a paternalistic legal system that denies you all power to commit yourself, you may, on feeling regret, wish for a little paternalism to protect you in the particular circumstance. In other words, while you are glad that you can make binding promises, you may wish that you were not bound by the particular promise that you made. What circumstances cause promisors to change their minds?

"The matter does not appear to me now as it appears to have appeared to me then," said Baron Bramwell when confronted with the argument that he should follow one of his earlier dicta.[4] Why might Bramwell have changed his mind? Was his earlier dictum to be regretted as soon as uttered— perhaps because of faulty logic or misunderstanding of the law? Or was it only later to be regretted—perhaps because of subsequent events or a change in his views? There are lots of reasons for changing your mind and wanting not to be bound by a promise. Most of them do not excuse reneging:

plainly it will not do to simply change your mind on further reflection. Much of contract law is devoted to identifying the reasons that do excuse reneging, and the resulting rules are of great practical importance.[5]

We need not explore these rules in detail because our interest is in the freedom to renege, even if done capriciously and without excuse. Nevertheless, it will be instructive to sketch the outlines of these rules, because, unless they apply, a promisor's only justification for reneging is that the promise is simply not binding.

In addition, it is a fair guess that the more paternalistic the courts are in allowing promisors excuses for reneging on binding promises, the more willing they will be to find binding promises in the first place. If, at the other extreme, courts rarely excused those who made binding promises, courts would be hesitant indeed to find binding promises. A variation on this theme appears when we come to gift promises (Chapter 8), but for now it is enough to observe that the shift, though glacial, is clearly toward greater tolerance of reneging and in this sense in the direction of paternalism. Today few people, in the words of one scholar, "see much wrong in admitting to a change of mind, and the law indeed goes out of its way to recognize a man's right to change his mind and extricate himself from certain contracts," such as marriage.[6]

Regret, as I use the term here, describes the sensation of distress that you feel on concluding that you have done something contrary to your present self-interest, something that does not accord with your present preferences.[7] But merely making a decision, without taking a second step, is no real cause for regret; it is the second step that causes regret. What caused Odysseus regret when the Sirens sang was not his decision to stay his course but his second step—having his men tie him to the mast.

Since your resolutions do not tie you to the mast, the step of resolving to carry out some decision will not lead to regret. But the step of promising to carry out that decision may well do so. Before you take that second step you must make another decision—a *subsequent* decision to promise to carry our your *initial* decision. In looking for reasons for regret it is to this subsequent decision that we must look. Why was your subsequent decision to promise flawed?

In answering this question it is useful to divide situations into two categories, depending—as in the example of Bramwell—on whether the passage of time plays a role.[8] In situations in the first category, time plays no role in occasioning regret. Your decision to make your promise did not reflect your existing preferences, and your promise was to be regretted when made, though you may not have realized this until later. Time did not have to pass for you to have a reason for changing your mind. In this category are cases of what I call *unfairly influenced* decisions, *uninformed* decisions, and *ill-considered* decisions. In situations in the second category, regret comes only with the passage of time. Your decision to make your promise reflected your existing preferences, and your promise was only later to be regretted because the decision no longer reflected your preferences. Time had to pass for you to have a reason for changing your mind. In this category are cases of what I call *improvident* decisions and *obsolete* decisions. These five categories are not exclusive, and a decision may be flawed in more than one respect—as when it is, say, both ill considered and improvident.

To start, consider situations in which your decision did not reflect your existing preferences, so that time played no role. There are three possible reasons for such situations.

First, you may find that because of coercion or misrepresentation your decision was unfairly influenced. Protests on these grounds are especially compelling and so universal as to be recognized even in the law of nations.[9] When coercion is claimed, there is a trend toward allowing excuse. The doctrine of duress, once limited to threats of wrongs sufficient to inspire what a thirteenth-century writer termed "fear . . . in a resolute man,"[10] has been relaxed to include a variety of less extreme forms of coercion, called economic duress or business compulsion.[11] And if the relationship between the parties to the contract is one of trust or confidence, such as that between husband and wife or physician and patient, excuse may be based on the less demanding doctrine of undue influence.[12] The same trend can be seen when misrepresentation is claimed. Courts are increasingly inclined to characterize a mere failure to disclose as a misrepresentation and to grant relief for misrepresentations that are innocent rather than intended to mislead.

But courts have been unwilling to go beyond these traditional grounds and entertain arguments that a decision is unfairly influenced because poverty or ignorance affected it, though such circumstances may play a role in the application of the traditional grounds. Even under the modern doctrine that allows a promisor to escape from an "unconscionable" undertaking, courts commonly require some "substantive" unfairness (such as an extreme limitation of remedies for breach) in a contract term itself in addition to "procedural" unfairness (such as high-pressure sales techniques) in the manner in which the promise was obtained.[13] The fact that your choices were limited when presented with a printed "contract of adhesion" and asked to "take it or leave it" is not by itself an excuse.[14]

Second, you may discover that because you did not know enough your decision was uninformed. Protests on this ground have not often been warmly received. If you realize, on receiving new information, that your decision did not take proper account of your preferences, you may sometimes have relief if your mistake was shared by the other party and goes to a basic assumption or, even where not shared, was so mindless as to be designated "clerical."[15] But you must often decide on the basis of such information as you already have or can conveniently acquire, and you are expected, by and large, to bear the consequences of not having enough. Courts are not so paternalistic as to require that you have perfect information in order to make a binding promise, and it matters not that you may have misjudged your available resources, underestimated the burden of your performance, overestimated the value of what you are to receive in return, or overlooked another opportunity that would have better suited your preferences. The possibility of such error is seen as a cost that you have accepted.

Third, you may conclude that for cognitive or volitional reasons your decision was ill considered. You are unlikely to succeed on this ground, for you must generally take this risk. Sometimes the failure is cognitive: you fail to apply all that you know. It is a human failing to simplify the making of complex decisions by using rules of thumb, and these rules, however useful, may result in flawed judgment and irrational decisions.[16] Because we tend to underestimate future risks and overestimate the benefits of today, you may "fill the Cup" by eating another fudge sundae.[17] A distinguished former academic illuminates our propensity to Faustian bargains by pointing out that "the farther in advance you invite an academic to attend a conference, the likelier he is to accept; yet when the date of the conference finally rolls around, he may bitterly regret his acceptance."[18] Because of this tendency you may undervalue a lost opportunity while overvaluing out-of-pocket expense and so decline to buy for $900 a painting that, if it were yours, you would refuse to sell for $1,000.[19] It has even been suggested that too much reflection may impair our ability to make sound decisions, so that it may not be a good idea to analyze your preferences too carefully.[20] At other times the failure is not cognitive but volitional: you fill the Cup by eating that fudge sundae not because you do not know what you want but because you lack the will to choose accordingly.[21] Because you sometimes let your emotions control your decisions, you may promise to purchase a luxury item to satisfy a transient desire for status.[22] In your more reflective moments, you may yearn for a little paternalism to protect yourself from decisions that are not really in your best interests, but most such failings are not easily correctable by legal regulation. If you bid a half million dollars for the humidor sent by Milton Berle to John Kennedy, you are unlikely to find sympathy in court.[23]

Occasionally, however, paternalism prevails. Sometimes legislation provides for "cooling-off" periods to guard against impetuous decisions: a couple may have to wait before marrying; a legislature may have to have a second reading of a bill before enactment; a buyer in a door-to-door sale may have a three-day period to withdraw from the transaction.[24] Sometimes statutes protect consumers, employees, franchisees, and others from their ill-considered decisions by allowing them to renege on some of their promises for no reason at all. But for the most part the law leaves us with the risk of our ill-considered decisions. Just as the law is not so paternalistic as to require perfect information as a condition of making a binding promise, neither does it require complete rationality.

Now consider the effect of the passage of time. Promises are made in the face of an uncertain future. Even if your promise reflected your existing preferences, so that you had then no cause for regret, you might nevertheless have cause for regret after the passage of time. For this there are two possible reasons.

First, because you were poor at predicting external circumstances, you may find that they have changed and you have made an improvident decision. You may be unexpectedly presented with an attractive opportunity that is incompatible with the promise, as when, having promised to sell goods when the market was down, you now find that the market is up. Or something may have happened to make the expected return performance much less valuable, as when, having promised to buy goods when the market was up, you now find that the market is down. Because contracts are devices for dealing with uncertainty by allocating risks of future changes, courts have tended to be markedly less paternalistic when faced with excuses based on improvident decisions than when confronted with excuses based on uninformed decisions. A promisor is expected, on the whole,

to "suffer the slings and arrows of outrageous fortune"—
a proposition compressed into the Latin maxim *pacta sunt
servanda* (contracts are to be performed)—and so, with rare
exceptions, bears the risk of an adverse turn of the market, as
a gambler bears the risk of an unfavorable throw of the dice.

Some events, however, are sufficiently extraordinary to
be regarded as beyond the risks assumed by the parties. Excusing a promisor in such a situation may not be seen as
an exercise in paternalism at all but merely as the application of a legal rule designed to spare the parties the trouble
of inserting a provision to the same effect in their contract.[25]
Even the law of nations recognizes this under the doctrine
of *rebus sic stantibus* (things remaining thus), which may
excuse a nation from its treaty obligations if there has been
a "fundamental change of circumstances."[26] Under the Uniform Commercial Code a seller of goods may be excused for
nonperformance if performance has been made "impracticable by the occurrence of a contingency the nonoccurrence
of which was a basic assumption on which the contract was
made," as where a supervening government regulation prohibits delivery.[27] Here again there is a visible trend in favor of
tolerating excuses. What was once a requirement of impossibility has been watered down to one of impracticability. And
relief is granted for "frustration of purpose" if the event, instead of making one's own performance more burdensome,
makes the other party's performance nearly worthless.[28]

Furthermore, you are not usually saddled with your decision if your regret is caused by an improvident choice
of another party that has failed to perform, since a serious
breach will not only entitle you to damages but will excuse
you from performing.[29] A promisor's sense of betrayal on not
getting the expected return for a promise is recognized by
the law governing the promises of nations and the promises
of prosecutors alike.[30] And such excuses have become more
readily available to contracting parties through recognition
that each owes the other an obligation of good faith and fair
dealing in contract performance, even though that obligation

is not explicitly spelled out.[31] To this extent, courts grant relief from improvident decisions. But the working rule, applicable to most improvident decisions, denies relief.

Second, because you were poor at predicting your preferences, you may find that they have changed even though external circumstances have not, and that you have made an obsolete decision. Your change of mind stems from an internal change, such as an irresistible desire for sweet-singing Sirens or an evolving taste from rock to Bach.[32] But though you might sometimes be grateful for a little paternalism along these lines, courts are much less likely to grant relief in the case of an obsolete decision than in the case of an improvident one. And, by and large, this is so even though when your decision was made your preferences were malformed because you were in some way disadvantaged.[33]

This remains so despite the beguiling notion that over time a person may evolve into a "later self"—a distinct individual with different preferences that produce regret.[34] As Alice replied to the Caterpillar, "I know who I *was* when I got up this morning, but I think I must have changed several times since then" verifying La Rochefoucauld's maxim, "We are sometimes as different from ourselves as from other people."[35]

Although this recognition of personal development has found favor among some legal scholars, it has had no significant impact on courts.[36] Country-music star Willie Nelson, when asked about his four marriages, replied, "I've changed. I'm not the same guy that was married to this person or that person. . . . [E]ach of my wives have been married to a different person."[37] But contract law is not so forgiving. Even a financial disaster that not only alters one's preferences but leaves one unable to perform is dismissed as mere "subjective impossibility, that is, impossibility that is personal to the promisor and does not inhere in the nature of the act performed" and so is no excuse.[38]

Feeling like a different person may bring relief in one's own mind, but it will not bring relief from one's promises. As a prominent jurist concluded, for the purpose of "evaluating a proposal to allow elderly people to repudiate obligations made when they were young, it is more fruitful to think of the present and the future self as one person."[39] Contract law does give a child, on coming of age and in a sense becoming a "later self," a power capriciously to avoid earlier promises. But the child's preferences are regarded as imperfectly formed in the first place, and the change from child to adult is abrupt, on reaching the age of majority, not gradual, as in the archetypal case of a later self.[40] Even abrupt change is not always enough. Although the death of a promisor and the substitution of an executor or administrator may trigger reneging, it does not of itself affect contractual obligations. Nor does a sudden change in management or control of a corporation. If the state of Illinois' promise to Enricho was binding, the arrival on the scene of a new prosecutor, with a different attitude toward plea bargaining, would not justify the state in reneging.[41] By and large, one is accountable for one's own development, and the commitment that results from a promise is essentially unaffected by changes in preferences.[42]

You might try to avoid committing a later self by saying something like: "I promise to do thus-and-so, but only if my preferences do not sooner change to cause me to regret having made my promise." But a court would probably characterize this as an "illusory promise," too lacking in substance to result in commitment. Leaving the door this wide open for a later self to renege on a mere change of preferences deprives your "promise" of legal effect. I leave to a later chapter more effective ways of confining your commitments.

To sum up, only rarely will a court allow you to change your mind and renege on a binding promise, though there is a trend toward tolerance of reneging and in this sense toward paternalism. Before we look into why a promise should commit, it will be helpful to ask: What is a promise, and how does a promise express commitment?

CHAPTER THREE

How a Promise Expresses Commitment

Words of "prophecy, encouragement or bounty" by the Michigan legislature held not a promise. The two elements of a promise: a representation of a decision and an expression of commitment. Three questions about commitments: First, what is an expression of commitment? How courts tell whether you have made such an expression. Second, commitment as to what? How a promise can be beyond anyone's control. Third, commitment to whom? How a promise may result in a commitment to a third person, as Nettie Beman's promise did to Marion Seaver.

I earlier defined a commitment as a voluntary undertaking to do something in the future. Most commitments result from promises. But what is a promise, and how does it express commitment? In 1903 the Supreme Court of the United States had to decide whether the state of Michigan had made a commitment to a railroad. In 1893 the Michigan legislature had enacted a law levying a tax on railroads but providing that the law "shall not apply to any railway company hereafter building . . . a line . . . unless the gross earnings shall equal four thousand dollars per mile." The Wisconsin & Michigan Railway Company then constructed a line that qualified for this exemption. But in 1897 the Michigan legislature amended the 1893 law, changing the method for calculating earnings so that the railroad's line was no longer exempted.

The railroad challenged the validity of the 1897 amendment on the ground that it violated the provision of the Constitution of the United States that prohibits any state from enacting a law "impairing the Obligation of Contracts." The state responded that it had made no contract: despite the quoted language of exemption, it had made no promise and was therefore not committed. The Supreme Court, in an opinion by Justice Oliver Wendell Holmes, agreed with the state.

Holmes saw the question as "whether the State has purported to bind itself irrevocably or merely has used words of prophecy, encouragement or bounty, holding out a hope but not amounting to a covenant." He concluded that "in view of the subject matter, the legislature is not making promises, but framing a scheme of public revenue and public improvement." The quoted language of the law, therefore, "simply indicates a course of conduct to be pursued until circumstances or its views of policy change."[1] The state had made up its mind—it had made a decision—but it had done no more. How does a promise go beyond this and express commitment?

To begin with, a promise has two distinct elements, each saying something about an initial decision by the promisor but only the second involving commitment. First, a promise represents that the promisor has made an initial decision to do what is promised. A promise to do thus-and-so says: "I have decided to do thus-and-so." But this is not an expression of commitment, and it would not be inconsistent if the promisor, on later regretting the decision, refused to do thus-and-so. Second, a promise expresses the promisor's commitment to carry out the initial decision by doing what is promised at some future time despite a subsequent change of mind. A promise to do thus-and-so also says: "I will carry out my decision to do thus-and-so when the time comes even if I later change my mind and regret my decision to do it." In this there is an expression of commitment, and plainly it would be inconsistent if the promisor later refused to do thus-and-so.

The first element of a promise, a representation that a decision has been made, is a statement about the promisor's state of mind at the time of the promise. Because this initial decision is based on the promisor's existing preferences, it affords the promisee some basis for planning. A statement need not be a promise in order to do this, for even a resolution may afford others at least some basis for planning. Thus, though Michigan's 1893 law may not have contained a promise, it provided what Holmes called a "scheme of public revenue and public improvement" that presumably reflected the legislature's "views of policy"—its preferences at that time.

A promisor whose promise *mis*represents an initial decision fraudulently misrepresents an important fact concerning the promisor's state of mind. In the oft-quoted aphorism of an English judge of more than a century ago, "The state of a man's mind is as much a fact as the state of his digestion." [2] Courts therefore treat a promise made with no intention of performing it as a misrepresentation of fact, and such a promise can be the basis of liability for "promissory fraud" either in contract or in tort. The possibility of tort recovery is attractive to claimants because it may carry punitive as well as compensatory damages. The Supreme Court of California, for example, held that a California employer would be liable in tort for promissory fraud if, as alleged, it had lured an employee to leave his job in New York and move with his family to California by promises of permanent employment and salary increases that the employer did not intend to provide. The court explained, "A promise to do something necessarily implies the intention to perform; hence, where a promise is made without such an intention, there is an implied misrepresentation of fact that may be actionable fraud." [3]

Although a representation that one has made a decision may arouse expectations, as did Michigan's 1893 law, it says nothing about the future, and in this respect gives the promisee scant grounds for planning. For a promise to provide an effective basis for planning it must have a second element that speaks to the future. Our concern is with the second element of a promise: an expression of commitment. In the remainder of this chapter, I consider three questions. First, what is an expression of commitment? Second, as to what does it express commitment? Third, as to whom does it express commitment?

First, what is an expression of commitment to do something, as distinguished from a mere representation that a decision has been made to do that thing? This second element of a promise has proved more elusive than the first. Unlike a representation that a decision has been made, an expression of commitment does not assert that anything is a fact, so it cannot be either true or false. The expression is the *doing* of something as distinguished from merely the *saying* of something. In describing expressions of commitment, philosophers use the term "performative utterance," and evidence scholars use the term "verbal act," each to suggest that the expression is itself the performance of an action.[4]

If, for example, you say "I promise to sell you my ship *Argo*," you both say something and do something. What you say is that you have made an initial decision to sell me your ship. If what you say is false because you actually have not decided to sell me your ship, you make a fraudulent representation. What you do is make a commitment to sell me your ship even if you change your mind in the future. If you renege on your promise, you go back on that commitment.

In deciding whether an expression is one of commitment, courts commonly use an objective and not a subjective standard of interpretation, asking not what the promisor actually intended by the words in question but what a reasonable promisee would have understood by those words. Others are entitled to judge by appearances, and even if you do not mean to make a commitment you may be bound if a reasonable person in the circumstances would have understood you to be making one. As the Restatement (Second) of Contracts puts it, with evident circularity, a promise must "justify the promisee in understanding that a commitment has been made."[5] To this extent, for reasons to be addressed in Chapter 4, a commitment may not, strictly speaking, be voluntary. It is enough if you "purport"—to use Holmes's word—to limit your freedom to renege if you change your mind.[6]

Sometimes words alone are enough. So in interpreting a teachers' tenure law enacted by the Indiana legislature, the Supreme Court of the United States noted the act's repeated use of the word "contract" in concluding that teachers were justified in understanding that the word "was not used inadvertently or in other than its usual legal meaning." Unlike the case of the Michigan statute, "the policy therein expressed may [not] be altered at the will of the Legislature."[7] Even if your words are not enough, circumstances may make it reasonable to understand that an unspoken commitment was implicit in what you said. So in interpreting a letter from a third party to a creditor assuring the creditor that "we have every intention of meeting [the debtor's] obligation as soon as possible," the Supreme Court of Michigan concluded that this was a promise to pay the debt, alluding to the creditor's "forbearance to enforce payment" in return.[8] A promise need not invite or solicit reliance,[9] but a court may take into account the circumstance that the promisee would be likely to rely.

Expressing commitment is a matter of substance and not merely of form. Thus the Supreme Court of Iowa held that a buyer that "promised" to buy all the coal that it "would want to purchase" made no commitment because the buyer undertook only "to buy if it pleased, when it pleased, . . . to buy much, little, or not at all, as it thought best."[10] As we have seen, what the buyer made is called an illusory promise, which is a way of saying that it is no promise at all.

Now to the second question: As to what does the expression express commitment? If a commitment limits a promisor's later conduct, it follows that the expression of commitment must say something about the *promisor's* future action or forbearance. When you say, "I promise you thus-and-so," thus-and-so is ordinarily action or forbearance within your control and what you mean is that you will cause thus-and-so to happen. This is not necessarily the case, however, for sometimes thus-and-so is beyond your control and what you mean is that you will pay something if thus-and-so fails to happen. Even if thus-and-so is beyond *anyone's* control, as when you say, "I promise that it will rain tomorrow," your words may be taken as meaning, "If it does not rain tomorrow, I promise to pay you for your loss." And paying is within your control.

To make such a promise might seem rash, and courts have been reluctant to interpret language concerning events beyond your control as a promise, preferring to find mere words of "prophecy, encouragement or bounty." Fortunately for astrologers and other soothsayers who predict events beyond their control, no liability follows from an erroneous prediction. In a Minnesota case, a landlord sought to induce his tenant to put more cattle on the rented farm by saying, "I will see there will be plenty of water because it never failed in Minnesota yet." The tenant relied on the statement and bought more cattle, but the water failed, and the tenant sued. Had the landlord gone beyond prediction and expressed commitment? Even though the landlord was no rainmaker, an expression of commitment would have made him liable to pay for any loss caused by the lack of rain. The Supreme Court of Minnesota concluded, however, that the statement was a mere prediction that did not rise to the level of a promise because the indefiniteness of the language "rather characterized the talk more as . . . advice than a contract."[11] The landlord could have made a promise that rain would come had he done so in plain language, but because he had not done so he was not liable.

The judicial reluctance to interpret language concerning events beyond your control as more than a mere prediction does not extend to statements by a seller as to the quality of goods sold. Suppose, for example, that a seller says to a buyer, believing that it is so, "This bottle of elixir will cure what ails you." Although the power of the elixir is beyond the seller's control, in all likelihood a court will hold that the seller has made an expression of commitment—known as a warranty—and not a mere prediction. For breach of this warranty the seller will be liable if the elixir fails to cure what ails the buyer.[12]

And the third question: As to whom does the expression express commitment? A promise differs from a resolution, as we have seen, in that a promise is directed at another person, and it is that person, the promisee, to whom the commitment runs. You can keep your resolution to yourself, but you must communicate your promise to the promisee. As it has aptly been put, a promise is "essentially hearer-directed" and must be communicated to the promisee in order to result in a commitment.[13] You are therefore free to revoke your promise at any time before the promisee learns of it. And if you wish to be relieved of the commitment that results from your promise, it is the promisee to whom you must look for release. Implicit in Judge Benjamin Nathan Cardozo's assertion that "[t]hose who make a contract may unmake it" is the proposition that the promisee's assent is required for the unmaking.[14]

Even if a promise must be communicated in order to result in commitment, it does not follow that communication is needed in order to make every decision irrevocable. Thus, although there must be a manifestation of intention to create a trust, you can create a trust without communicating that intention to the beneficiary.[15] As the New York Court of Appeals explained more than a half-century ago, "The declaration need not be made to the beneficiary, nor the writing given to him; in fact his ignorance of the trust is immaterial."[16] This, however, was said in connection with a relinquishment, the creation of a trust, not a commitment.

Ordinarily your promise results in commitment *only* to the promisee. If I overhear you making a promise to a neighbor to give a block party, I can neither hold you to that promise nor release you from it. You committed yourself only to the promisee, the neighbor.[17] In exceptional circumstances, however, another person will be regarded as an intended beneficiary of your promise to whom your commitment also runs.

Here is a noted example. Nettie Beman, advanced in years and believing that she was about to die, had her husband, Albert, draw her will, but when it was read to her she was not satisfied because she wanted her house to go to a favorite niece, Marion Seaver, and the will left it to Albert during his life and then to a charity. Albert offered to write a new will, but Nettie feared that there was no time for that. So Albert then promised her that if she signed the will as it was he would leave Marion enough in his own will to make up the difference. Nettie then died, and Albert died soon after, but he left nothing in his will to Marion.

Was Marion entitled to enforce Albert's promise? The highest court of New York decided that she was.[18] Albert's promise, though made only to Nettie, expressed commitment to Marion as well as to Nettie. Nettie had gotten that commitment to Marion as part of her swap with Albert, so Marion as an intended beneficiary could hold Albert to his promise. Whether Albert would have had to look to Marion as well as to Nettie in order to be relieved of his commitment is for a later chapter.

But if a promise is an *expression* of commitment, why should such an expression result in *commitment?* What explains the power of a promise to commit the promisor?

CHAPTER FOUR

Why a Promise Should Commit

Why should you be committed by your promise? Rules of a game as a metaphor for rules of contract law; how a promisor assents to those rules. Older explanations focus on the promisor: moral obligation theory and will theory. The importance to you of the power to make a binding promise. Modern explanations focus on the promisee: an explanation based on expectation theory and one based on reliance theory. The objection of circularity as to both and some reasons for favoring a reliance principle.

In every promise there is an *expression* of commitment. But why should the promisor be *committed* by that expression?

The metaphor of a game is sometimes invoked to answer this question. Just as a purpose of the rules of a game is encouraging appropriate behavior by future players, a purpose of contract law is encouraging socially desirable conduct by future contracting parties. And just as players in a game are bound by conventions or rules established to maintain the game's integrity, contracting parties are bound by rules of law designed to uphold the practice of making promises.[1] In both spheres there is a concern for fairness in the participant's conduct (for a "level playing field"), for ease of administration (for "bright line" rules over "judgment calls"), and for internal consistency (for rules that make sense when tested against other rules). As the conduct of the game is shaped by its rules, the practice of promising is shaped by the law of contracts.[2] Without its rules, the game would not take place in the way it does, and without contract law, the practice of making promises would not be the same. It is therefore the desirability of the practice of promising, not that of keeping of individual promises, that justifies the law of contracts.[3]

The metaphor is not without flaw.[4] A player assents to

the rules of a game by agreeing to play, but whence comes a contracting party's assent to be bound by the rules of contract law?[5] Does merely uttering words like "I promise" suffice?[6] What of the party who does not mean to make a promise but is bound, as we have seen, under an objective standard because of the other party's reasonable understanding? Even a promise uttered in jest may result in commitment. As a Washington appellate court wrote, "If the jest is not apparent and a reasonable hearer would believe that an offer was being made, then the speaker risks the formation of a contract which was not intended. It is the outward manifestations of the offeror that count and not secret, unexpressed intentions."[7] One may be bound by the rules of contract law even if one did not mean to play that game.

For many lawyers it may be enough that the game and its rules are there—that the practice of promising not only exists but is the subject of an elaborate body of legal rules devised for that practice. But this has not ended the search for a deeper explanation of the promisor's power to make a binding promise. Over the centuries a variety of explanations have been earnestly debated. As the first chapter suggested, some explanations focus on the promis*or* and others on the promis*ee*. My own belief is that no single explanation will suffice and that the answer is a complex mix of explanations that focus on both promisor and promisee. The instances in which promises should be enforced are too varied to be shoehorned into the confines of a single rationale.

Older explanations focus on the promisor. At times it was argued that, because of its inherent sanctity, your promise imposes a moral obligation to honor the commitment that it expresses.[8] This view can be criticized on the ground that no legal system makes *all* promises enforceable. The legal enforcement of promises is costly, and the conception of sanctity of promises says little about which promises justify this cost of enforcement. At other times it was argued that your promise was an exercise of your will and that a person's will was in itself worthy of respect: to speak of keeping one's word is to suggest that the word itself has force.[9] This view can be criticized on the ground that there is as much an exercise of will in the case of your resolution, which does not result in a commitment, as in the case of your promise, which does.[10] But promises differ from resolutions (Chapter 1), and I later suggest in connection with promises to make gifts (Chapters 7 and 8) that it is a mistake to lose sight of the importance to *you* of your power to make a binding promise. This power is the basis of what I call the intention principle, under which the intention to be legally bound is a basis for commitment.

More recent explanations focus not on the importance of the power to you as promisor but on its importance to the promisee—on what Papinian called "someone else's disadvantage" (Prologue). The most common explanations rest on disadvantages of two kinds. The first is the promisee's loss of those *expectations* that reasonably arose from the promise. The second is the promisee's loss through *reliance* that was reasonably induced by the promise. Neither of these explanations takes account of the importance that your power to make a commitment may have to *you* as promisor independently of its importance to the promisee.

Because both of these explanations require reasonableness on the part of the promisee, both invite courts to use the objective standard of interpretation described in Chapter 3. A promisee whose expectations are aroused or whose reliance is induced is entitled to judge by outward appearances, and a promisor may therefore be bound to what a reasonable person in the promisee's position would have understood even if it was not what the promisor intended. Although you may not have made up your mind to make a commitment, you may find yourself committed.

When you say "I promise to do thus-and-so," your promise causes the promisee to expect that you will in fact do thus-and-so. Therefore, the first explanation runs, the law should protect that expectation. In 1763, Adam Smith wrote that the "obligation to performance which arises from contract is founded on the reasonable expectation produced by a promise."[11] A promise may also cause the promisee to rely on the promise. Therefore, the second explanation runs, the law should protect that reliance. A contemporary English scholar has written: "Few would today deny that . . . the fact that promises tend to be relied upon, that they positively invite reliance, is one of the chief grounds for the rule that promises should be kept, and that contracts should be legally enforceable."[12] Both explanations have been faulted for circularity.

Words of "prophecy, encouragement or bounty," like those of the Michigan state legislature (Chapter 3), may arouse expectations, but one should know that the law does not protect such expectation. How does a promise differ? Courts do not protect one's actual expectations but rather one's justifiable expectations, and under the objective standard this requires that the expectation be reasonable. How could Enricho reasonably expect the state to perform its promise *unless* he was aware at the outset that the law protects expectations by enforcing promises? Because the reasonableness of one's expectation turns on what one has a legal right to expect, the argument based on expectations assumes what it tries to prove—that the law protects expectation. Differently put, if we assumed a society in which the law gave *no* protection whatsoever to expectations aroused by promises, promisees would simply discount the value of those promises to take account of the greater likelihood of disappointed expectations, just as persons named in wills discount the value of being named. As a writer on wills observed, "It is possible that a system of law might be imagined in which a will was irrevocable, ... but this is not the way that we think or talk about the legal institution of the will."[13] It is circular to base the conclusion that the law *should* protect one's expectation on the premise that the law *does* protect it.[14]

The explanation based on reliance is subject to a similar objection. A mere prediction may induce reliance, but one should know that such reliance is not protected. How does a promise differ? How could Enricho reasonably rely on the state's promise *unless* he was aware at the outset that the law protects reliance by enforcing promises? As a scholar wrote more than a century ago, "It is difficult to say that one is deceived who . . . has seen fit to rely upon a promise which the law in advance notifies him is void."[15] Because the reasonableness of one's reliance turns on whether reliance results in a legal right, the argument based on reliance assumes what it tries to prove—that the law protects reliance. Again, because it is understood that wills are revocable, a person named in a will cannot reasonably rely on being named in a will. It is also circular to base the conclusion that the law *should* protect one's reliance on the premise that it *does* protect it.

These objections have not gained a wide following outside academe. They ignore the certain outcry from those in the workaday world if the value of a promise had to be as deeply discounted as it would if the law did not protect the resulting expectations or reliance. The circularity argument overlooks the possibility that, regardless of legal consequences, a promise may arouse expectations or induce reliance because the promisee supposes that the promisor will be encouraged to perform by extralegal restraints.[16] In the Minnesota case involving a newspaper's confidentiality agreement (Chapter 1), the court first concluded that the parties had not intended the agreement to be legally enforceable as a contract. The court then went on, however, to conclude that the newspaper's source could reasonably have relied on the promises of confidentiality because they "were intended by the promisors to be kept" as a matter of "honor" and of "morality" and as "required by professional ethics."[17] Neither predictions nor wills are subject to comparable extralegal restraints.

There is appeal to an explanation based on the expectations that a promise usually arouses in the promisee. Failure to perform a promise often results in a kind of psychological harm, and there is at least some life to the notion that the promise imposes an obligation on the promisor to prevent that harm by fulfilling the promisee's expectations. It has even been argued that in cases like Enricho's, the "severity of the psychological injury in the form of disappointed expectations is particularly great . . . because of the seriousness of the consequences and the nature of the resources and expertise arrayed against" criminal defendants.[18]

But though a promise may arouse expectations, it is not easy to see why it should result in commitment if the promisee has as yet done nothing in reliance on it. The claim that commitment is justified as a means of avoiding the promisee's psychological harm fails to explain why some promises are unenforceable in the face of disappointed expectations, as is generally true for promises to make gifts (Chapter 8).[19] The claim also fails to explain why other promises are enforceable when there is scant chance of disappointed expectations, as in the case of the lender who takes ample security in the expectation that the borrower's promise will *not* be performed because—as Shylock of Antonio— "his means are in supposition."[20]

Recent decades have witnessed growing support for the view that your power to make a binding promise turns on the reliance it induces, rather than the expectations it arouses, in the promisee.[21] Enricho's claim that the state's promise was enforceable is compelling because of his reliance on that promise, not because of the expectations that it may have aroused. If protection of reliance is not logically inescapable, it is at least practically beyond question. People in the workaday world want to and do rely on promises and have come to view promises as reliable. Legal protection of reliance on them is seen as essential. Hence a *reliance* principle, under which a promise results in a commitment if the promisor should reasonably expect the promisee to rely on it and if such reliance ensues.[22]

Such a principle will not only protect past reliance but will encourage future reliance, and economists inform us that one purpose of enforcing promises is to encourage reliance that takes the form of a party's investment in specific relationships, investment that will make that party better off if the other party performs the contract but worse off if the other party does not.[23] In later chapters I consider whether the emphasis on the reliance principle has occasioned neglect of alternative bases for enforcement (Chapters 7, 8, and 9).

We now turn to the legal rules that govern promises. How do they distinguish between promises that result in commitment and promises that do not? How do they protect reliance in such a way as to encourage reliance in the future? Is actual reliance necessary for commitment? The reader should not be startled if the legal rules seem, at least on the surface, to bear little relation to the preceding discussion of theory.

CHAPTER FIVE

When a Promise Does Commit

Amelia Hopper finds that she has made a commitment to sell land to Peter Mattei for his shopping center. When does a promise have this result? Two traditional legal bases for enforcement: the seal and consideration and their historical origins. The use of the seal as a formality, how its force rested on the intention principle, and how the abolition of its efficacy led to the demise of that principle. The growth of the doctrine of consideration, including recognition of a promise as consideration and development of the "bargain" test. How halfhearted application of the doctrine of consideration has relegated it to a technicality.

When, according to the *law*, does your promise commit you to do what you have promised? Peter Mattei believed that Amelia Hopper's promise had committed her to sell him a piece of land that he wanted for a shopping center. Because Peter worried about not getting enough tenants, he had conditioned his own promise to buy on his agent's obtaining, within 120 days, leases that were "satisfactory" to Peter. When, before the 120 days were up, Amelia changed her mind and refused to sell, Peter, satisfied with the leases, sued her.

Amelia argued that all she had gotten in return for her promise was Peter's illusory promise—which he could have wriggled out of simply by claiming that the leases were not satisfactory to him. According to the law, she insisted, such a promise was not "consideration" for her promise and so her promise did not commit her. The trial judge agreed and entered judgment in Amelia's favor.

Peter appealed, and the Supreme Court of California reversed the judgment, holding that his was not an illusory promise and that there was consideration for her promise after all. Why was it essential that she receive something called "consideration" for her promise? And what was that consideration?

We have seen some reasons why promises should be enforced—why a promisor should not be able to renege at every caprice (Chapter 4). The transition to the *legal bases* for enforcing promises is not a smooth one. A stranger to contract law might well be dismayed by the apparent inconsistency between the rationale for enforcement on the one hand and the legal bases for their enforcement on the other. Until well into this century contract law generally acknowledged only two such bases: the formality of the seal and the doctrine of consideration. At least at first blush, both might seem ill suited to the task of singling out enforceable promises if the power of a promise resides in the reliance it induces in the promisee.

The formality of the seal dates back to medieval times, when a promisor melted wax onto a document that recited the promise, made an impression of the promisor's emblem on the wax, and delivered the document with its wax seal to the promisee. The seal was thus an efficient means for giving legal effect to promises that might otherwise have had at most moral force. The promisee did not have to swap anything for the promise, nor did the promisee have to rely on the promise. The institution of the seal recognized the promisor's interest in being able to make a commitment. The force of the seal resided in the fact that the promisor had chosen to adopt it as a formality. The resulting commitment was based on the intention principle, which recognizes the importance to you of your power to make a commitment and bases that power on your expression of your intention to do so. Because, as we have seen, every promise involves an expression of intention, courts used the formality of the seal to distinguish those promises that were binding under the intention principle from those that were not.

What does it mean to say that the seal was a formality? For our purposes, a formality is a ritual procedure—a ceremonial manner of doing things—involving particular acts or special words that a person can use to produce a desired legal consequence.[1] Rules requiring formalities do not turn on substance, and this gives them a gamelike quality. Form dominated substance in the case of a sealed document representing a debt. Take away the form and the legal consequences were gone: tear off the seal and the debt was discharged, regardless of what was intended. But leave the form and the legal consequences remained: pay the debt without canceling or destroying the sealed document and the debt was not discharged, again regardless of what was intended.[2]

Most legal systems know formalities as a means of distinguishing between transactions that are in some respect effective and transactions that are not. Common ingredients of the prescribed ritual include a writing, an oath, a seal, and witnesses—sometimes with official status. French law traditionally went to remarkable lengths in providing a formality for an effective gift or promise of a gift. "When the Code spoke of authentication before 'notaries' this is what it meant, for *two* notaries were required, and if only one could be found, then two other unlicensed persons must replace the missing notary to serve as witnesses. The donor and normally the donee would also be present. After the terms of the transaction had all been written down, one of the notaries must read the whole document 'aloud' to the group and all were required to sign. The only thing missing was an indication whether the meeting must open and close with prayer."[3] Why should a ritual such as this one or the one involving a seal give legal effect to a transaction?

Scholars have lavished much ink on the functions of legal formalities.[4] For our purposes, two functions are paramount. One is "evidentiary"—the function of providing trustworthy evidence of the existence and terms of the promise in case of controversy. The other is "cautionary"—the function of bringing home to the promisor the significance of promising by encouraging reflection on its consequences—preventing ill-considered decisions by prompting apprehension of future fears. Requiring a formality is therefore an exercise in paternalism, intended to serve the promisor's "own best interests."

In medieval England a wax seal may have performed these functions tolerably well. But in the United States few people owned or used a seal, and the ritual deteriorated to the point that wax was dispensed with and printing houses simply decorated the signature lines of their standard forms with the printed letters "L.S." for *locus sigilli* (place of the seal). Perfunctory invocation of the rules for sealed documents called into question the seal's utility in making promises enforceable. By the early part of the twentieth century state legislatures had largely abolished the seal's efficacy. Whether they were rash in so doing will be left for later. If the cautionary function of the seal showed an undercurrent of paternalism, the abolition of the efficacy of the seal showed a tide and signaled the demise of the intention principle, at least as far as the enforcement of promises was concerned. The legislators who deprived promisors of the power to make binding commitments by following a simple ritual must have concluded that it was no longer in promisors' "own best interests" to have such a power.

The doctrine of consideration, the second basis for enforcing promises, did not evolve until the fifteenth and sixteenth centuries. The doctrine came to require a swap: a promisor had to receive something—often called a quid pro quo—in exchange for the promise. This meant that some promises that might have been regarded as having moral force but were not part of a swap would not commit the promisor unless made under seal.

In describing what had to be swapped for the promise it was common to say that the thing received in exchange for the promise had to be a *detriment* to the *promisee*.[5] If, for example, a homeowner paid you in advance for your promise to repair a house, the payment was an obvious detriment to the homeowner, the promisee. Had anyone been concerned with finding reliance as the basis for enforcing your promise, it would have been easy to find it in the payment by the homeowner—the detriment to the promisee.

But the reliance principle could not explain the full reach of the doctrine of consideration, for the thing swapped for the promise was not always an actual performance, such as the payment of money. Especially in commercial contracts, what was swapped was often a return promise of some performance in the future, such as a promise to pay money, resulting in what is called a bilateral contract. How could a return promise qualify as a detriment to the promisee? After all, the promise made in return for your promise would not be enforceable unless it too was supported by consideration, and that consideration would have to be *your* promise, the very promise whose enforceability is in question. If, for example, we ask whether a homeowner's promise to pay is consideration for your promise to repair a house, we must ask whether the homeowner's promise is a detriment to the homeowner, and it would seem that this would not be so unless that promise were enforceable. But the homeowner's promise to pay would be enforceable only if, by the same reasoning, the builder's promise to build were enforceable, and this reasoning would bring us full circle. Now had anyone been concerned with finding reliance as the basis for enforcing your promise, it would not have been so easy to find it in the mere return promise of the homeowner—a difficulty that I explore in the next chapter.

English judges, however, scarcely blinked a collective eye when, toward the end of the sixteenth century, they leapt from the proposition that a performance could constitute consideration to the proposition that a promise to render that performance could do the same. In the words of a leading legal historian, "What seems remarkable to the modern lawyer is the way in which the doctrine that a promise can count as a good consideration comes into the law in this quiet and unobtrusive way."[6] Once this had happened, the notion of detriment to the promisee became remarkably attenuated.

In its first Restatement of Contracts, the American Law Institute gave the quietus to that notion and sanctified a new concept of consideration. The Restatement required only that what was received in exchange for the promise—the performance or return promise—must have been bargained for by the promisor.[7] Under this "bargain" test, a promise merely had to be swapped for its consideration. If promises are enforceable because of the expectations they raise, there is some sense in the bargain test, for bargaining tends to raise expectations.

Although most courts now espouse the Restatement's bargain test, the change has produced scarcely a ripple outside of academe. Since your objective in making a promise is usually to swap it for something from the promisee, the bargain test is usually satisfied without serious question. And since you do not usually need to bargain for something unless it is a detriment to the promisee, if the new test of bargain is satisfied, so usually is the old one of detriment.[8] Although it has become fashionable to style the bargain test as a "bargain theory," this seems an unwarranted elevation of what is ostensibly merely a test. Substituting the requirement of bargain for that of benefit or detriment was just another step in the historical process of attempting to describe those promises that courts enforce. Proponents of the test would have been startled to hear it called a theory.

Legislative abolition of the efficacy of the seal enhanced the importance of the judicially shaped doctrine of consideration, which then reigned as the sole survivor of the two traditional bases for enforcing promises. The requirement of consideration had already been subjected to attack on the ground that it unjustly limits the class of enforceable promises. Back in the eighteenth century, the great English judge Lord Mansfield had unsuccessfully attempted to dispense with the requirement by advancing the heresy that the "ancient notion about the want of consideration was for the sake of evidence only: for when it is reduced into writing . . . there was no objection to the want of consideration."[9] When the seal was deprived of its effect, these attacks might have been expected to gain momentum. Statutes were enacted in a few states to give twentieth-century currency to Mansfield's eighteenth-century proposal by making a signed writing "presumptive evidence of consideration," but the demise of the intention principle occasioned no mourning and evoked no sentiment in favor of some other formality.[10]

During the twentieth century the attitude of the American legal establishment toward formalities was ambivalent. Judges generally favored substance over form, for example, invoking the concept of reliance as a means of undercutting the writing requirement of the statute of frauds. Legislators, however, were favorably disposed toward formalities, imposing a requirement of a writing for a variety of kinds of contracts, ranging from contracts between couples living together to those between physicians and their patients.[11] But unlike the seal, which provided a threshold test for enforceability, these twentieth-century formalities are cumulative requirements, piled onto the substantive requirements for enforceability to protect defendants from suspect claims. Nowhere has there been sustained pressure to find a formality that would substitute for the seal as a basis for enforcing promises. As we will see, the situation has been different in areas not involving promises but where the seal also played an important role (Chapters 13 and 15).

The lack of pressure to find a substitute for the seal can be ascribed in good part to an attenuated doctrine of consideration, stretched to its limits as the result of a disinterested judicial attitude toward its demands—except, as we shall see, where promises to make gifts are concerned. Despite scholarly fascination with the "bargain theory," the requirement of a bargained-for exchange never assumed great practical significance in commercial life. Judges have rarely displayed much enthusiasm for such rigors as might have been imposed by the requirement of a bargain. Commercial cases almost invariably involve swaps that meet the bargain test, and in such cases the typical judicial attitude ranges from complacency to apathy. Amid the multitude of cases reciting bromides about the doctrine of consideration, in only a handful does the doctrine have any bite. An instance in which the doctrine has been applied with such zeal as to give the doctrine a bad name will be treated later, but this instance involves relinquishments, which are not our present concern (Chapter 15). Judges are less likely to see the doctrine of consideration as a bar to the enforceability of promises than as a hurdle to be overcome or circumvented and have shied away from monitoring agreements by ingenious application of the doctrine. Here are two, one involving the *substance* of the agreement and the other the *process* by which it was reached.

Courts have long declined to invoke the doctrine of consideration in order to monitor the substance of the agreement, inspiring the hyperbole that even a peppercorn can be consideration. "A cent or a pepper corn," said the Supreme Judicial Court of Maine early in the nineteenth century, "would constitute a valuable consideration."[12] This engorged theory of consideration fits well with the Restatement's bargain test: even a peppercorn, if you bargain for it, will suffice to make your promise enforceable. Although many courts continued to mouth the requirement that there must be a detriment to the promisee, there was little substance left in the requirement. The notion of reliance had become so attenuated as to be scarcely recognizable.

And if a peppercorn will suffice, so will a promise of a peppercorn: even a relatively insignificant promise on one side will support a much more substantial promise on the other. So the notion of reliance had become doubly attenuated—first by tolerating a mere peppercorn as sufficient detriment, and second by tolerating a mere promise as sufficient detriment.

What, then, if your promise appears to commit you to perform but leaves performance to your sole discretion? While courts once condemned such promises as illusory and therefore unfit to support a return promise, courts today tend through inference to flesh out the promise so that it can serve as consideration. In a leading New York case, for example, Lady Duff-Gordon, an English fashion designer, promised Otis Wood the exclusive right to market clothes bearing her label in return for his promise of a percentage on what, if anything, she sold.[13] She argued that because his promise contained no undertaking to sell anything, it was illusory and could not support her promise of an exclusive right. But New York's highest court, in a landmark opinion by its most illustrious member, Judge Benjamin Nathan Cardozo, avoided striking down for lack of consideration what appeared to be a serious bargain. After examining the nature of the transaction the court imposed on Wood an "implied" undertaking to devote "reasonable efforts" to selling clothes with her label, and this was consideration for her promise.

In Peter Mattei's case the court achieved a similar result by fleshing out an undertaking instead of adding one. The Supreme Court of California rejected Amelia's contention on the ground that what was meant was dissatisfaction with the leases and not the contract. Peter's dissatisfaction would at least have to be in good faith—honest even if not reasonable; he could not wriggle out of doing anything simply by *dishonestly* claiming that he was not satisfied with the leases. Peter's promise was therefore not illusory and was consideration for Amelia's return promise.[14]

How would the doctrine of consideration apply to Enricho's case if it were argued that the state's promise was illusory because it was conditioned on the prosecutor's satisfaction with Enricho's cooperation? Faced with this question, a federal Court of Appeals analogized to the reasoning in Peter Mattei's case and concluded that even if satisfaction with the cooperation of the accused was left "to the sole discretion of the prosecutor, that discretion is limited by the requirement that it be exercised fairly and in good faith."[15] The state's promise would thus not be illusory, and unenforceable. But might not Enricho's promise be illusory, and so not consideration for the state's promise, because he could surely have avoided his duty to plead guilty had he chosen to do so? Curiously, no court seems to have advanced this reasoning. Perhaps there is an analogy to the promise of a minor, which can serve as consideration for a return promise even though the minor can avoid it simply by disaffirming it after coming of age.[16] Such promises are dubbed voidable rather than merely void. The disinclination of courts to monitor the substance of agreements in the name of consideration supports the conclusion that neither promise is illusory.

In recent years courts have also shown a disinclination to monitor, in the name of consideration, the process by which the agreement was reached. Take, for example, the cases involving at-will employment. It is generally accepted throughout the United States that, unless the parties otherwise agree, both employer and employee are free to terminate the employment at will, with the result that the promises of both are illusory. Nevertheless, an employer's promise of employee rights made to the employee at the moment of hiring is supported by consideration—the employee's actually beginning to work. And an employee's promise not to compete made to the employer at the moment of hiring is supported by consideration—the employer's actually allowing the employee to begin work.

If, however, such a promise by either employer or employee is not made until after employment has begun, the bargain test of consideration is not often met. Mere continuation of employment, by either employer or employee, is not consideration unless bargained for, and rarely is there the slightest suggestion of any bargaining. The employer's promise is commonly made by the routine distribution of a handbook to all employees, and the employee's promise by the routine signing of a printed form prepared by the employer.

Nonetheless, many courts have concluded, with only superficial attention to the requirement of bargain, that such promises are enforceable. As the Supreme Court of Tennessee observed in a case involving employees' covenants not to compete, the argument that there is no consideration because there is no bargain "threatens to vitiate any agreement between an employee already working and his or her employer." It concluded that "because of the length of employment of each [employee], the covenant is binding against them."[17]

This judicial disinclination to monitor agreements for either substance or process prompted Justice Oliver Wendell Holmes to suggest that "consideration is as much a form as a seal."[18] This suggestion misconceives either the nature of the doctrine or the nature of a formality. The doctrine of consideration provides no ritual that can be invoked at will by a promisor who desires to make a binding commitment. A promisor could make a binding commitment in the days of the seal by going through the convenient ritual of affixing a seal, but a promisor cannot make a binding commitment today by going through the motions of a sham bargain.

Halfhearted application of the doctrine of consideration has often made it seem a technicality if not a formality. If the cost of enforcing promises justifies limiting enforcement to those promises that have some socially useful purpose, it is difficult to see how a technicality that can be met with a peppercorn accomplishes this purpose. At least as far as swaps are concerned, promises made with a serious intention to be legally bound generally turn out in practice to be supported by consideration. To this extent, recognition of an intent principle as an alternative to the doctrine of consideration would have scant effect. Paternalism plays no role here. Rare is the transaction in which there lingers the slightest doubt that the requirement of consideration is met, and even rarer the transaction in which, with a little good legal advice, any lingering doubt cannot be dispelled. As we shall see, the main exceptions to these generalizations are promises to make gifts, for it is these that the doctrine marks off for unenforceability. It is these promises that have been most affected by the abolition of the efficacy of the seal.[19]

Before turning to promises to make gifts we take up another instance in which it has been suggested that courts have shown excessive tolerance in finding consideration—an instance that appears to present a conflict between the traditional legal bases for enforcing your promise and the rationale for doing so discussed in the preceding chapter.

CHAPTER SIX

A Surrogate for an Enigma

Why should the promisee's mere return promise, with no reliance, suffice to commit the promisor? W. O. Lucy's promise to buy a farm commits the Zehmers to sell it. Eileen O'Connell's promise to take David Quick in marriage commits her to take him. The enigma of the unperformed bilateral agreement. The explanation that expectation should be protected in order to protect reliance, treating assent as a surrogate for reliance under an assent rule. Criticisms and defenses of this explanation. The suspicion that a principle other than the reliance principle is at work. Three other examples of assent rules: contract repudiation, contract beneficiaries, and in good faith purchase.

Why should your promise commit you if the promisee has done no more than make a return promise, without relying on your promise? Suppose that Enricho Navarroli promised only to plead guilty, not to cooperate as an undercover agent, and that the state reneged right after the exchange of promises, before Enricho had done anything in reliance. If contract law applied, the state would be bound as soon as the parties swapped promises, but the Supreme Court of the United States has held that the state would not be bound unless Enricho performed his promise by pleading guilty.[1] Does this holding conflict with the general principles that underlie the accepted rules of contract law?

Under contract law a mere exchange of promises—without any reliance—is enough to bind both parties. But what underlies this bright-line rule? If the power of a promise to bind the promisor is seen as based on the expectations that it induces in the promisee, the rule makes sense enough. But if reliance is the touchstone of commitment, it is odd that contract doctrine should stubbornly cling to the notion that a promisee's mere assent suffices to bind the promisor. Most

people would agree that an exchange of promises should result in commitment: a deal, after all, "is a deal," relied on
or not. But why should a party that has done nothing whatsoever in reliance on the other party's promise—performing,
preparing to perform, or even forgoing other opportunities—
be entitled to enforce that promise?[2]

Most commercial agreements are bilateral, involving
swaps of reciprocal promises, and this question of the enforceability of the unperformed bilateral agreement is one
of the law's perplexing enigmas. Consider two cases from
opposite ends of the world, the first a contracts case and the
second not.

The contracts case arose in Virginia when W. O. Lucy
went to a restaurant owned by A. H. and Ida Zehmer, hoping
to buy their farm. After talking and drinking, they exchanged
promises. The Zehmers signed a restaurant check on the
back, where A. H. had written: "We hereby agree to sell to
W. O. Lucy the Ferguson Farm complete for $50,000, title sat-
isfactory to buyer," but as soon as W. O. put it in his pocket
and offered A. H. $5 to seal the bargain, A. H. protested,
"I don't want to sell the farm." Had A. H. reneged in time?
W. O. went to court to find out, and the Supreme Court of Virginia held that the answer was no: the Zehmers were already
bound by their promise, even though there was no possibility that W. O. had relied on it in the few seconds between
the exchange of promises and A. H.'s protestation.[3] But why?

The other case arose in Australia. Eileen O'Connell
and David Quick, fellow employees, were—coincidentally—
drinking in a hotel and discussing the institution of marriage. David suggested that they get married, Eileen agreed
and collected her things, and they got a license and found
a clergyman, who began the marriage ceremony. Eileen and
David exchanged promises, repeating the marriage vow, but
as soon as the ring reached Eileen's knuckle, she threw it on
the ground, protesting "I will not marry you," and ran out.

Had Eileen reneged in time? Four years later David went to court to find out, and the Supreme Court of Victoria held that the answer was no: Eileen was already bound by her promise, though there was no possibility that David had relied on it in the few seconds between the exchange of promises and Eileen's protestation.[4] But why?

We have already seen that English judges did not ask "why" when, beginning in the sixteenth century, they shaped the doctrine of consideration (Chapter 5). The exchange of promises became an important mechanism for allocating risks between parties whose attitudes toward or estimates of those risks differed, as well as for protecting reliance by a party who would otherwise have been reluctant to act. There was scant reason to rethink what judges had decided in the sixteenth century, since the enforcement of unperformed bilateral contracts, even if wholly unperformed, has long accorded with the average person's sense of justice.[5] But when academics began to suspect that reliance might be the true basis for enforcing promises, *they* began to ask why, a question that has had an enduring fascination.

For me, the most satisfying answer is still the one proposed by Lon Fuller more than fifty years ago: "To encourage reliance we must . . . dispense with its proof."[6] Promising is an important activity because a promise affords the promisee a basis for planning. But a promise will be of little use as a basis for planning unless it can be relied upon, and protecting a promisee's expectation is the most effective way of protecting a promisee's reliance. Although the law could protect reliance by enforcing promises only if the promisee proved reliance, reliance is difficult to prove, and promisees might hesitate to rely on promises out of fear that the burden of proving reliance would complicate or prevent enforcement. Some promisees might even feign or engage in wasteful reliance with a view to making legal sanctions available.

Difficulties of proof become acute when a party's reliance is negative—consisting not in doing something but

rather in refraining from doing something.[7] W. O. might rely
on A. H. and Ida's promise by refraining from arranging to
buy another farm. David might rely on Eileen's promise by
refraining from arranging to marry another person. Economists call these opportunity costs. In Robert Frost's imagery,

> Two roads diverged in a yellow wood,
> And sorry I could not travel both
> And be one traveler, long I stood . . .[8]

Frost concluded that his choice "has made all the difference." But how could one know? Such negative reliance is
hard to prove. In addition, we are told that it produces regret that is particularly acute. "The road not taken causes far
more suffering than a wrong turn."[9]

Thus, the argument runs, a promisee should not be asked
to produce proof of negative reliance—of the road not taken.
It is enough that W. O. *may* have had opportunities to buy
other farms and David *may* have had opportunities to find
other wives. And so A. H. and Ida were committed though
they reneged before W. O. could possibly have passed up
any opportunity to buy another farm, and Eileen was committed though she reneged before David could have passed
up any opportunity to find another wife. Better to favor the
few who have not relied than to vex the many who have relied but will have trouble proving it. A bright-line rule based
on assent, it turns out, both protects expectation and at least
covertly recognizes reliance.

In our system of contract law, attuned as it is to the availability of substitutes on a market, the kind of negative reliance commonly envisioned is refraining from arranging for
a similar substitute on a market.[10] In such cases economists
view the enforcement of contracts as desirable because it en-
ables parties to shift market risks. Contract law characteristically assumes that at the time a contract is made, a promisee
has access to a similar substitute on a market, just as it assumes—as will emerge in Chapter 11—that on breach an ag-

grieved promisee has access to such a substitute on a market.

Negative reliance does not necessarily involve a similar substitute. One might, for example, claim to have passed up an opportunity to further one's education in reliance on a promise of a profitable business opportunity. But arguments based on such claims are generally more speculative and therefore less appealing than those involving a similar substitute. To put it differently, though proof of lost opportunities is always difficult to produce, the strength of a promisee's claim based on unproven lost opportunities turns in good measure on the plausibility of the assertion that the promisee would have found and seized some supposed opportunity. Seldom is the plausibility as great as in the case of a similar substitute. Would Frost's assertion that his choice "has made all the difference" have been as convincing had he lost the opportunity to stop and go fishing rather than to take a similar road?

This reasoning leads to the conclusion that the claims of reliance that should be accepted without proof are those that are hard to prove because negative and that are plausible because based on the on the availability of similar substitutes. Choosing the moment of assent produces a bright-line rule that binds the promisor at the earliest moment that the promisee could possibly have a claim based on such reliance. Reliance before assent would not be justifiable.[11]

It can be argued that a promisor should have a chance to rebut the presumption of reliance by proving that the promisee had not relied before the promisor reneged.[12] Perhaps the promisor can show that there was no opportunity to be lost—that there was no other road to take. If a close friend promises a smoker $1,000 in return for the smoker's promise to give up smoking, the friend may be able to show that the smoker lost no opportunities because the smoker had none to lose—no one else would have made such a contract with the smoker.[13] Or perhaps the promisor can show that in fact no opportunity was lost—that though there were two roads both could have been taken. If the owner of a building has promised a neophyte builder $100,000 in return for the builder's promise to renovate the building, the owner may be able to show that the builder lost no opportunities because the builder would have snapped up all available opportunities to enlarge its struggling business.[14]

A federal appeals court seems implicitly to have accepted such reasoning in holding that a buyer cannot recover for a product's failure to live up to the seller's claims if there was no alternative product available that would have done so—no similar substitute available. Suppose, the court hypothesized, that a seller "represents to a man who is beginning to go bald that use of the [seller's] product will prevent the loss of his hair." If the balding man contracts to buy the product but the seller fails to deliver it, would the seller be liable for the loss of the balding man's hair?[15] No, answered the court, if, "as appears to be the case, nothing will reverse or prevent baldness." The logical rationale for this "alternative product" doctrine is that if no alternative product was available, then there was no lost opportunity to obtain a similar substitute, and so no reliance of the kind commonly envisioned as present but unprovable.

Other courts, however, have been reluctant to fashion rules enabling a party to rebut a presumption of reliance.[16] Negative proofs are hard to make, and the difficulties that courts would face in administering such rules make them unappealing. On the whole, it is easier for a court to determine whether there has been assent than to determine whether there has been reliance—or the absence of reliance. A bright-line rule based on assent also helps the parties to know where they stand: W. O. to know whether to look for another farm and David to know whether to look for another wife. Perhaps something is to be learned from the metaphor of the game, where bright-line rules without exceptions allow players to go on with a minimum of controversy and delay. Three strikes and you're out, regardless of the peculiarities of batter or pitcher. So, too, there is good reason for a rule based on assent that brooks no exception.

If one comes to the enigma of the wholly unperformed and otherwise unrelied-on bilateral agreement with the conviction that the enforceability of promises should be based on reliance rather than assent, assent then acts as a surrogate for reliance under traditional contract law, taking the place of reliance. This surrogacy is the basis of an *assent* rule that is, as we have seen, justified by the practical advantages of a rule based on assent over one based on reliance. This does not mean that reliance should never be protected in the absence of assent, for we shall see later that this is not so. It means only that there is justification for a rule under which assent acts as a surrogate for reliance and protects unprovable reliance.

This reasoning also provides an explanation for the hypothetical case of Enricho Navarroli and the wholly unperformed plea bargain, for when he made his bargain with the state there was no similar substitute for the state's promise. He could not have lost an opportunity to negotiate with another prosecutor, there being no other. He would therefore have to prove even negative reliance if it was not a similar substitute for the state's promise. What chance would he have of proving, for example, that he relied on the state's promise by not hiring a more high-powered lawyer? [17] Because plea bargains can be clearly marked off from other agreements, enforceability of the state's promise cannot be justified by the difficulty of drawing lines along the continuum of contract disputes. To recur to the metaphor of the game, Enricho was not playing the game of contracts but a different game, that of plea bargains. And since unprovable reliance in the form of the loss of a similar substitute is not likely in that game, there is no reason to apply the accepted rule of contract law that unperformed bilateral agreements are enforceable. Unlike David's situation, which was analogous to W. O.'s, Enricho's situation in the hypothetical case of the wholly unperformed plea bargain is distinguishable, and the analogy does not hold.

It should not be supposed that assent is a formality under the assent rule, for it is not merely part of a ritual but an element in a substantive rule as a substitute for another element, that of reliance. This can be seen from the willingness of courts to spell out assent from facts where assent is not explicit—a willingness that would be inappropriate if assent were merely part of a ritual.

The rationale that assent is a surrogate for reliance in connection with the enforcement of promises gains some support from the use of assent as a surrogate in other connections. Here are three other instances of assent as a surrogate for reliance. Two, involving repudiations and contract beneficiaries, come from contract law, and one, involving "value" in good faith purchase, comes from personal property law.[18]

First, assent serves as a surrogate for reliance in determining when it is too late to retract a repudiation. Suppose that before the time for performance you repudiate the contract by refusing to perform and then change your mind and seek to retract the repudiation. Is it too late to do this?

Fairness dictates that, once the other party has changed position in reliance on your repudiation, it is too late for you to nullify it, and it is generally held that the other party's assent has the same effect.[19] The Restatement (Second) of Contracts explains that though it is the aggrieved party's material change of position in reliance on the repudiation that makes it unjust for the repudiating party to retract the repudiation, "it is undesirable to make the injured party's rights turn exclusively on such a vague criterion," and in the interest of certainty that party "may therefore prevent subsequent nullification by indicating to the other party that he considers the repudiation final."[20]

Here an assent rule is harder to justify than in the case of the unperformed bilateral contract. Reliance on a repudiation might be negative, as by failing to get ready to perform the contract, but is more likely to be affirmative, as by arranging for a substitute contract or eliminating the need for any contract. In any event, it will not consist of forbearance from arranging a substitute and will not be so difficult to prove as when lost opportunities are involved. Perhaps a claim of reliance that is not negative and so is too weak to suffice in creating a right in the first place can nonetheless suffice to bar retraction of a repudiation. Similar difficulty in justifying a bright-line rule arises when an offeree rejects an offer and then seeks to accept (Chapter 18) and when a party with a power to avoid a contract has made a statement of disaffirmance and then seeks to affirm (Chapter 19).

Second, assent acts as a surrogate for reliance in determining when a beneficiary's rights are vested. Return to the case of Marion, Nettie, and Albert (Chapter 3), and suppose that Nettie had lived on for several more months and, angered at Marion's failure to visit her, made a new agreement with Albert under which he would leave the promised sum to a favorite nephew instead of Marion. Would this new agreement have cut off Marion's right to enforce Albert's earlier promise?

Fairness dictates that, once Marion has changed position in reliance on Albert's earlier promise, it is too late for Nettie and Albert to nullify it, and the Restatement (Second) of Contracts adds that Marion's assent has the same effect.[21] The commentary explains that this twist rests "on the probability that the beneficiary will rely in ways difficult or impossible to prove."[22] The Reporter elaborated on this during the discussion on the floor of the American Law Institute, stating that the addition of assent was "justified on the ground that there is a possibility—and, indeed, in many of these situations, a very high probability—of reliance at that point, and often the reliance will take the form of a failure to act, a failure to make other arrangements," the sort of negative reliance that is particularly difficult to prove.[23] The Institute viewed assent as a surrogate for reliance.

Here, as in the case of the repudiation, the justification

for an assent rule is less compelling than in the case of the unperformed bilateral contract. Had Marion been a creditor rather than a donee beneficiary (had Nettie owed Marion a debt), it would be easy to suppose that, as the Reporter suggested, when Marion found that Albert had promised to pay Nettie's debt, the "inevitable consequence" would be that Marion would "relax [her] efforts to collect" from Nettie—a similar substitute for collecting from Albert.[24] But Marion was a donee beneficiary, and her reliance seems less plausible since she could have accommodated any number of prospective donors, and no other donor's gift would have been in any sense a substitute for Nettie's gift, a point to which I return in Chapter 13. If Marion claimed to have given up a dissimilar substitute, such as finding work to earn a comparable sum, this claim would be less plausible, and if she claimed to have taken positive steps in reliance on Albert's promise, she could more easily prove those. Perhaps a claim of reliance that though negative is not plausible, and so is too weak to suffice in creating a right in the first place, can nonetheless suffice in turning an existing but vulnerable right into a vested one.[25]

Assent rules are not confined to contract law. Consider as a third example one from personal property law. Ordinarily a buyer of personal property—say a watch—gets only the rights to the property that the seller had. Thus even an innocent buyer of a watch from a seller who has obtained it from its owner by *theft* gets no more than the thief had. If, however, the seller has obtained the watch by *fraud,* the innocent buyer does get more than the seller had. The defrauded owner, by giving possession to the seller, is to some extent responsible for clothing the seller with the appearance of ownership. A doctrine sometimes known as that of ostensible ownership protects a buyer who has relied on this appearance by paying for the watch. The buyer, who is said to have given "value," can keep the watch.[26]

But suppose that the watch is not bought but is taken by one of the perpetrator's creditors as security for a debt?

Statutory law makes it clear that the creditor has given value and therefore stands in as good a position as the buyer.[27] The creditor might have relied on the appearance of ownership if the security of the watch induced the creditor to forbear from enforcing the debt.[28] But the rule is an assent rule that does not require that the creditor show actual reliance: the mere possibility of such negative reliance suffices. Here the plausibility of the claim of such reliance is enhanced by the specificity of the opportunity asserted to have been lost—the opportunity to enforce the perpetrator's debt. Once again, assent acts as a surrogate.[29]

Despite these analogous assent rules, a skeptical reader may be tempted to ask whether the justification for the use of assent as a surrogate is not sometimes too tenuous to be taken seriously where the enforceability of promises is in issue. One might balk at the conclusion that, since a peppercorn can suffice as consideration, a lost opportunity for a suitable substitute for a peppercorn will also suffice. If, in return for the Zehmers' promise to sell their farm, W. O. had promised only a peppercorn, would a skeptical reader be convinced by the argument that when W. O. made his contract with the Zehmers that he had passed up the opportunity to buy another farm for his peppercorn? Yet under the attenuated doctrine of consideration, the Zehmers' promise would still have been enforceable regardless of how tenuous W. O.'s claim to possible reliance.

Surely there is reason to ask whether this attenuated doctrine of consideration, supported by the reliance principle and its corollary, the assent rule, provides a rational basis for the entire universe of enforceable promises. So we now look for other principles on which enforceability might be based. In the next two chapters, I consider this question in connection with promises to make gifts.

CHAPTER SEVEN

Wanting to Make a Commitment (Reprise)

Mary Yates Johnson pledges to make a gift of $5,000 to Allegheny College. Why you might decide to make such a gift. Why you might want to defer making it and, if so, why you might want to commit yourself to make it. An undercurrent of paternalism in the unenforceability of promises to make gifts. A questionable justification based on the difficulty providing for regret. How the doctrine of consideration was stretched so that Mary Yates Johnson was committed.

Earlier I asked why you would want to make a commitment—to put your will in chains for the future. The answer then was *self-interest:* to get what you want from someone else as part of a swap. But that is not always the answer. Consider the case of Mary Yates Johnson, who in 1921 decided to give $5,000 to Allegheny College's fund drive and then signed a "pledge" in which she promised to give the money at a later time.[1] Why would one promise to make a gift? Before asking why one makes such a promise, it may be well to ask why one makes a gift. Is it pure altruism—an unselfish regard for the interests of others?

Altruism unalloyed, as in the classic case of the saintly person who gives a fortune to a beggar, is a rare if praiseworthy commodity.[2] Saint Anthony, we are told, "was twenty years old when he heard these words of Jesus read in the church: 'If thou wilt be perfect, go sell what thou hast, and give to the poor!' At once Anthony sold all his goods, gave the profit to the poor, and went off to the desert to become a hermit."[3] Today, however, most significant gifts are made either to someone in one's family or circle of friends or to a charity. Those who make them are not motivated solely or even primarily by altruism.

According to fundraisers for higher education, "The most promising models of donor behavior favor exchange over pure altruism: They say donors are motivated by receiving 'goods' in exchange for gifts, and a repeated disequilibrium leaves donors with a need to respond to recognition and acknowledgement with even more gifts."[4] To say that one asks for nothing in return is not to say that one *expects* nothing in return. Thus when real estate developer Samuel LeFrak promised to give $10 million to the Guggenheim Museum in New York City, he said that he made the promise "with no strings attached"—that he asked for nothing in return. But it was understood that he expected to see his name on the outside of the museum's rotunda, and it surely came as no surprise when he was reported to be rethinking his decision after the New York City Landmarks Preservation Commission refused to approve this form of recognition.[5]

Such an expectation of an enhanced reputation is only one of many reasons for making a gift.[6] One might expect to gain tax advantages, as when one gives to a college with the understanding this will reduce one's liability to the Internal Revenue Service.[7] One might expect better treatment in the hereafter, as when one gives to a favorite relative out of fear that death is near. One might expect the respect—even admiration—of one's peers, as when one decides to give to one's law school in response to a classmate's entreaties.[8] One might expect an indirect benefit, as when one gives to the botanical garden, in the expectation that it will be a more agreeable place to visit. One might expect love and affection, as when one gives to one's intended with an anticipation that one's intended will show suitable gratitude. A decision to give often results from a complex mixture of these and other motives sometimes difficult to identify.[9] But though one may get something in return for one's gift, one does not get it as the result of a swap. Though there is exchange, there is no bargain.

Whatever reasons Mary had for her initial decision to give $5,000 to Allegheny College, hers was not a decision to make a present gift. Why defer the gift?[10] Perhaps she did not have $5,000. Perhaps she had $5,000 tied up in collectibles. Perhaps she could get a tax advantage by deferring the transfer of the $5,000. Perhaps she thought that she could earn a higher rate of return on the $5,000 than the college could. Perhaps she was unsure of her initial decision to give $5,000 and hoped to keep her options open. Whatever the explanation, the $5,000 was not to be paid until thirty days after her death.

Our first question remains: Why would Mary have made such a *promise?* If she wanted to make a deferred rather than a present gift, why not simply tell the college that she had made a firm but nonbinding *resolution* to make a gift of $5,000? A resolution would afford the college some basis for planning and yet would make it plain that Mary was free to change her mind. Indeed, in 1924 Mary did change her mind and notified the college that she was reneging on her promise.

After Mary's death the college sued her estate on her promise. The *Allegheny College* case, as it came to be known, culminated in an opinion by Judge Benjamin Nathan Cardozo, writing for New York's highest court. The estate was represented by Robert Jackson, later a member of the Supreme Court of the United States, who argued that Mary's pledge was no more binding than a resolution—"a pledge only in the evangelical sense of an unctuous and ceremonial, but unenforceable resolve in the present to do good in the future."[11] But her pledge was not a mere resolution, like the pledge of the California political candidate (Chapter 1). It was an expression of commitment to *another* who was in a position to enforce that commitment—it was a promise to Allegheny College.

Nevertheless, the common law long treated promises to make gifts as no more binding than resolutions. Since nothing is swapped for such a promise, it is not supported by consideration and is therefore, as common law judges saw it, not enforceable.[12] At one time a promisor could make the promise enforceable by the use of a seal, but the effect of the seal had been abolished in New York long before Mary's pledge.[13] Promises to make gifts were sometimes described as "sterile" to suggest the insignificance of their role in commercial life.[14] The role of such promises in contemporary society, however, is anything but insignificant, as any museum, university, or religion will attest.[15]

Granted, the reasons for enforcing a promise are less compelling when the promise is not part of a swap. Consider first the interest of the promisee. When you swap your promise, the promisee may rely on it by losing opportunities for similar substitutes, but this is not so when your promise is not part of a swap. In the *Allegheny College* case, Cardozo hypothesized that if A promises B a gift, B may have "renounced other opportunities for betterment in the faith that the promise will be kept."[16] It is unlikely, however, that the college lost any opportunity to obtain a similar substitute from another donor. It would surely have seized all other opportunities, for there was no practical limit to the number of donors whose names it could perpetuate. As long as the college did not have to give anything in return for Mary's promise, its assent to the promise did not cost it the opportunity to receive any other gift.[17] Perhaps the college, by its delay in reliance on Mary's promise, lost the opportunity to use its limited funds for a more modest project, but this is not the loss of a similar substitute. Although it might be supposed that during the three years before Mary reneged the college had relied on her promise in some affirmative way that would have been more easily demonstrable, the college treasurer stated at the trial, "We could not establish the fund and have students coming expecting to receive from it until we had it."[18]

But now consider the interest of the *promisor*. Perhaps your worth in the eyes of others or in your own eyes would not suffer greatly if you could not commit yourself by promising to make a gift. You could still commit yourself by swapping promises. But why should it be true, as Robert Jackson argued, that the "whole aspect of the transaction forbids any conclusion that [Mary Yates Johnson] intended to assume a legal obligation by the agreement in suit"?[19] There are some compelling reasons why Mary might have wanted to commit herself by promising to make a gift.

Look back to the time that she made the promise. To the extent that she was motivated by altruism, she had an interest in maximizing the benefit to the college.[20] Had she actually made a gift by handing over $5,000, that gift, being complete and irrevocable, would have been worth its face value of $5,000 to the college. Even if she had made a legally binding promise the college would have had to discount it some to take account of the difficulty of enforcement should she renege. But it would have had to discount a nonbinding resolution even more deeply because of the greater likelihood that she would renege and because of the impossibility of enforcement.[21] In two situations she might have been particularly eager to commit herself in order to dispel the college's uncertainty.

First, if there was a significant chance that the college would mistrust her resolution as not representing an actual decision to make the gift, she might have wished to dispel that misapprehension and enhance the value of the prospect of her gift by committing herself.[22] Had Allegheny College regarded Mary as untrustworthy, she might have wanted to make a binding promise to make a gift rather than a nonbinding resolution.

Second, if there was a significant chance that the college would overestimate the likelihood that she would change her mind, she might have wished to dispel the misapprehension. Had Allegheny College considered Mary excessively capricious, she might have preferred a binding promise to make a gift rather than a nonbinding resolution. Because, as a matter of law, the promisor's death has the same effect as a capricious revocation, the promisor's death may be of no less concern to the promisee than the promisor's caprice. Litigation over promises to make gifts frequently arises following the promisor's death, when a rule that denies effect to the promise favors not the promisor but those who will share in the promisor's estate. Because the executor or administrator of the decedent's estate has a fiduciary obligation to resist questionable claims on their behalf, extralegal sanctions have no effect. Thus the promisor may be particularly eager to dispel the promisee's uncertainty in the event of death.

Just as there are reasons why you might want to be bound by a promise that is exchanged in a swap, there are reasons why you might want to be bound by a promise that is not. If you have such an interest in being able to commit yourself to make gifts, why should the law deny you that power? Should there be no way for a person who has a serious and considered desire to make an enforceable promise to make a gift that will satisfy that desire? Should there be no alternative to the reliance principle and its corollary, the assent rule?

It is difficult to suppress the suspicion that there is an undercurrent of paternalism here. Would having the power to commit yourself to make a gift be in your "own best interests"? If you had the power, what would limit your profligacy? Could you not commit yourself to give everything that you would acquire during the rest of your life? It may be remembered that a profligate Fyodor Dostoevsky once gambled nine years of his future output on his ability to write a novel of at least 160 pages by a deadline only several months away.[23] More than a century ago the philosopher John Stuart Mill explained his one exception to his prohibition against paternalism—selling oneself into slavery—on the ground that "by selling himself for a slave, [a person] abdicates his liberty; he forgoes any future use of it beyond that single act," thereby defeating the "very purpose which is the justification of allowing him to dispose of himself."[24] So, in the case of your promise, it might be argued that such a profligate exercise of the power to commit yourself would leave you with no future use of that power, defeating the very purpose of allowing you the power in the first place.

A variant of this argument is the basis of an attempt to rationalize the traditional rule that denies you that power. Promises that are part of swaps are significantly different from promises that are not, the argument runs, because it is much less common to qualify the latter to take account of regret.[25] Where promises are exchanged, there is often a bargaining process during which past regrets fuel our apprehension of future fears and promisors naturally consider qualifying their promises by, for example, retaining a power to terminate on the occurrence of stated events that may cause regret. But where there is no exchange, it is argued, there is no comparable bargaining process during which promisors are likely to qualify their promises to take account of regret. If such unqualified promises were binding, parties might even be discouraged from making them.[26] Paternalism, therefore, counsels that promises to make gifts should be denied enforcement.

But this difference between promises that are exchanged in swaps and those that are not is questionable.[27] It is reported that entrepreneurs often drive hard bargains when they make gifts and that donors increasingly attach strings to gifts to higher education.[28] As one fundraiser put it, "You want to feel your gift has impact, and know how it will be used in fairly exacting detail."[29] And the assumption that bargaining generally accompanies exchange ignores the prevalence of adhesion contracts, where in most exchanges there is no bargaining whatsoever over conditions. Finally, even if a difference exists, courts could reduce its impact by creating implied qualifications for promises in cases of gifts just as they have done in other cases. In any event, the argument proves too much because, as we will see, the law now recognizes that promises to make gifts are binding in some exceptional situations, and in these situations, questions of qualifications cannot be avoided.

But before we look at those exceptional situations, let us return to the *Allegheny College* case. In treating Mary Yates Johnson's promise as one to make a gift, Robert Jackson had not counted on Cardozo, whose ingenuity in finding swaps to avoid the strictures of the doctrine of consideration has already been noted. The college had taken advantage of what fundraisers call a "naming opportunity." Under the Estate Pledge that Mary signed, the gift "was to be known as the Mary Yates Johnson memorial fund, the proceeds from which shall be used to educate students preparing for the ministry." In addition, in 1923, two years after her promise and a year before her repudiation, she had paid the college $1,000. So, wrote Cardozo, "by implication [the college] undertook, when it accepted a portion of the 'gift,' that in its circulars of information and in other customary ways when making an announcement of this scholarship, it would couple with the announcement the name of the donor."[30] Her promise of $5,000 was not made, as Samuel LeFrak's promise of $10 million was, "with no strings attached." In return for her promise the college had swapped its implied promise "to perpetuate her name," and she was therefore committed because her promise was supported by consideration—since even a peppercorn would suffice. Cardozo thus used the assent rule to atone for the demise of the intention principle, pushing the already attenuated doctrine of consideration to its limits. It is difficult to imagine what opportunity for a similar substitute the college had lost by making its deal with Mary, but courts do not inquire closely into such matters, as we saw in the example of the neophyte builder (Chapter 6). One wonders if in all the years that students have dutifully studied this case there has never been one who exclaimed, "Surely, Judge Cardozo, you cannot have been serious!"

In some legal systems, such as the French and German, where special rules govern the category of "gift promises," judges may have to puzzle over how to characterize promises made with mixed motives.[31] Because we have no such category, our common law judges have no need for such exercises in characterization. What is critical is not that a promise is gratuitous but that there is no consideration for the promise. As Holmes put it, "A man may promise to paint a picture for five hundred dollars, while his chief motive may be a desire for fame."[32] The swap must not be a sham, but it need not be the promisor's principal motivation. Mary's principal motivation may have been altruism, but there was enough of a swap to make her promise enforceable.

What better evidence to confirm our earlier suspicion that consideration has become a mere technicality? A fundraiser for a small California museum is reported to have remarked that if major pledges were to come in, the promisor would probably have to agree to receive something in return for the promise, such as the naming of a gallery after him or her.[33] The distinction between promises that are part of swaps and promises that are not has lost whatever significance it may once have had, making the rule that denies enforceability to gratuitous promise hard to defend and, as Cardozo demonstrated, tempting to avoid.

Despite the general rule that promises to make gifts are unenforceable, there are some exceptions. In the next chapter I examine those exceptions and consider the merits of the general rule.

CHAPTER EIGHT

Enforceable Promises to Make Gifts

Exceptional promises to make gifts that are enforceable: promises to perform "moral obligations" and promises that have been relied on. The continuing role of paternalism. Restatement of Contracts §90 and its modification in the Restatement (Second) for charitable subscriptions, dispensing with reliance without requiring a formality. The intention principle and the Model Act. Jack Tallas tries to make a commitment to give $50,000 to his friend Peter Dementas. A plea for an appropriate formality. Support in the example of estoppel by deed. Some questions about how to deal with regret.

Some exceptional promises to make gifts are enforceable. The two most important exceptions involve promises to perform a "moral obligation" and promises that have been relied on. An undercurrent of paternalism is evident in both. I begin with the moral obligation cases.

Suppose that, after a debt has been barred by the statute of limitations, the debtor makes a new promise to pay the debt without getting anything in return for that promise. The new promise would seem to fall within the general rule that promises without consideration are unenforceable. It is, in effect, a promise to make a gift. But courts have long viewed the promise as one to perform a moral obligation, if not a legal one, and have made an exception to the general rule.[1] Even a paternalistic judge is unlikely to be troubled by this exception, since the most profligate promisor can commit no more than the amount of the barred debt.

There is now good authority for extending this exception to many other situations in which a someone promises to perform what might be regarded as a moral obligation. For example, a person who is rescued by another is ordinarily under no legal obligation to the rescuer even if the rescuer has been injured during the rescue. And a promise by the person rescued made after the rescue would not be supported by consideration and therefore would not be enforceable under the general rule. But the promisor may be seen as owing a moral obligation to the injured rescuer and the promise enforced under the exception devised for the debt barred by the statute of limitations.[2] In formulating this rule, the Restatement (Second) of Contracts states that a "promise made in recognition of a benefit previously received by the promisor from the promisee is binding to the extent necessary to prevent injustice" and adds that the promise is not binding "to the extent that its value is disproportionate to the benefit."[3] Again, the law's paternalistic concerns are assuaged by the thought that the promisor's power to commit the future is limited by the benefit received in the past.

Scholars have attempted to rationalize this exception on a variety of grounds. It has been emphasized that the promise reenforces the claim that there is an obligation.[4] Conversely, it has been suggested that the obligation reenforces the claim that there is a promise.[5] And it has been claimed that in such cases the promisor is better able to negotiate conditions of the promise than in the case of the usual promise to make a gift.[6] It seems both simpler and more convincing to say that because in the moral obligation cases the promisor's power to commit the future is limited, courts are able to recognize the promisor's interest in making a binding promise without the paternalistic concern for profligacy that underlies the general rule.[7]

To this extent courts recognize the intention principle. As was suggested earlier, it is a mistake to lose sight of the importance to the promisor of the power to make a commitment, and the moral obligation exception recognizes that importance and supports the intention principle (Chapter 4).

Other decisions enforcing promises to make gifts turn on the fact that the promise has been relied on. Suppose that in the *Allegheny College* case (Chapter 7) the college had

proved that it had relied on Mary Yates Johnson's promise of
$5,000. Would her promise have been enforceable even if it
had been made "with no strings attached"? Cardozo went out
of his way to say that it would have been, concluding that
"there has grown up of recent days a doctrine that a substitute for consideration or an exception to its ordinary requirements can be found in what is styled 'a promissory estoppel.' . . . Certain . . . it is that we have adopted the doctrine
of promissory estoppel as the equivalent of consideration in
connection with our law of charitable subscriptions."[8]

His dictum was surely influenced by what was to become Restatement of Contracts §90, for its text had been considered at the annual meeting of the American Law Institute
the year before the decision in the *Allegheny College* case.
It read: "A promise which the promisor would reasonably
expect to induce action or forbearance of a definite and substantial character on the part of the promisee and which does
induce such action or forbearance is binding if injustice can
be avoided only by enforcement of the promise." The promisor is commonly said to be "estopped" (that is, precluded)
from reneging on the promise as a result of the promisee's
reliance, hence the term "promissory estoppel." This rule
may encourage inefficient action by promisees seeking to
make promises enforceable. Furthermore, applying this rule
in particular cases often raises difficult questions of what
a promisor might "reasonably expect" to be induced by a
promise and whether "such action or forbearance" has been
induced.[9] And if these questions can be resolved, what are
courts to make of the language that limits enforcement to
cases in which "injustice can be avoided only by enforcement of the promises"?[10]

In spite of these questions, courts have welcomed Section 90 during the more than half a century since it appeared—roughly the period during which the seal has been
deprived of its effect. It is now plain that the reliance principle applies to promises to which, because there is no swap,
the assent rule does not apply. Not only is a promise that is

part of a swap enforceable on the promisee's assent, to take account of the mere possibility of reliance by the promisee, but a promise that is not part of a swap is enforceable on a showing of actual reliance by the promisee.

What has become of the law's paternalistic concerns? The present version of Section 90 offers this solution: "The remedy granted for breach may be limited as justice requires." Under this provision a court may limit the promisor's liability to the extent of the promisee's reliance (see Chapter 11). For the present it is enough to note that this discretion permits a court to limit to the amount of the promisee's proven reliance the power of even the most profligate promisor's power to commit the future. As in the moral obligation cases, the law's paternalistic concerns are assuaged by the thought that the promisor's power is not unlimited.

There may, however, still be more than a spark of life left in the intention principle in connection with promises to make gifts. To the formulation of the doctrine of promissory estoppel in Section 90 there has now been appended an exception of liability for charitable subscriptions (promises to make gifts to charities), an expansion that is difficult to rationalize otherwise. The exception dispenses with any requirement of reliance in the case of charitable subscriptions, making them "binding . . . without proof that the promise induced action or forbearance." [11] The exception thus marks off promises made to charities from promises made within the family. Its practical impact is less than it might at first appear, since courts had long been creative—after the fashion of Cardozo in the *Allegheny College* case—in warping the doctrine of consideration to enforce charitable subscriptions. [12]

The exception for charitable subscriptions has played to mixed reviews. In 1989 a New Jersey intermediate appellate court supported the exception in holding a living donor committed by a $2,000 admitted oral pledge, emphasizing society's interest in such sensible displays of altruism. Reliance, the court observed, "is a questionable basis for enforcing a charitable subscription . . . because in reality, a charity does not rely on a particular subscription when planning its undertakings. . . . The real basis for enforcing a charitable subscription is one of public policy—that enforcement of a charitable subscription is a desirable social goal."[13] But in the same year the Supreme Judicial Court of Massachusetts held that the promisor's estate was not committed by a $25,000 oral charitable subscription. The inclusion of the promised sum in the promisee's budget did not amount to reliance, and the court declined to dispense with the requirement of reliance.[14] Even assuming that the court would follow the exception for charitable subscriptions in an appropriate case, the court saw no injustice in refusing to enforce the decedent's oral promise after his death. In general, judicial response has been varied.[15] Courts have been less than pellucid in assessing such important factors as whether the promise was written or oral and whether the promisor reneged before death or simply died.[16]

Scholarly efforts to justify the exception have been varied. The judicial assumption that public policy in favor of charitable giving supports enforceability of charitable subscriptions can be faulted on the ground that the enforceability might discourage such giving by increasing the cost to the donor of making pledges. Instead, it has been suggested that the exception may rest on the large size of many charitable pledges and the related desire of the donor to spread out payment over time.[17] Or that in a charitable setting as contrasted with a family setting there is more opportunity for a donor to bargain over conditions and that extralegal sanctions are less likely to be effective.[18] Whatever its rationale, the exception is a conspicuous example of the intention principle.

Oddly, the exception for charitable subscriptions requires no formality. Admittedly no such requirement is imposed for a promise to perform a moral obligation or a promise that has been relied on, but there the magnitude of the moral obligation or the extent of the reliance limits a promisor's liability. The exception for charitable subscriptions has no such limit and yet it does not require even a signed writing like that executed by Mary Yates Johnson. Before the abolition of the seal, a promisor could make a binding promise to make a gift by using that formality. The promisor's power to make such a promise was unlimited since the cautionary function of the formality was supposed to curb possible profligacy. As has already been observed, the main impact of the abolition of the seal has been on promises to make gifts because of the lax judicial attitude toward consideration in other contexts. The effect was thus profoundly paternalistic with respect to such promises, perhaps reflecting a decline in the belief that individuals know their "own best interests." Because the seal was seen as having become so trivialized that it no longer had the desired cautionary function of distinguishing promises made after adequate reflection, there is no longer any formality that a promisor can use to make a binding promise.

The demise of the seal evoked no threnody, but it did prompt an attempt to provide a different formality through a Uniform Written Obligations Act. The act embodied the intention principle and enabled a promisor to make a binding promise by signing a writing containing an "express statement, in any form of language, that the signer intends to be legally bound." Its drafter, Samuel Williston, explained that "it seems to me it ought also to be possible that if a man makes a promise, knowing that it is gratuitous, and, nevertheless, purposes to have it legally binding, he shall have it so."[19] But this attempt to resurrect the intention principle failed when only Pennsylvania and Utah adopted the act and Utah later repealed it. Utah's code commissioners concluded, in a whimsically paternalistic outburst, that there was "no more vicious statute in the written laws of any civilized nation" since it would "enable confidence men and swindlers to enforce written promises . . . which they may obtain from the unwary . . . and to take from such unfortunate persons a defense that has been recognized . . . in the courts of all civilized nations since the dawn of history."[20] The act was renamed the *Model* Written Obligations Act, and in almost all states the promisor's power to make a binding promise to make a gift remains restricted to the exceptional situations mentioned here, no matter how justifiable the promisor's purpose or how serious the promisor's intention to be legally bound. No existing formality is adequate to the task of removing this restriction.[21]

At one extreme, the exception for charitable subscriptions restores the promisor's power with respect to such promises to what it was before the abolition of the seal—but without even the requirement of a signed writing like that in the *Allegheny College* case to perform a cautionary function. At the other extreme, general adherence to the common law rule means that no formality whatever will suffice to enable a promisor to make a binding promise to make a gift in, for example, a family setting.

Consider the case of Jack Tallas, an immigrant from Greece who wanted to make a gift of $50,000 to Peter Dementas, a close friend of fourteen years who had been of help to Jack during that time. Jack dictated a memorandum to Peter in Greek promising to leave him $50,000 in his will, kept the Greek document, retyped it in English, notarized the English version with his own notary seal, and delivered the documents to Peter three days later. Jack died six weeks later, leaving a substantial estate but nothing to Peter. Too bad for Peter, decided an appellate court in Utah: there was no consideration for Peter's promise.[22] A peppercorn would have sufficed, but there was none. Indeed, had Utah not repealed its Written Obligations Act, Jack's promise would have been enforceable even absent consideration. Jack's intention to be legally bound could not have been clearer. Should no formality have been available to give legal effect to that intention? If the seal has been trivialized, should not a signed writing plainly showing Jack's intention have been sufficient?

If the technicality of a peppercorn will suffice to make a promise binding, why not the formality of a signed writing? This would, to be sure, require legislation. But as Samuel Williston put it, "It is something, it seems to me, that a person ought to be able to do, if he wishes to do it,—to create a legal obligation to make a gift. Why not? . . . I don't see why a man should not be able to make himself liable if he wishes to do so."[23] In the same vein, a distinguished comparatist has asked whether "for a legal system which lacks the institution of a notary in the civil-law sense, it is wholly impossible to create *a fair equivalent* of a civil-law-style notarial document," and whether a document signed with the advice of counsel and filed in a public place might be such a fair equivalent.[24] I share this sympathetic view of the intention principle, though I doubt that the formality need be so elaborate. A Canadian commission has recommended a simpler formality, proposing enactment of a statute providing that a signed, witnessed writing take the place of the seal.[25]

Whatever the appropriate formality, the abolition of the seal without the substitution of some other formality seems rash. To deny the power to make enforceable promises on the ground that an appropriate formality cannot be fashioned seems absurd. The power to make binding charitable subscriptions should be limited by imposing some formal requirements. At the same time, promisors should be given back the power that they once had on complying with some formal requirements, to make binding promises to make gifts to others than charities. The Restatement (Second) view that would allow Jack to make a binding oral promise to give everything he had to his church but that denies him the power to make a formal promise to give $50,000 to his friend seems indefensible. (It seems even more indefensible in light of Jack's power, discussed in Chapter 13, to make a binding oral declaration of trust that would have given Peter the right to the $50,000, assuming that Jack had it at the time.) Although there may be no need to require a formality when the existing exceptions for moral obligations and reliance apply, the use of a formality would avoid the difficult questions often posed in connection with those exceptions.

Support for an effective formality can be found in a somewhat esoteric quarter. Suppose that a vendor gives a purchaser a warranty deed purporting to convey full ownership of land even though the vendor's ownership is subject to an outstanding interest held by another person. If the vendor later acquires that interest, the purchaser automatically acquires it under a doctrine misleadingly styled "estoppel by deed." (Unlike other forms of estoppel, this one requires no reliance.) The result could be explained by treating the vendor's purported conveyance of full ownership by warranty deed as an implied promise to convey the outstanding interest if the vendor later acquired it. This promise could be enforced by the purchaser who paid for it, and a court will simply treat the promise as if it had been performed without requiring that the purchaser bring a suit to enforce it.[26]

But suppose that the deed is given as a gift to a donee who has not paid for it. It would seem that the result would be different because the implied promise to convey is now a promise to make a gift. Such authority as there is, however, is that the doctrine of estoppel by deed applies in this situation too, even though nothing has been paid for the promise.[27] Here, as before, circumstance places a limit on profligacy. The doctrine of estoppel by deed, even if applied to gifts, will not enable a donor to squander a lifetime of rewards. But a more convincing rationale for the rule is surely the intention principle, the more so because of the formality of the source of the promise—a deed that must be delivered. A century and a half ago the United States Supreme Court recognized the principle behind the doctrine of estoppel by deed:

"Where a man has entered into a solemn engagement by deed under his hand and seal as to certain facts, he shall not be permitted to deny any matter which he has so asserted."[28]

If promises are to be enforced under the intention principle, courts will have to rethink the objective standard conventionally used in contract interpretation (Chapter 3). That standard makes sense only as long as enforceability turns on expectation or reliance (Chapter 4). As a distinguished English jurist pointed out, "When construing a statute or will, you are considering the intentions of one body only—be it Parliament or a testator. When construing a contract, be it in writing or by word of mouth, you are considering the intentions of two parties—who have agreed together on the terms that shall bind them."[29] When the "intentions of one body only" are in question, the appropriate standard is a subjective one. Thus, for example, in interpreting a will, a court will seek to ascertain "the very disposition which the testator wanted to make."[30] Similarly, a subjective rather than an objective standard is appropriate for promises enforceable under the intention principle. This includes promises to make gifts now enforced by courts under the exceptions for promises to perform moral obligations and promises of charitable subscriptions, although it is unclear that courts have recognized that this is so.

In contrast with the case in which the Supreme Court of Michigan concluded that the words "we have every intention of meeting this obligation" amounted to a promise (Chapter 3), consider the case of the executor of an estate who gave a college a signed pledge card with very similar words: "I/we intend to subscribe to the College Founders Fund the sum of Five Thousand——no/100 Dollars." The Supreme Court of Iowa concluded that these words were a "mere expression of intention," not a promise. Had the court found a promise, its enforceability would have been based on the exception for promises of charitable subscriptions and therefore on the intention principle. The appropriate standard of interpretation would have been a subjective one, under which the question would have been whether the executor intended to make a promise, quite without regard to whether the Fund may reasonably have thought that he did. It seems unlikely that the court perceived this point, though it may nevertheless have reached a correct result.[31]

Furthermore, if some promises to make gifts are binding, questions will arise as to when, if ever, a promisor is free to renege on even a binding promise to make a gift. These questions will be unavoidable as long as there are exceptions to the general rule; and enlarging the category of binding promises will only increase their frequency. I suggested earlier that the less tolerant a legal system is in excusing promisors from their promises, the more hesitant courts would be in finding promises to be binding (Chapter 2), so excuses must be fashioned if courts are to enforce more promises to make gifts.

Those who make such promises are no more immune from regret than are other promisors. When Richard H. Barclay, a seventy-two-year-old self-made real-estate developer, died without paying $600,000 of the $1 million he had promised the University of California for a new theater, the university found itself enmeshed in a legal battle with his widow, who protested that her husband's estate could afford to pay no more than $250,000 because he had suffered heavy losses shortly before his death.[32] One might therefore expect that the same courts that have lavished so much attention on rules to deal with regret in cases of swaps would have paid some attention to the analogous questions posed under promises to make gifts. But up to now they have not done so and, in light of the many exceptional circumstances in which promises to make gifts turn out to be binding, it behooves one who makes such a promise to fashion explicit provisions that take account of the possibility of regret. (While it might sometimes be prudent to make only a promise to use "best efforts" to make the gift, this is not usually what is intended.)

Any proposal to enlarge the category of binding promises must therefore address the question of how courts should deal with regret when the promisor has been silent.[33] In broad outline, the reasons for their regret are not very different from the reasons we considered earlier in the case of persons who swap their promises. Sometimes time plays no role: the promisor's decision when made was to be regretted because it was unfairly influenced, uninformed, or ill considered (Chapter 2). Sometimes time plays a role: the promisor's decision, while not to be regretted when made, turns out to be improvident or obsolete (Chapter 2). When, in the words of Section 90, can "injustice . . . be avoided only by enforcement of the promise"?

When time plays no role, doctrines shaped for swaps may be adaptable here. In cases of unfairly influenced decisions, the doctrines developed to deal with misrepresentation and coercion seem applicable to both kinds of promises, for promises to make gifts may also be unfairly influenced by the promisee. Although Mary Yates Johnson's lawyer complained that his client had been subjected to the "social pressure of not being outdone in virtue by others,"[34] those established doctrines would give no bases for relief. In cases of uninformed decisions, the rules developed for mistake could be adapted to cases of gifts, as when one turns out to have been mistaken about the supposedly favorable tax consequences of one's promised gift. But should the law be as intolerant of the claim that one misjudged available resources in promising to make a gift? Mary's surviving contemporaries are said to have suggested that she reneged "because she was concerned about her capacity to both pay the college and to leave enough to her daughter so that her daughter could in turn aid her impoverished cousins, the Yates."[35] If such a claim seems insufficiently extreme to justify her reneging, what of a claim based on concern for the promisor's *own* welfare? In cases of ill-considered decisions, should the law ignore—as it does in the case of swaps—the claim that cognitive failure led the promisor to undervalue future risks or that volitional failure produced a transient desire to enhance the promisor's status, resulting in the promise of an extravagant gift (Chapter 2)?[36]

When time plays a role it is more difficult to see how traditional doctrines could be adapted to promises to make gifts. Courts could still deny relief based on obsolete decisions, as when a "later self" regrets having promised $5,000 to the Society for the Promotion of Rock and would rather give it to the Association for the Advancement of Bach.[37] But in cases of improvident decisions, should courts continue to turn a deaf ear to excuses such as those based on medical emergencies, financial reverses, and even unexpected competing business opportunities? Should one who promises to make a gift be taken to have assumed such risks? Should Samuel LeFrak be taken to have assumed the risk that the Landmark Preservation Commission would not approve the LeFrak name on the exterior of the Guggenheim Museum's rotunda? Is even a devastating reversal of fortune to be ignored? As far back as the second century, the Roman emperor Antoninus Pius established the rule that "those who are sued in order to secure a liberality [that is, a gratuity] are to be condemned for what they can afford."[38] An analogy might be found in cases defining the implied right of a donor to recover a gift *causa mortis* after making an unexpected recovery.[39] Courts might find contemporary inspiration in an Israeli statute that allows a promisor to retract a promise to make a gift, even after reliance, "if the retraction is warranted . . . by a considerable deterioration in the [promisor's] economic situation."[40]

And what if the excuse goes to the promisee's failure to live up to the promisor's expectations?[41] How can the rules constructed to deal with the effects of the other party's breach in the case of a swap be adapted to such a situation? What if one is shocked at inefficient food distribution by one's chosen charity? Startled at the unavailability of one's expected tax deduction? Dismayed by recovery from the illness one supposed to be terminal? Irritated at the insensitivity of one's law school classmates to one's generosity? Displeased by the emphasis of the botanical garden donee on carnivorous plants?[42] Or outraged at the unexpected ingratitude of one's intended? How, if at all, should the law take account of regret in such situations? Is it significant that the promisee has at least some responsibility for the promisor's regret? An analogy might be found in decisions addressing the implied right of a jilted fiancé to recover the gift of an engagement ring.[43] And at least some of these situations would fall within the further provision of the Israeli statute that allows a promisor to retract a promise to make a gift, even after reliance, "if the retraction is warranted by disgraceful conduct towards the [promisor] or a member of the [promisor's] family."

A coherent set of answers has yet to be developed in the United States.[44] Answers are needed even now because of the exceptions for moral obligation and reliance. And the need for answers will increase as the category of binding promises is enlarged, as has been attempted in the case of charitable subscriptions. As was observed earlier, it is a fair guess that the more tolerant a legal system is of reneging on binding promises, the more likely it will be to treat promises as binding. It follows that the future expansion of the category of binding promises to make gifts will depend on the fashioning of excuses to take account of regret. Some lessons can be learned from ways that courts have confined and softened commitments in connection with swaps, matters taken up in Chapters 10 and 11.

Having seen how a promise can be the basis for commitment under the reliance principle and the intention principle, we now ask whether a promise is the only possible basis for commitment.

CHAPTER NINE

Commitment Without Promise

*How the PSC's promise to take care of William Overlock in-
creased his dependence on them. Cases in which courts base
commitment on conduct without promise though it would be
better to spell out a promise. Other cases in which this cannot
be done and commitment must be based on the effect of the
conduct in increasing another's dependence on the promisor.
How a stepfather's conduct increased his stepdaughters' dependence on him. A dependence principle formulated. The "happy
campers" cases, the intention principle, and the enforceability
of resolutions.*

We have been concerned with how promises result in commitment. Now we ask whether a promise is *needed* for commitment. Partisans of a "relational" basis for commitment
fault traditional contract law for what they see as an excessive emphasis on promise to the detriment of a recognition
of commitment based not on promise but on the relationship
between parties.[1] But when is there commitment without
promise?

Consider the case of the unfortunate William Overlock,
who was severely injured in a fall while working as a line-
man for the Central Vermont Public Service Company (PSC).
Some concerned citizens planned to take up a collection for
his benefit, but they abandoned their plans when the PSC
promised them that it would take care of William for the rest
of his life. The PSC then changed its mind and reneged on
its promise. William sued the PSC, but the Supreme Court
of Vermont held that he could not enforce the promise.[2] The
promise had not been made to William but to the concerned
citizens. Although he might have been an intended beneficiary of the promise, as we saw in Marion's case, the promise
was not an enforceable one.[3] Section 90, as it appears in the

Restatement (Second) of Contracts, gives effect to reliance by third persons as well as by the promisee, but the court did not regard the concerned citizens' abandonment the kind of "detrimental reliance" necessary to result in commitment under the reliance principle.[4] The concerned citizens sustained "no real loss," for they merely "did not undertake a solicitation for funds for a gift" to William. William failed to argue that the PSC was liable on the quite different ground that its promise, even if not enforceable as a promise, was nonetheless *conduct* of a sort that increased William's dependence on the PSC. Should not such conduct commit the PSC to at least use reasonable care to see that William's situation was not worsened?

When conduct results in commitment, this is usually because a promise is spelled out in the conduct. A promise need not be in words. A player can manifest commitment to follow the rules of a game simply by starting to play: one cannot with impunity abandon the bridge table in the middle of a rubber. If I say, "I'll give you $100 if you promise to drive us to Peoria," and you start to drive us in that direction without saying anything, your conduct may be taken as a promise to drive us to Peoria that amounts to an acceptance of my offer.[5] But your conduct in starting to carry out a decision is not usually taken as manifesting your promise to keep on in spite of a change of mind. Even if you have decided to drive to Peoria and have gone halfway, you are still ordinarily free to turn back and go instead to South Bend. As a scholar suggested, "The burghers who set their watches by Emmanuel Kant's walks relied on him but could not have been heard to complain if Kant had altered his habits."[6] And as a court explained in a more commercial context, although a seller of defective goods begins repairing them so that by its "deeds it has assumed what would otherwise be the buyer's burden of mitigation . . . , if at some point the seller makes it clear to the buyer that it has ceased trying to correct the breach, the suspension of the buyer's duty to mitigate damages ends, and he must arrange for the repairs himself."[7]

Occasionally, however, a court will hold that you are not free to discontinue what you have started. In a memorable dictum, Chief Judge Benjamin Nathan Cardozo, speaking for New York's highest court, said: "The hand once set to a task may not always be withdrawn with impunity though liability would fail if it had never been applied at all."[8] Although this is commonly stated as a principle of tort law, in most cases it adds little or nothing to the principles of contract law that govern promises. Nor does it lend much support to a relational basis for commitment.

Suppose that a railroad decides to maintain a watchman at a grade crossing, though it is not required to, and after a while drivers come to rely on this. If the railroad changes its mind and discontinues the practice, is it liable if a driver, relying on the practice, is struck by a train?[9] Or suppose that the government decides to maintain a lighthouse, though it is not required to, and after a while ships come to rely on this. If the government changes its mind and discontinues the practice, is it liable if a ship, relying on the practice, runs aground?[10] Or suppose that a city decides to maintain guards at school crossings, though it is not required to, and after a while parents of schoolchildren come to rely on this. If the city changes its mind and discontinues the practice, is it liable if a child, left unaccompanied by a parent, relying on the practice, is struck by a car?[11] In each instance the court held that the hand once set to the task could not be withdrawn with impunity and saw liability as based in tort, not contract.

The announced rule of tort law is that one who undertakes gratuitously to render services for the protection of another's person or property becomes committed, if the other relies on the undertaking, to perform the undertaking with reasonable care and is liable in tort for a failure to do so.[12]

What does this add to what we have already seen? There is no need for recourse to a relational basis for commitment here. In each of the cases described the court could easily have treated the undertaking as a promise spelled out from conduct, the continued setting of the hand to the task. Since in each case the promise was relied on, the court could then have imposed liability under the reliance principle.

Liability on this reasoning is not only well established but is free of two constraints that hobble the tort rule. First, it is doubtful that the tort rule applies if there has been no beginning of performance of the undertaking.[13] Second, liability under the tort rule is limited to physical harm to persons or things and does not extend to economic loss. It is unclear why claimants ignore the possibility of a promise as the basis of liability and persist in involving a more constricted tort rule.[14] To my eyes, commitment based on a promise would be preferable for liability in such cases. There is, however, a similar type of situation in which commitment cannot be based on a promise but could be grounded in tort—the situation of William Overlock.

Suppose that you are on a crowded beach and see a drowning swimmer. By and large, even in this case, you are not liable for inaction, and it is up to you to decide whether to attempt to make a rescue or to do nothing. At the law's most extreme, "no ordinary bystander is under a duty to attempt the rescue of a child from drowning in what he knows is shallow water."[15] But suppose that you decide to go to the rescue—you dive in, start to tow the drowning swimmer toward safety, and then decide to leave the swimmer to drown. A court could view your conduct as amounting to a promise to try to finish the rescue, and it could be shown that others on the crowded beach might have gone to the rescue had you not done so.[16] But even such reliance by the others would not have sufficed to result in commitment based on your promise according to the court in William Overlock's case, because it was not the kind of "detrimental reliance necessary."[17]

Might there not be liability on a different ground? Remember Papinian's admonition that "No one can change his mind to someone else's disadvantage." In going to the rescue you discouraged others from doing so and increased the drowning swimmer's dependence on you. Should you nonetheless have been free to change your mind to the drowning swimmer's disadvantage?

Tort law recognizes, at least to a limited extent, that such conduct may give rise to a commitment to use reasonable care to see that the drowning swimmer is not put in a worse position than before that conduct. According to the American Law Institute's Restatement (Second) of Torts, a person "who, being under no duty to do so, takes charge of another who is helpless adequately to aid or protect himself is subject to liability to the other for any bodily harm caused to him by . . . the actor's discontinuing his aid or protection, if by so doing he leaves the other in a worse position than when the actor took charge of him."[18] After you decide to take charge and begin to do so, it is too late to change your mind. You become committed to at least use reasonable care not to leave the drowning swimmer in a worse position than before.[19] If the beach had been deserted, of course, the consequences of your aborted rescue would have been entirely different.

Your commitment is not based on promise but on conduct that increases another person's dependence on you. This becomes apparent if we assume that the drowning swimmer is unconscious, for, as we have seen, a promise needs a promisee, and an unconscious person cannot be a promisee (Chapter 3).[20] Although resolutions do not ordinarily result in commitment, here your commitment might be seen as arising from a resolution that benefited the drowning swimmer (Chapter 1). In such situations a relational basis for commitment would be advantageous, since tort law is hobbled by the constraints that we saw earlier.

First, it is unclear whether taking charge under the rule of tort law covers a mere promise expressed in words where there has not yet been any performance of that promise.[21] If it does not, no commitment would result if you simply shouted "I will save you," and all the others left the beach to do other things.[22]

To one familiar with contract law, where conduct that takes the form of expression in words is generally a more reliable guide to intention than is nonverbal conduct, this limitation makes no sense. In William's case, the PSC's promise was surely more effective in increasing William's dependence on the PSC by causing the concerned citizens to abandon the collection than conduct consisting of a series of payments would have been. Yet it is doubtful that the tort rule would have resulted in commitment because the PSC had not begun performance.

Second, the tort rule covers only bodily harm and not economic loss, as in William's case.[23] Again, to one familiar with contract law where commitment protects economic loss as well as other kinds of harm, this limitation is difficult to justify. This is especially so in William's case, in which the economic loss consisted of the loss of financial support to enable him to cope with bodily harm. Yet William would have been denied recovery under the tort rule because no bodily harm resulted from his increased dependence.

Commitment of this kind has been recognized in the absence of bodily harm, however, in another context. Suppose that a woman has a child by her first husband, gets a divorce and is given custody of the child, marries her second husband, who treats his stepchild as his own, and then divorces the second husband. Ordinarily, the stepfather's liability for support of the child ceases at the breakup of the marriage, and the child must turn to her natural father for support payments. But suppose that the second husband not only treats the stepchild as his own but acts in such a way as to discourage the child's natural father from having contact with the child and succeeds in alienating the natural father. Might a court hold that the stepfather, having alienated the natural father from his child and increased the child's dependence on the stepfather, is bound by a commitment to the child?

The Supreme Court of New Jersey answered this question in the affirmative in 1984. Jay, the second husband, had lived with Gladys and her two daughters for seven years, during which, Gladys alleged, he "induced the girls to rely on him as their natural father." In so doing, he "had prevented and cut off the girls' relationship with their natural father," Ralph, who had supported Gladys and the children before going to prison on a narcotics charge several years before Gladys's second marriage. When, after Ralph's release from prison, he sent a check to the children, Jay tore it up to avoid being "tied to his illegal activities." Jay also opposed any visits by Ralph. Faced with Jay's opposition, Ralph eventually stopped trying to visit or send money to the children. Noting that a stepparent is ordinarily under no support obligation after divorce, the court said that such an obligation will be imposed "only when a stepparent by his or her conduct actively interferes with the children's support from their natural parent. . . . The stepparent must take positive action interfering with the natural parent's support obligation to be bound." [24] Under the rationale suggested here, because Jay's conduct had the effect of increasing the children's dependency on him, he was committed to use reasonable care to avoid leaving them in a worse position than they were in when that conduct began. [25]

In summary, tort law regards conduct as resulting in commitment in two kinds of situations. In the first, one's conduct is seen as manifesting an undertaking to use reasonable care, and when another relies on that undertaking, commitment results. The setting of the hand to the task expresses commitment, and the hand may not be withdrawn after reliance. I believe that because the basis of this commitment is effectively a promise, it would be better to view it as based on promissory estoppel, under the rubric of contract law. In the other kind of situation, one's conduct has the effect of increasing another's dependency, and the result is a commitment to use reasonable care to avoid leaving the other in a worse position than when the conduct began. Once dependency is established, the hand may not be withdrawn if the result would be to worsen the other's situation. Here the basis of commitment is not a promise but increased dependence. In conventional terms, liability under this dependence principle falls under the rubric of tort law, though it might be preferable to assign a relational basis.[26]

Rubrics aside, one might well ask whether the reliance principle is not simply a variation on the broader theme of the dependence principle. A promise is one kind of conduct, and by relying on a promise the promisee becomes dependent on the promisor. Loss of an opportunity in reliance on a promise inevitably increases dependency. If W. O. relied on A. H. and Ida's promise by refraining from arranging to buy another farm, he became more dependent on them. If David relied on Eileen's promise by refraining from arranging to marry another wife, he became more dependent on her.

Before leaving the subject of commitment without promise, it will be of interest to consider a few cases in which such commitment has arisen in quite another context. In these cases, employees threatened by discharge have sought to enforce disciplinary procedures described in handbooks distributed by their employers. Can an employee who happens not to have seen the handbook nevertheless hold the employer to the procedures it sets out for dismissal? Ruling against such an employee would create chance distinctions among employees depending on distribution of the handbook, but ruling for the employee would require the court to find some doctrine other than consideration (for there has been no bargain) or promissory estoppel (for there has been no reliance). When Kenneth Bankey lodged a complaint based on the handbook distributed by his employer,

Storer Broadcasting Company, the Supreme Court of Michigan resolved this dilemma by concluding that "an employer who chooses to establish desirable personnel policies, such as a discharge-for-cause employment policy, is not seeking to induce each individual employee to show up for work every day, but rather is seeking to promote an environment conducive to collective productivity. The benefit to the employer of promoting such an environment, rather than the traditional contract-forming mechanisms of mutual assent or individual detrimental reliance, gives rise to a situation 'instinct with an obligation.' " [27] In the court's view the employer was committing itself in its self-interest in order to have "happy campers" as employees. The relational aspect of this line of reasoning is evident.

Nearly a century after Holmes concluded that the Michigan legislature's statement of "policy" concerning tax relief resulted in no commitment to the Wisconsin & Michigan Railway Co. (Chapter 3), the Supreme Court of Michigan concluded that the employer's statement of "policy" gave rise to a commitment. The court was fastidious in describing the employer's undertaking as a "commitment" and not as a "promise." [28] In this it was correct, since a promise must be communicated to a promisee. Under the reasoning of the Supreme Court of Michigan, the employer would presumably have been no less committed if *none* of the employees had actually read the handbook so that no promise had been made to anyone.

Similar reasoning has been advanced to justify the occasional cases that have allowed a person to recover a reward although the person was unaware, at the time of performing the act to be rewarded, that a reward had been offered. "Standing offers of rewards made by governmental bodies . . . may be regarded as intended to create a climate in which people do certain acts in the hope of earning unknown rewards." [29] Thus a municipality may commit itself to follow such a policy in order to have "happy—and cooperative— campers" as inhabitants. As in the handbook situation, the commitment would arise even if no inhabitant was aware of the offer of a reward.

Since there is no increased dependence on the part of employees or inhabitants in the handbook and reward cases, the results cannot be justified on the ground of the dependence principle. The explanation must be the intention principle. But here, in contrast with the cases of promises to make gifts, no communication of intention to the beneficiary is required. The law accords to a party the power to make a commitment in that party's own self-interest as long as the intention to make that commitment is plain. To this extent the law recognizes as a commitment an undertaking that is like a resolution, with the significant exception that here there is a beneficiary who is in a position to complain if it is not carried out (Chapter 1).[30]

There are, however, some important differences between the reach of commitments that are based on promises and those that are not. To these differences I now turn.

CHAPTER TEN

The Reach of a Commitment

What is the reach of a commitment? How promises are confined by provisions for reasonable efforts and for termination. How termination provisions may be limited by warning requirements and by even-handedness requirements. Some illustrations, including the happy-campers cases and the Winstar *case.*

If you are committed, what is the reach of your commitment? I suggested earlier that the more tolerant a legal system is in allowing promisors excuses for reneging, the more likely it will be to find that promises are binding (Chapter 2). So too, the more ways you can confine your promise, the more likely you will be to agree to be bound by it. Peter Mattei might not have agreed to be bound by his promise to Amelia Hopper if he had not been able to hedge that promise by conditioning it on his agent finding leases "satisfactory" to him. We have seen that one justification for the refusal oᴸ courts to enforce promises to make gifts is the assumed impracticality of hedging such promises (Chapter 7).

When one speaks of a commitment, therefore, it is important to consider the scope of the commitment. Between the extremes of commitment and no commitment there is much middle ground where pangs of regret are at least mollified though not eliminated. A contract drafter, beset when expressing a commitment by apprehension of future fears, may seek to gain this middle ground by using language that confines the commitment. A court in fashioning a commitment may seek to gain this middle ground as well. How may commitments be confined?

A common way of confining a commitment is to limit the undertaking to one to use "reasonable efforts."[1] In the case of the New Yorker who had exclusive rights to market the designs of an English fashion designer, it will be recalled that his commitment as crafted by the court was limited—not a commitment to achieve any specific result but only to use reasonable efforts to market her designs (Chapter 5). Courts commonly limit the commitments of a range of professionals —from surgeons to private eyes—to reasonable efforts.

Another common way of confining a commitment is by giving a power of termination. Instead of saying simply "count on me," you might say "count on me unless I tell you that it's all off." However, giving a promisor an unqualified power to terminate will, as Peter Mattei's experience suggests, make the promise illusory (Chapter 3). Thus, where a license agreement for the manufacturer of a soft drink provided that the licensee could terminate at any time, a federal Court of Appeals held that the licensee's promise was illusory because the licensee "could at any time cancel the contract."[2] It is therefore important that the power to terminate be qualified somehow. A common way to do this is by a warning requirement. Instead of saying "count on me unless I tell you that it's off," you might say "count on me unless I warn you in advance that it's off." If, for example, the licensee's power of termination had been qualified by making it effective only thirty days after the licensee gave notice, the licensee would then have been bound for at least thirty days, and its promise would not have been illusory.

A warning requirement of this kind involves a compromise between the interests of the promisor and the promisee in the event of the promisor's regret. The promisor wants to reduce the cost of reneging, and the promisee wants to reduce the cost due to reliance. By settling on a thirty-day warning, the licensee can renege effective in thirty days. But the licensee is committed for at least that period and so bears some of the cost of reneging. The licensor, on the other side, can take appropriate steps after receiving the warning to avoid some of the costs of reliance. But the licensor will still have to bear other costs of reliance that cannot be avoided even with the warning—such as costs already sunk in the venture and costs of arranging a substitute.

Warning requirements need not be explicit. They are often read in by courts, as in the happy-campers case (Chapter 9). When Kenneth Bankey was fired after working for more than twelve years as a salesman for Storer Broadcasting Company, he sued Storer and took his case all the way to the Supreme Court of Michigan. Kenneth argued that he was protected by Storer's Personnel Policy Digest, which stated that an employee could be discharged only "for cause." Storer replied that two months before firing Kenneth it had revised its Digest to eliminate the "for cause" requirement. The Supreme Court decided, as already explained, that the "benefit to the employer" of promoting "an environment conducive to collective productivity" was alone sufficient to make a promise in a handbook binding (Chapter 8). The question then was: Could Storer modify this commitment *unilaterally*, without Kenneth's consent? The court concluded that it could because Storer's commitment was subject to a power of termination.[3] From Storer's point of view, this power allowed it to avoid regret if it changed its mind after deciding on a discharge "for cause" policy.

That power was, however, qualified by a warning requirement. Storer had to give affected employees reasonable notice of any change in its commitment under the Digest. "Fairness suggests that a discharge-for-cause policy announced with flourishes and fanfare at noonday should not be revoked by a penny whistle trill at midnight."[4] From the employees' point of view this gave fair warning, allowing them to avoid further reliance on the "for cause" policy. Once Kenneth had received Storer's warning he could no longer claim that he was relying on the policy by remaining in Storer's employ instead of seeking another job.

Often, as in Kenneth's case, the reliance that a warning fends off is negative and consists of lost opportunities to make alternative arrangements. The promisee's main interest in having a warning is that it will help in making alternative arrangements—in Kenneth's case, finding another job.[5] Courts often read in warning requirements to accommodate this interest. A physician, while free to terminate a relationship with a patient, is required to give reasonable notice so that the patient can make suitable alternative arrangements.[6] Similarly, a lawyer, while free to terminate a relationship with a client, must give the client reasonable notice.[7] Warning requirements have also been read in two situations of commercial importance.

The first situation is that of the contract of indefinite duration for sale of goods, in which one party can terminate at any time, but there is no explicit requirement of notice. Despite the absence of an explicit requirement, the Uniform Commercial Code requires that "reasonable notification be received by the other party,"[8] notification that, according to the official commentary, "will give the other party reasonable time to seek a substitute arrangement."[9] Thus, in a Kentucky case in which a distributor terminated a beverage distributorship agreement with a subdistributor on only six days' notice, the court held that "fairness and equity" required more notice, in order to "afford the party losing the contract an opportunity to make appropriate arrangement in lieu thereof by dispersing inventory, adjusting work force, exploring probable alternatives, and in general, 'getting his house in order' to proceed in absence of the former relationship."[10]

A second and more controversial situation is that of the long-term financing agreement between bank and borrower under which the borrower may ask for periodic advances that the bank is not obligated to make. Despite the absence of an explicit provision, some courts have imposed a requirement that the bank give reasonable notice to the borrower before refusing to continue its practice of making periodic advances. In a leading—if controversial—federal Court of Appeals case, the agreement gave the borrower a $3.5 million line of credit to finance its wholesale and retail grocery business. Loans were secured by the borrower's inventory and accounts receivable, with all the borrower's receipts to go into a "blocked account" to which the bank had sole access. When the bank then, without notice, refused a requested advance of $800,000 that would have brought the balance nearly to the limit, the borrower sued, claiming that the sudden discontinuance of financing resulted in the collapse of its business. The court pointed out that the "blocked account" mechanism left the borrower "without operating capital until it had paid down its loan," putting its "continued existence entirely at the whim or mercy" of the bank. Looking by analogy to the Code's notice rule for contracts for the sale of goods, the court concluded that the "obligation to act in good faith would require a period of notice to [the borrower] to allow it a reasonable opportunity to seek alternate financing, absent valid business reasons precluding [the bank] from doing so."[11]

The examples discussed so far have involved warning requirements in promissory commitments. Warning requirements are also found where conduct results in a nonpromissory commitment. The result is to lighten markedly the burden of the commitment, as can be seen in three earlier illustrations from (Chapter 9). The railroad that has committed itself by maintaining a watchman at a grade crossing may leave the crossing unattended if it uses reasonable care to warn drivers; the government that has committed itself to maintain a lighthouse may let the light go dark if it uses reasonable care to warn ships; and the city that has committed itself to maintain guards at school crossings may leave parents of schoolchildren to their own devices if it uses reasonable care to warn parents. Here, as in many instances of promissory commitments, one is bound only to warn if one wishes to change one's mind.

Imposing a warning requirement is not the only way to qualify a power of termination. A less common way is imposing an evenhandedness requirement. The Supreme Court of Michigan fashioned just such a requirement in Kenneth

Bankey's case. After imposing a warning requirement, the court went on to hold that "an employer may make changes in a written discharge-for-cause policy applicable to its entire work force or to specific classifications without having reserved in advance the right to do so." But this would not permit "the temporary suspension of a discharge-for-cause policy to facilitate the firing of a particular employee in contravention of that policy."[12] If the employer changes its mind it may exercise its power of termination, but it is expected to act evenhandedly.

It is not unusual to find requirements of evenhandedness imposed by agreement in contracts between private parties. A buyer of goods under a long-term contract may agree to buy at the seller's "posted" price—the publicly advertised price at which the seller sells to other similar buyers. The buyer thus takes the risk of price hikes, as long as they are evenhanded. Such a buyer may also agree to a "most favored nation's" clause—a clause that entitles the buyer to the most advantageous terms granted by the seller to any other buyer. The buyer thus takes the risk of a change in terms, as long as they are, in this respect, evenhanded. But it is less common to find them imposed by courts and legislatures.

The common law imposed no requirement of evenhandedness on a debtor in failing circumstances. Even if insolvent, the debtor was free to treat some creditors more favorably than other similar creditors. Early in the nineteenth century, the United States Supreme Court observed that a "debtor may prefer one creditor, pay him fully, and exhaust his whole property, leaving nothing for others equally meritorious."[13] The idea that it is objectionable for a debtor that owes a number of creditors to satisfy the claim of one creditor in preference to the others, at a time when the debtor lacks sufficient assets to satisfy the claims of all creditors, came into state and federal law by statute and is now firmly embedded in the bankruptcy laws.[14] A debtor who is insolvent or who is about to become insolvent must deal even-handedly with all creditors.

A requirement of evenhandedness is also imposed by statute on a seller who has promised to sell goods to a number of buyers and who is excused in part because the partial destruction of the goods has made full performance impracticable. Just as the insolvent debtor must deal evenhandedly with all creditors, the disabled seller must deal evenhandedly with all buyers. According to the statute, the seller must, in a "fair and reasonable" manner, "allocate production and deliveries among his customers."[15]

In a few instances, as in Kenneth Bankey's case, even-handedness requirements have been imposed by courts rather than legislatures. Thus, in interpreting standardized agreements, courts often observe a requirement of evenhand-edness, interpreting the agreement "wherever reasonable as treating alike all those similarly situated, without regard to their knowledge or understanding of the standard terms of the writing," since in assenting to such terms one "normally assumes that others are doing likewise and that all who do so are on an equal footing."[16] A party that does business with a number of customers using the same standard-form contract is thus held to the same meaning of the contract language as to all customers.

An interesting example of judicial recognition of the importance of evenhandedness is the sovereign acts doctrine, which attempts to reconcile two apparently conflicting principles as they apply to government contracts.[17] On the one hand, a contracting party may be excused from performance that has become impracticable, as when it is prevented by a supervening act of government (Chapter 2). On the other hand, a contracting party is not excused by impracticability that is self-inflicted. When, if ever, is the government as a contracting party excused from performance that has become impracticable because it has been prevented by its own supervening act? In 1925 the United States Supreme Court answered that "the United States when sued as a contractor cannot be held liable for an obstruction to the performance of the particular contract resulting from its public and general acts as a sovereign, [for, though] 'sovereign acts performed for the general good may work injury to some private contractors, such parties gain nothing by having the United States as their defendants.'"[18] In 1996 the Supreme Court was called on to apply this sovereign acts doctrine, and the principle of evenhandedness on which it rests, in the *Winstar* case.

During the financial crisis that beset savings institutions (known as thrifts) in the early 1980s, the Federal Home Loan Bank Board provided incentives to induce profitable thrifts to take over failed ones. The incentives included a change in accounting standards that permitted the resulting institution to treat what was a deficit in capital as an asset known as "supervisory goodwill." In the mid-1980s profitable thrifts were induced by this change to acquire failed thrifts, acquisitions that would not have been possible without supervisory goodwill, because the resulting institutions would not have met the board's minimum capital requirements.

In the late 1980s, in the wake of a second financial crisis, Congress enacted the Financial Institutions Reform, Recovery, and Enforcement Act (FIRREA), which severely limited the use of supervisory goodwill, described in the House Report as one of the board's "accounting gimmicks." Threatened with enforcement proceedings for failure to meet minimum capital requirements, the thrifts sued the United States, contending that the "government," through the board, had promised to allow them to use supervisory goodwill, and that the government, through Congress, had reneged on that promise by enacting FIRREA.

The government countered with the argument that enactment of FIRREA was a public and general sovereign act that excused its performance of that promise under the sovereign acts doctrine. Since enactment of FIRREA would have excused a private party on the ground of impracticability had it made the same contract (Chapter 2), the government maintained that it too was relieved of the consequences of the Bank Board's improvident decision.

A splintered Supreme Court held for the thrifts, and a plurality opinion rejected the government's argument based on the sovereign acts doctrine, reasoning that "if the Government is to be treated like other contractors, some line has to be drawn . . . between regulatory legislation that is relatively free of government self-interest and therefore cognizable for the purpose of a legal impossibility defense and . . . statutes tainted by a governmental object of self-relief."[19] The plurality opinion added that the requirement of generality "will almost always be met where . . . the governmental action 'bears upon [the government's contract] as it bears upon all similar contracts between citizens.'"[20] The government is not liable if, in obstructing its own performance, it does so as to bear "upon all similar contracts" evenhandedly. Although the *Winstar* case is surely not the last word on the meaning of "public and general acts," it sheds at least some light on one judicially imposed requirement of evenhandedness.

The requirement of evenhandedness in the context of the sovereign acts doctrine may draw some theoretical support from a model of decision-making put forward by scholars who view the individual as a collection of many decision makers, with responsibility for making choices rotating among them. They analogize to a principal who has many agents. So one farsighted "planner" has a series of myopic "doers." The doers exercise direct control over decisions, and the planner exercises indirect control by influencing each doer's decision.[21]

Almost without exception, however, the law makes no allowance for such internal divisions. If, according to agency law, one of the doers has the authority to bind the individual, the planner is powerless to override the doer's decision once the doer has made a commitment. Thus a farsighted member of a partnership is powerless to override a myopic partner's decision to make a commitment on behalf of the partnership. Similarly, a farsighted division of a corporation is powerless to override a myopic partner's decision to make a commitment on behalf of the corporation.

But, as the *Winstar* case illustrates, the government is subject to different rules. If Congress is viewed as the far-sighted planner and the Bank Board as a myopic doer, the case stands for the proposition that the planner can override the doer's decision even though the doer has made a commitment on behalf of the government. But it can do this only if it acts as a planner should—evenhandedly by an act of either the executive or legislative branch that is "public and general." A requirement of evenhandedness, in the sense in which I will use it, insists that a promisor who has made similar promises to a number of promisees deal fairly with each promisee in relation to the others, not unjustly prefer-ring any one to the others. And, as the *Winstar* case shows, requirements of evenhandedness are sometimes imposed by law. Both legislatures and courts have imposed such require-ments.

Other illustrations of a judicially imposed requirement of evenhandedness can be supposed. Should not such a re-quirement be imposed on a municipality that establishes a policy of paying rewards to those who capture criminals? Should not such a requirement be imposed on a department store that announces a policy of accepting without question the return of goods purchased? The appeal of evenhanded-ness can be felt in many situations involving happy campers.

Before leaving commitments for relinquishments and preclusions, we must consider how commitments are soft-ened as well as confined.

CHAPTER ELEVEN

The Strength of a Commitment

How strong is a commitment? What will it cost to renege on it? Eugene V. Klein contracts to buy a G-II jet from PepsiCo and learns that "committed" does not imply compulsion. The limited availability of specific performance and the preference for an award of money damages. The expectation measure of money damages and its limitations. The alternative of a reliance measure and its appropriateness for reciprocal promises and gratuitous promises. What "committed" means in cases of plea bargains.

If your promise commits you, you will experience regret if you change your mind and decide to renege. The strength of your commitment can be measured by the extent of that regret in terms of the costs, both legal and extralegal, of reneging.[1] Our concern is with the legal costs. What will a court do to you if you fail to honor your commitment?

Eugene V. Klein found out. After a search he learned that PepsiCo owned a used G-II Gulfstream corporate jet—just the one he wanted—and PepsiCo promised to sell it to him for $4.6 million.[2] When, a week later, PepsiCo changed its mind and reneged, Eugene went to a federal district court and persuaded the trial judge to grant specific performance, ordering PepsiCo to deliver the promised G-II.

In many legal systems, notably those descended from Roman law, the trial judge would have been correct. Under French law, for example, courts routinely order recalcitrant sellers to deliver goods.[3] But when PepsiCo appealed, a federal appeals court held that the trial judge erred in granting specific performance, a remedy that "is inappropriate where damages are recoverable and adequate." Though Eugene "would have to go through considerable expense to find a replacement," since prices had started to rise, "price increases alone are no reason to order specific performance." And, though there were only three "roughly comparable" G-IIs on the market, PepsiCo's G-II was "not unique"—all the more so because Eugene had argued that "he wanted the plane to resell it at a profit." Money damages "would clearly be adequate" to compensate him for the enhanced cost of a G-II on the risen market.[4]

Eugene thus discovered what many other promisees have learned—that a variety of rules of contract law operate to soften the commitments of promisors. Along with your celebrated freedom to make contracts goes a considerable freedom to break them should you change your mind. Commitment is not a matter of yes or no but a matter of degree, enforced by a cascading array of remedies, some specific and some substitutional. Among the specific are those that disable the promisor from reneging on the promise, those that execute the promise without the aid of the promisor, and those that compel the promisor to perform the promise. Among the substitutional are those that award a sum of money based on the expectation interest, the reliance interest, or the restitution interest. In the discussion that follows, remedies have been arranged along a descending scale with the more exacting ones first.

Odysseus was so firmly bound to the mast that he was disabled from succumbing to the Sirens' song. But only rarely is a recalcitrant promisor so firmly bound to the promisee as to be disabled from reneging on a promise. Thus whereas the state of New Jersey had by statute promised bondholders that it would refrain from acts that might impair the value of the bonds, the Supreme Court of the United States held that an attempted repeal of the statute was invalid and therefore without effect. Because repeal would have impaired a contractual obligation in violation of the Contracts Clause of the Constitution, the state of New Jersey was as firmly bound as was Odysseus.[5] More often, however, a court will not disable the promisor from reneging on the promise but rather will seek to assure that the promise is performed.

In some situations the court can do this by executing the promise without the promisor's aid. If the promise is to convey ownership of property, a court may enter a decree divesting the promisor's title to the property and vesting it in the promisee, with the same effect as if the promisor had voluntarily conveyed the property.[6] Because "equity treats as done that which ought to have been done," it was at least in theory within the court's power to have granted specific relief by divesting PepsiCo of the title to the G-II and vesting it in Eugene.[7]

In practice, however, equity traditionally acts on the person, and a court will more often grant specific relief by ordering the recalcitrant promisor to perform the promise, on pain of civil and even criminal sanctions for contempt of court. But as Eugene learned on PepsiCo's appeal, even this remedy is considered exceptional. Anglo-American law has a strong preference for substitutional relief over specific relief. (In sale of goods cases, as we shall see, this gives heightened importance to delivery [Chapter 12].) For reasons partly historical, courts have declined to order performance if, as in the case of a G-II that was not "unique," money damages are seen as "adequate."

In recent years, courts have shown a willingness to relax the strictures of the adequacy rule and to order performance, and the United States has ratified a treaty governing international sales that embodies just such a remedy.[8] Nonetheless, relief is still usually substitutional rather than specific. As Karl Llewellyn wrote, "A contract is no equivalent of performance; rights are a poor substitute for goods."[9]

At least in theory, substitutional relief would not have to be limited to a sum of money. One might, for example, imagine a court ordering PepsiCo to deliver a substitute G-II to Eugene. Money is the currency of substitutional relief, however, and, as far as the law goes, if you renege on a promise the measure of your regret is usually expressed in dollars. There remains much truth in the assertion of Oliver Wendell Holmes that "the duty to keep a contract at common law means a prediction that you must pay damages if you do not keep it,—and nothing else."[10]

The question then becomes: How to calculate the sum of money to be awarded as substitutional relief? For the most part, its calculation in contract cases is directed not at *compulsion* of *promisors* to *prevent* breach but rather at *relief* to *promisees* to *redress* breach. A court will not ordinarily impose punitive damages on a recalcitrant promisor. The concern is not with the question: How can promisors be made to keep their promises? Rather it is with the question: How can people be encouraged to deal with those who make promises?

The usual response to that question is to award damages based on the "benefit of the bargain" of which the promisee has been deprived, a measure of damages that is called the *expectation* measure because it is intended to protect the promisee's expectation. Courts thus attempt to put the promisee in as good a position as the promisee would have been in had the contract been performed, that is, had there been no breach.[11] They ask: How much better off would the aggrieved party have been if the promisor's commitment had been met? (This does not measure the aggrieved party's regret, which would be the difference between the value of the choice that was made to deal with the promisor and the choice that was not made and is therefore regretted.)[12]

In Eugene's case, the answer to this question might depend on what he planned to do with the G-II. Damages must be proved with reasonable certainty,[13] and if Eugene wanted it to start a charter business, uncertainty in calculating his lost profit might preclude recovery. If he wanted the G-II for purely recreational use he might have even more difficulty in proving damages with reasonable certainty. If, as he argued, he wanted the G-II jet for the purpose of resale, he could probably establish damages based on the loss of the profit that he expected on that resale. To say that such an award of money damages could protect Eugene's expectation of performance is, however, to use "expectation" in a somewhat curious sense.[14] Had PepsiCo's promise been performed, Eugene would have been in possession of PepsiCo's G-II, and, as we shall see, PepsiCo would generally have been powerless to get it back (Chapter 12).

The expectation measure often softens a promisor's commitment by enabling the promisor to commit what is called an "efficient breach." A promisor that overlooked a better opportunity and later regrets this uninformed decision can break the contract, seize that opportunity, compensate the promisee for lost expectation, and still be better off than if the contract had been performed. This is so because the expectation measure bases recovery on the loss to the promisee and not on the gain to the promisor. Since the promisor values its gain more than the promisee values its loss, the economist styles the breach as "efficient." So when PepsiCo changed its mind and decided that it would be better to break its contract with Eugene, forgo the purchase price, and pay him damages based on his expectation, its breach was an efficient one.[15]

Indeed, the expectation measure sometimes softens commitments in startling ways. Suppose that in making a promise you have grossly underestimated the cost of your performance, which you now realize will greatly exceed the increase in value to the other party. You can avoid some of the consequences of your uninformed decision by reneging and paying damages limited to that increase in value. Imagine a builder that made a $35,000 mistake in contracting to do excavation for $100,000. How much will the mistake cost the builder? The builder thought that the work could be done for $85,000, leaving a $15,000 profit, but now finds that it will cost $120,000, resulting in a $20,000 loss. The owner, in turn, who contracted to pay the $100,000, thought correctly that the work would improve the value of the land by $10,000. On discovering the truth before beginning work, the builder can renege and pay the owner only $10,000 as damages. Although the builder made a $35,000 mistake and would have lost $20,000 by performing, the measure of the builder's regret is only $10,000.

Important limitations on the expectation measure of damages help further to lessen the pangs of regret. One of the most important of these is that there is no recovery for loss that the promisee could reasonably have avoided, a limitation which operates somewhat like a warning rule.[16] A promisor who has a change of mind and decides to renege can, in effect, warn the promisee to incur no further costs in reliance on the contract and to take appropriate steps to arrange a substitute. The sort of warning rule discussed earlier, however, confines the promisor's commitment so that a promisor that has given the required warning has not broken the promise and is not liable for the promisee's unavoidable reliance, including any costs of arranging a substitute (Chapter 10). Here, on the other hand, the rule only softens the commitment—despite a warning, the promisor has broken the promise and is liable for the promisee's unavoidable reliance, including any costs of arranging a substitute. Thus, Eugene could have recovered any additional amount that it would have cost him to buy a substitute G-II jet on a risen market.[17] But he could not have recovered damages based on his lost resale profit to the extent that he could have avoided that loss by buying—even on a risen market—one of the three "roughly comparable" G-IIs and reselling it instead of PepsiCo's.

Expectation is not the only possible measure of recovery. An alternative is to award damages designed to put the promisee in the position that the promisee would have been in had no contract been made, rather than the position that the promisee would have been in had the contract been performed. Because this protects the promisee's reliance, it is called the reliance measure. It is nearly always less generous than the expectation measure, even with all the limitations on expectation.

At first it might seem that reliance is a fairer measure than expectation. As a practical matter, to be sure, expectation is sometimes easier to measure than is reliance. But in theory, why should a promisee be compensated for more than reliance? What has become a conventional answer is much the same as that given earlier in response to the enigma of the unexecuted bilateral agreement. Reliance includes lost opportunities. But since lost opportunities are hard to prove, expectation is a surrogate measure for reliance.[18]

The buyer who buys goods on the market for $100 and so passes up the opportunity to buy similar goods at the same price from another seller sustains a reliance loss of $25 if the seller refuses to deliver after the market has risen to $125 and the buyer is forced to cover at that price. But $25 is also the measure of the buyer's expectation, taking into account the limitation of avoidability just described in connection with the G-II. Thus if one assumes such a market, the expectation measure is a perfect surrogate for the reliance measure, taking loss opportunities into account. And even when the expectation measure does not have this coincidence with the reliance measure, it produces the apparently satisfying result of forcing the promisor to take into account the contract's value to the promisee when calculating the effects of breach, thereby enhancing the promisor's incentives to perform and encouraging people to deal with promisors.[19]

This reasoning does not, however, apply to promises to make gifts, and it has been argued that, at least where reliance is the basis for enforcing such a promise, the promisor's liability should be limited to the reliance measure.[20] The result would be a commitment confined by the sort of warning rule described in connection with the limitation of avoidability. Suppose that you promise to pay me $10,000 in the hope of encouraging my interest in music, and in reliance on your promise I quit my part-time job and begin to take guitar lessons. If you renege after I have relied to the extent of only $1,000, my reliance recovery would be only that amount, and if I continued to take and pay for guitar lessons even after you had warned me that you did not intend to pay, I could not recover for that avoidable expense. But it may be no simple matter to calculate my reliance interest, which includes my loss from quitting my part-time job. And it is even easier to calculate my expectation interest than if you had exchanged your promise for my return promise because there is no un-rendered return performance on my part to be accounted for.

Furthermore, the reliance measure is unsuitable if the promise is enforceable under the intention principle rather than the reliance principle.[21] This is so for a promise enforce-able because it is one to perform a moral obligation. Since no reliance is required, the obvious choice is the expectation measure, limited by the extent of the moral obligation. It is also so for a promise enforceable under the Restatement Sec-ond's exception for charitable subscriptions. Again, since no reliance is required, the obvious choice is the expectation measure. And it would also be so for a promise enforceable because of a formality if the institution of a formality were to be resurrected. Liability would have to be based on expecta-tion. Charitable subscriptions—and promises supported by formalities—typically involve situations in which the threat of the expectation measure may have the desirable effect of inducing promisors to limit their promises by conditioning them to take account of the possibility of regret.[22] Further-more, in such situations promisors may want promisees to have the benefit of promises fully enforceable to the extent of the expectation measure.

Yet another remedy is sometimes available. A Roman jurist nearly two thousand years ago opined that it is fair "by nature . . . that no one become richer by the loss and in-jury of another."[23] Accordingly, today a promisor can be re-quired to make restitution by disgorging whatever has been received from the promisee, restoring the promisor to the position in which the promisor was before the contract was made. Sometimes this can be be done by a form of specific relief—specific restitution, in which the exact thing received is ordered to be returned. More often it is done by awarding the aggrieved promisee a sum of money equal to the value of what should be disgorged: a sum called the restitution measure. Such relief may be available in case of a complete refusal to perform or another serious breach that justifies termination of the contract.[24] If, for example, Eugene Klein had given PepsiCo a deposit of $1 million on its G-II jet, he could have recovered this when PepsiCo reneged. While restitution requires the promisor to disgorge the benefit received, it does not compensate the promisee for lost expectation nor for reliance—except to the extent that, as in the case of the $1 million deposit, the reliance may have conferred a benefit. It does not "enforce" the promise. Its attractiveness to the promisee is largely limited to situations in which the contract is a "losing" one, in the sense that the promisee's expectation turns out to be a loss rather than a gain.

Under the restitution measure, as it is applied in contracts cases, the benefits that the promisor must disgorge are limited in an important respect, as can be seen from the contrasting case of Frank Snepp. On going to work for the Central Intelligence Agency, Frank signed an agreement that recited that he was "undertaking a position of trust" and in which he promised not to publish any material relating to the CIA without its "specific prior approval." After leaving the CIA, Frank published *Decent Interval,* a book about CIA activities in South Vietnam, without submitting it for CIA approval. The government sued Frank to enforce the agreement, though it conceded that the book contained no classified material and would have been approved had it been submitted. If the expectation measure had been applied, the government would have recovered nothing since, as the Supreme Court of the United States explained, the "actual damages attributable to a publication such as Snepp's generally are unquantifiable."[25] But Frank's case was exceptional because he had recited that his was a "position of trust," and the court held that this was no mere contract. Frank owed a fiduciary obligation, and it was therefore proper to require him to "disgorge the benefits of his faithlessness"—his profits from *Decent Interval,* including $60,000 in advance payments.

This generous notion of benefits is, however, limited to actions against fiduciaries, such as agents and trustees, whose breaches are seen as faithlessness. Had Frank's commitment been merely contractual, the government could not have recovered his profits. Under contract law, the benefit to the promisor is not seen as including gain that is not conferred on the promisor by the promisee. In contrast to the case of the $1 million deposit, conferred on PepsiCo by Eugene, the profits from *Decent Interval* were not conferred on Frank by the government. Were contract law otherwise, commitments would not be softened by the possibility of committing an efficient breach.[26]

Return now to Enricho Navarroli's case and consider an accused's remedies for breach of a plea bargain (Prologue). Suppose that Enricho had swapped his promise to plead guilty for the state's promise, but that after Enricho had pled guilty the state had reneged. Which of the remedies just listed are available to an accused in Enricho's position?

At the most exacting extreme, although a court would not prevent the state from reneging or execute the state's promise itself, a court could grant specific performance, protecting the accused's expectation by ordering the state to perform its promise.[27] As for substitutional relief, the less exacting remedy of damages measured by either the expectation or reliance interests would not be available against the state.[28] The only alternative to specific performance is the least exacting remedy of restitution, which here would allow the accused to "get back" the benefit conferred on the state by withdrawing the plea of guilty. This would not only protect the accused's restitution interest by forcing the state to disgorge the benefit received, on the ground of its complete refusal to perform, but would also protect the accused's reliance interest by returning the accused to the position the accused was in before making the plea bargain.[29] If the accused now regards the plea bargain as an ill-advised "losing contract" and would rather that it not be enforced, this may seem preferable to the more exacting remedy of specific performance.[30]

As in contracts cases, the choice of remedy is initially in the hands of the injured party—here the accused. So the Supreme Court of Washington has held that the accused's "choice of remedy controls, unless there are compelling reasons not to allow that remedy."[31] Courts have therefore generally been willing to grant specific performance when the accused has requested that remedy. In granting an accused's request for specific performance, the same court reasoned that "specific performance is the only adequate remedy available to the defendant," who is "entitled to the benefit of his original bargain."[32]

Courts have, however, been more reluctant to grant requests by the accused for restitution, particularly when the passage of time has resulted in the loss of evidence or witnesses, making prosecution of the case more difficult.[33] This reluctance is akin to that shown by courts in comparable contracts cases.[34] When plea bargains are involved, some courts have left matters largely to the discretion of the trial court.[35]

Having concluded our discussion of commitments, we take up relinquishments and preclusions.

Interlude

Whatever Rousseau may have thought of the absurdity of the will's putting itself in chains for the *future* (Prologue), the *present* is an altogether different matter. This is reflected in the distinction made between a commitment, an undertaking to do something in the future, and a relinquishment or preclusion, a surrender of something in the present.[1] Relinquishments and preclusions are like commitments and unlike resolutions in that there is someone to complain in an adversary system of an attempt to reverse a relinquishment or preclusion (Chapter 1). However, two salient characteristics distinguish relinquishments and preclusions from commitments.

First, whereas commitments speak to the future, relinquishments and preclusions speak to the present. The significance of this difference lies in the appealing notion that we are more competent in ordering our present actions than our future ones (Chapter 2). While we see relinquishments and preclusions as Now and For Sure, we see commitments as When and If. Society may impose limits on our buying for credit rather than for cash because we tend to underestimate future risks and make commitments based on ill-considered decisions. If Mary Yates Johnson gives Allegheny College

$5,000 right now she is likely to be more reflective than if she promises to give Allegheny College $5,000 thirty days after her death (Chapter 7). A perceptive scholar has pointed out that the law has a general tendency to draw a distinction "between a present consent and a consent to some future action," adding that "it is in the case of a present consent that the economic assumptions about the consumer knowing his own best interest are at their strongest."[2] The force of a present consent is implicit in the New Testament story of Esau who "sold his birthright for a single meal, and . . . although he wanted afterwards to claim the blessing, he was rejected; though he begged for it to the point of tears, he found no way open for second thoughts."[3] If, then, we are better able to protect ourselves against the possibility of second thoughts in cases of relinquishments and preclusions than in cases of commitments, paternalism argues in favor of distinguishing between the two.

Second, whereas you can commit what you acquire in the future, you can surrender only what you have. This important restraint on relinquishments and preclusions is expressed in a Latin maxim, *nemo dat quod non habet* (one cannot give what one does not have), that seems intuitive. Mary Yates Johnson could not have given $5,000 to Allegheny College unless she had the $5,000 to give. But she could have promised to give $5,000 even though she had not so much as a penny. For this reason, too, paternalism argues in favor of distinguishing relinquishments and preclusions from commitments.

What of the distinction between relinquishments and preclusions? Often when you surrender something you intend to do exactly that—to surrender it. When you *give* a collection of manuscripts to a university, *declare* that you hold a painting in trust for a friend, or *cancel* a debtor's $10,000 note, you intend to surrender something. In such cases your expression of intention is not unlike your expression when, by promising, you make an expression of commitment. You take a first step by making an initial decision to surrender something, you take a second step to carry out your decision, and then you change your mind—you regret having taken the second step of surrendering. I use the term "relinquishment" to refer to such situations in which surrender is not only voluntary, in the sense that the second step was within your control, but intentional, in the sense that surrender was what you intended when you took the second step.

But this is not always so. Sometimes you surrender something without intending to do so. When you *ratify* a contract made as a teenager, *represent* that a companion is the owner of your emerald ring, or *refrain* from protesting a neighbor's use of your land, you may have no intention of surrendering anything—your initial decision relates to something quite different. But after taking a second step to carry out your decision, you change your mind—and then you regret having taken your second step because of a legal rule under which your second step—ratifying, representing, or refraining—results in surrender of something that you do not want to surrender. I use the term "preclusion" to refer to situations in which surrender is voluntary, in the sense that the second step was within your control, but not intentional, in the sense that surrender was not what you intended when you took the second step. Preclusions do not always involve a change of mind. Sometimes the second step—as where you refrain from protesting your neighbor's use of your land—is not the result of a decision but of inadvertence or sloth. A likely reaction is "Oops!" Although such cases are also governed by the rules for preclusions, our concern is with cases in which there has been a change of mind.

In Part II of this book my concern is with the extent to which a surrender is irreversible. Can you reverse what you do if you *give* a collection of manuscripts to a university, *declare* that you hold a painting in trust for a friend, *cancel* a debtor's $10,000 note, *ratify* a contract made as a teenager, *represent* that a companion is the owner of your emerald ring, or *refrain* from protesting a neighbor's use of your land?

Sometimes the passage of time makes a surrender irreversible. Astrophysicist Stephen Hawking has written of an imaginary time in which you could not only go forward but could "turn round and go backward."[4] But you cannot do this in real time, as Robert Frost's traveler realized after having taken the road less traveled. In real time your surrenders are often irreversible because you cannot turn back the clock. Sometimes the nature of what you have surrendered makes it so: if you allow me to invade your privacy, that is irreversible. Sometimes the manner of your surrender makes it so: if you throw away your chocolates, that is irreversible. It is otherwise for commitments. If you have done no more than promise to allow a surgeon to remove your appendix, it is not too late to change your mind and revoke your promise. Your undertaking is revocable. Once you have allowed the surgeon to operate, however, it is too late to change your mind and reclaim your lost appendix. Your surrender is irreversible.

If another person is involved, as in the case of the surgeon, you might argue that your consent was not effective—that, for example, your decision to undergo the operation was the result of a decision that was unfairly influenced or uninformed. But even so, you would have no more than a right to damages against that person. You could not reverse your surrender, for even an award of damages against the surgeon would not restore your appendix to you.

I will not be concerned with situations like those just described in which, whatever the law might be, it is too late for you to change your mind and reverse your surrender. My concern will be limited to situations in which it is not too late, as where you have given your chocolates to an abstemious friend who has not eaten them. In Part I, I asked when you are no longer free to follow your every whim and caprice because you have made an undertaking that is binding as a matter of law; now I ask when you are no longer free because you have made a surrender that is irreversible as a matter of law.

In searching for general principles among the rules that govern relinquishments and preclusions, one must slog through a morass of legal jargon. In doing so, I have tried to bring some rationality to such terms as discharge, waiver, estoppel, laches, election, ratification, affirmance, and prescription.

The first five chapters of Part II deal with relinquishments in the contexts of performance (Chapter 12), gift (Chapters 13 and 14), discharge (Chapter 15), and waiver (Chapter 16). Here we see the vigor of the intention principle, no longer overshadowed by the reliance principle. As a prominent federal judge commented, "I do not know of any branch of the law . . . in which a renunciation of a legal entitlement is effective only if the other party relies to his detriment."[5] The final four chapters deal with preclusions in the contexts of estoppel and laches (Chapter 17), of rejection (Chapter 18), of election (Chapter 19), and of prescription (Chapter 20). Here, in addition to revisiting the reliance principle, I introduce an anti-speculation principle, a public interest principle, and a repose principle.

PART II

Relinquishments and Preclusions

CHAPTER TWELVE

Relinquishment by Performance

What if PepsiCo had delivered its G-II jet and then sought to reclaim it from Eugene V. Klein? How performance is a watershed, so that a seller after delivering goods to the buyer cannot usually reclaim them. Comparison with the enigma of the wholly unperformed bilateral contract and the concept of efficient breach. A different solution in French law. Explanation of our law in terms of the intention principle. The effectiveness of contrary agreements and some exceptions.

We have now seen how, though you may be bound by your promise as soon as you receive a return promise, you can usually pay damages instead of performing: you are not so firmly bound that you cannot commit an efficient breach. Though PepsiCo had promised to sell Eugene V. Klein its G-II jet for $4.6 million, a court would not force PepsiCo to give up the G-II when it changed its mind.

All this changes and irreversibility sets in once you perform your promise. Of course, the irreversibility is sometimes inherent in the nature of your performance—singing in an opera or painting a house, for instance. But even if this is not so, performance is generally irreversible as a matter of law. If PepsiCo had delivered the G-II to Eugene before changing its mind, its delivery would have been irreversible and PepsiCo could not have gotten the G-II back. Our law begins with the premise that by delivery the seller relinquishes its power over the goods. Performance is thus an important watershed: before performance the seller can renege and retain the goods; after performance the seller cannot renege and get them back.

What we saw earlier was that as long as PepsiCo had not given up possession of the G-II, Eugene could not compel

PepsiCo to do so. What we see now is that once PepsiCo gave up possession of the G-II, PepsiCo could not get it back. This would have been so even if PepsiCo's decision to sell the G-II had turned out to be improvident because Eugene had failed to pay the $4.6 million after taking delivery of the jet. Significant as performance is, what the seller loses by performing is only its remedy as an unpaid seller to seek satisfaction from the goods themselves, not its remedy as an unpaid seller to bring a lawsuit to recover the price. PepsiCo could still sue Eugene and get a judgment for the unpaid price of $4.6 million, but it could not get back the G-II. As your right to damages against the surgeon who removed your appendix would not give you back the appendix, PepsiCo's right to recover the price from Eugene would not give PepsiCo back the G-II.

Why should performance without more be critical? We have seen the argument that a promise should not result in commitment unless the promisee can prove reliance on the other party's promise. As it can be argued that PepsiCo should be committed to sell the G-II only if Eugene can prove reliance on PepsiCo's promise, it could also be argued that PepsiCo should be barred from reclaiming the G-II only if Eugene can prove reliance on PepsiCo's giving up possession. Why has no such argument been made?

We have also seen the argument that it is desirable to permit a promisor, on a change of mind, to renege on the promise and seize a better opportunity, as long as it can compensate the promisee for lost expectation and still be better off. Why should it be too late for PepsiCo to commit such an efficient breach because it has given up possession of the G-II to Eugene? Would not a breach by PepsiCo be as "efficient" after PepsiCo gave up possession as before?

Not all legal systems regard performance as a watershed. Under French law, if Eugene failed to pay the $4.6 million after taking possession, PepsiCo would be able, with the aid of a court, to get the G-II back.[1] And as we have already seen, if PepsiCo attempted to commit such a breach *before* delivery, Eugene would have a right under French law to specific relief and a court would order PepsiCo to deliver the G-II. Thus both before as well as after delivery, giving up possession lacks the significance under French law that it has under our own.

In our own system, delivery not only bars a recalcitrant seller from retaking the goods as a means of committing an efficient breach against an aggrieved buyer, but it also bars an aggrieved seller from retaking the goods as a remedy against a buyer in breach. The bar can be disadvantageous in two situations: first, when the buyer has become insolvent and the seller prefers the goods to a claim for the price against the insolvent buyer,[2] and second, when the contract has turned out to be a losing one for the seller and the seller would prefer the goods because they are worth more than the price.[3] If asked to explain why there should be such a bar, a common law lawyer might answer by saying that the seller has a "possessory lien"—a right to retain possession of the goods to secure payment—and that because this right is "possessory" it is lost when the seller gives up possession. This, of course, is no explanation at all. The answer to the question is that the significance of performance rests on the intention principle.

To begin with, performance has the described effect only if, as in the case of the G-II, it is pursuant to an agreement that shows the parties' intention that it have that effect. PepsiCo's contract with Eugene showed the parties' intention that PepsiCo relinquish its power over the G-II on delivery. Delivery would not have this effect if PepsiCo delivered the G-II for a more limited purpose—under what is termed a bailment—with the understanding that the G-II was not ultimately to become Eugene's. For example, if PepsiCo had delivered the G-II to Eugene in order to let him test it before deciding whether to buy it, PepsiCo's giving up possession would have barred PepsiCo from getting the G-II back only for the period of the test and not afterward. And if PepsiCo had delivered the G-II to Eugene under a lease, giving up possession would have barred PepsiCo from getting the G-II back only for the term of the lease and not afterward. In both of these situations PepsiCo would not only have retained a power over the G-II at the end of the term of the agreement but the right to regain possession of the G-II in the event of a breach of the terms of the agreement.[4]

From this it follows that performance does not have the effect described if the parties make it clear that they have a different intention. If PepsiCo had agreed to deliver the G-II to Eugene in return for $4.6 million in cash, PepsiCo would not have lost its power over the G-II if Eugene had failed to come up with the $4.6 million. When a buyer of cotton failed to come up with the cash for the cotton, the Supreme Court of Tennessee held that because the "intention of the parties controls," the seller could get the cotton back. "Looking to the intention of the parties, which is the governing principle, we are satisfied that [the seller] purposed to transfer title to the cotton only upon receiving cash therefor. . . . We are therefore of the opinion that title to said ten bales of cotton never passed from [the seller] to [the buyer]."[5] The Uniform Commercial Code preserves the right of an unpaid cash seller to reclaim the goods.[6] Sellers often express their intention not to relinquish their power over goods on delivery by providing for a security interest in the goods. Had PepsiCo delivered the G-II to Eugene on secured credit, it would have had the right to reclaim the G-II if Eugene had failed to pay the balance of the price.[7] A court will honor the parties' understanding that performance is not to have its usual effect.

Furthermore, even if it was the seller's intention to relinquish power over the goods on delivery, there are some exceptional situations in which the seller can reclaim them. In an early chapter I suggested that regret might result from decisions of five kinds—those that were unfairly influenced, uninformed, ill considered, improvident, or obsolete—and pointed out that, in differing degrees, the law allows you to renege on a promise made as a result of such a decision (Chapter 2). The law is not as forgiving if you have delivered goods under an agreement of sale. As we have already seen, you cannot reclaim the goods if you changed your mind on discovering that your decision was improvident because the other party defaulted. But you can reclaim the goods if your decision to deliver them was unfairly influenced or, in some situations, uninformed.[8] This is because you are not regarded as having had the required intention. Thus if PepsiCo's decision was unfairly influenced, because it was induced by Eugene's false representation, or if it was uninformed, because it was based on a mistake of both parties as to a basic assumption, PepsiCo might avoid the transaction and resume ownership of the G-II.

Because the effect of delivery is subject to agreement to the contrary, graphically illustrated by the case of the cash sale, and may be subject to avoidance on the ground of an unfairly influenced or uninformed decision, it is plain that the bar that results from delivery is firmly rooted in the intention principle. This is not to say, however, that this is the only relevant principle. The public interest principle (see Chapter 19) also works in favor of treating performance as critical. Treating possession as "nine-tenths of the law" relieves the legal system of the burden of arranging the return of goods to a seller that has decided to commit an efficient breach. Were the law otherwise, courts would have to either compel buyers to return goods or permit sellers themselves to retake goods. It may seem better to surrender to inertia and leave well enough alone on the ground that whatever interest society has in encouraging efficient breach is outweighed by society's interest in the simple and efficient administration of justice, achieved by simply not disturbing the status quo.

As discussed in this chapter, relinquishment is limited to power over the goods that are the subject of the performance and does not extend to any right to damages against the other party. In the following chapter we see a more dramatic application of the intention principle, resulting in the relinquishment of all rights.

CHAPTER THIRTEEN

Relinquishment by Gift

Edgar Degas gives a painting to Henri Rouart and then seeks to retouch it. Two characteristics that distinguish a relinquishment by gift from a commitment to make a gift. The relevance of the requirement of delivery; delivery seen as a formality. Ethel Yahuda's attempt to make a gift to Hebrew University fails as a self-declared trust, though no delivery is required. The erosion of the requirement of delivery by the acceptance of a writing as an alternative. The retention of the restraint on giving what one does not have. The donor's power to take account of the possibility of regret and the extent to which courts will do so if the donor does not.

Recall Jack Tallas's unsuccessful attempt to make an enforceable promise to leave $50,000 in his will to his friend Peter Dementas (Chapter 8). The French painter Edgar Degas, who was known for changing his mind, did things differently. While visiting the home of Henri Rouart, a friend who had bought one of Edgar's pastels, Edgar was seized with what Henri's son later described as "his habitual and imperious urge to retouch." When the artist finally prevailed on his friend to let him take the pastel, it was never seen again. Edgar "had to confess his crime: the work entrusted to him for a few retouches had been completely destroyed." To atone, the artist decided to give his friend his now-famous painting *Danseuses à la barre,* which now hangs in New York's Metropolitan Museum of Art. Unlike Jack Tallas, Edgar Degas delivered his gift. Then he changed his mind. The scene includes a watering can, used to dampen the sawdust on the dancers' practice floor—the shape of the can mimicking the shape of one of the ballerinas—and the artist repeatedly protested, "That watering can is definitely idiotic, I simply must take it out." But having learned from experience, Henri never allowed Edgar to retouch it, and, in a piquant if apocryphal version of the story, kept the picture padlocked to his wall so that the artist could not once again change his mind and take it.[1]

Edgar Degas, who had been for a time a student of the law, would not have needed much familiarity with that subject in order to surmise that, once he had handed over the painting to Henri as a gift, voilà, it was too late to change his mind and retake it—even for retouching. Indeed, had Edgar taken what was once his painting, padlocked or not, without Henri's consent, Edgar would have been liable for his wrong.[2] Unlike Jack Tallas, who had unsuccessfully attempted to commit himself to make a gift, Edgar Degas had succeeded in giving the painting, and his right to it had passed immediately and irrevocably on his delivery of it with the requisite intention. In the law of gifts, as in the law of relinquishments in general, the focus is on the intention of the donor, not the reliance of the donee. According to the Restatement (Second) of Property, the "underlying requirement to effectuate a donative transfer is the intention on the part of the donor that some interest in property of the donor move from the donor to the intended donee."[3] One who has made such a transfer should let it stand if it was done with manifested intent. For much the same reasons that you might like to be able to make commitments, you might also like to be able to make relinquishments. No reliance or possibility of reliance on the transfer need be shown, for the principle here is the intention principle.

In trying to understand this concern with intention rather than reliance, it is important to realize that Edgar Degas' gift differs in an important respect from the kinds of transactions that we have focused on so far. Edgar's decision to give the painting to Henri was reflected in a consent to a present transfer of ownership rather than in a promise to transfer ownership in the future. Instead of making a commitment, Edgar consented to relinquish the right to the painting that he had at the time of his consent. Relinquishments are often paid for in some fashion, but our interest is in relinquishments that, like the gift by Edgar Degas, are gratuitous. As is true for relinquishments in general, a gift has two salient characteristics that distinguish it from a promise to make a gift in the future.

First, a gift speaks to the present. The gift of the painting, once made, was over and done with, which even the capricious artist would have been likely to sense. He might not have regarded a promise to make a gift as having the same finality. But Edgar Degas had taken a step that Jack Tallas had not—Jack had only promised to make his gift, while Edgar had actually made his. And if in doing so Edgar was better able to guard against the possibility of regret than he would have been in making a promise, there is less reason for a legal system given to paternalism to protect him from his own improvidence.

Second, a gift is limited to what one has. Here, as in the case of relinquishments generally, *nemo dat quod non habet:* Edgar Degas could not give what he did not have. Even a profligate as well as remorseful artist, minded to atone for the destruction of the pastel by purporting to give Henri Rouart a lifetime's output of paintings, would thus be powerless to so squander his future by means of a gift. By a promise, however, the artist might purport to commit not only his present inventory of paintings but also all that he would produce in the future.

In addition to having these two salient characteristics, a gift ordinarily has, like other relinquishments, the practical advantage of being self-executing, whereas in all but the most exceptional cases a commitment requires a remedy (Chapter 11). Once there has been delivery, nothing is ordinarily needed by way of remedy. To give effect to Edgar Degas' gift to Henri Rouart, a court need only decline to allow the artist to maintain a suit to retake the painting—and give his friend the same rights that any owner has to prevent interference by others with the owner's property. Things would

be different, however, if the artist had promised his friend
to give him the painting, for the promise would not be self-
executing. In order to enforce the promise, a court would
have to either compel Edgar to perform or hold him liable
for damages for not performing. Jack Tallas's promise to give
$50,000 to Peter Dementas could only have been enforced
by a court if it granted Peter a judgment against Jack's estate.
Judicial inertia, then, may argue in favor of upholding a gift
but not a promise of a gift.

It is a primordial notion that a gift requires delivery.[4]
In Islamic Law it is buttressed by the words of the Prophet,
who is reported to have said that a gift is not valid without
delivery.[5] In thirteenth-century England it found support in
Bracton, who wrote that a "gift is not valid unless livery follows."[6] The requirement of delivery received modern sanction in England in the nineteenth century[7] and has been generally accepted in this country.[8] Under the common law it
was *only* when Edgar Degas delivered the painting to Henri
Rouart that the artist was barred from changing his mind and
reneging. A statement by Edgar to Henri that he was making a
gift to Henri and that the painting was now Henri's would not
suffice. By insisting on delivery, courts make sure that gifts
are self-executing; if a mere declaration of gift were enforceable, a court would have to devise a remedy for enforcement.

The requirement of delivery comports with the two salient characteristics of relinquishments. First, delivery brings
home to the donor the fact that the gift is completed in the
present and leaves nothing to the future. A mere declaration
of gift would speak to the future, as does a promise. Second,
delivery can only be made of what one has. One can deliver
no more.

Legal scholars usually emphasize the first of these in
rationalizing the requirement of delivery. The essence of a
gift is the intention to make a present transfer of ownership.
Delivery, these scholars say, is a desirable formality, not only
providing some evidence that there was the intention to

make a present transfer but also exerting a cautionary impact to assure that the intention was the result of reflection and deliberation.[9] Not only did the presence of the painting on Henri Rouart's wall serve as some evidence that Edgar Degas had indeed made Henri a gift, but the wrench of delivering of the painting to his friend may have made even the capricious artist realize that it was too late to change his mind. This paternalistic reasoning has more than parochial appeal, for, if one were to apply French law to the artist's gift, one would reach a similar conclusion. Although French law traditionally required an elaborate formality of notarization for gift transactions (Chapter 5), a variety of creative subterfuges have now vastly eroded the requirement of notarization, and one of these is the recognition of delivery as a substitute for notarization.[10] Given this history, it is scarcely surprising that contemporary French scholars, like their American counterparts, view delivery as a formality designed to fulfill evidentiary and cautionary functions.[11] Thus under French law, as under common law, the gift of the painting would be effective once the painting had been delivered.

The central role that delivery has played in the law of gifts tends to obscure the fact that it is the intention to give that is the essence. The law's insistence on some formality is understandable since the donee often asserts the claim of a gift after the purported donor has died. But the relevant principle is the intention principle, and delivery is merely a formality that manifests the intention to give. Why should it be the *only* formality that will suffice to manifest that intention?

The law's insistence on delivery to the exclusion of any other formality is difficult to justify in the face of cases holding that the requirement is satisfied if the recipient of the gift happens already to be in possession of the personal property that is the subject of the gift when the owner of the property orally manifests the intention to make the gift.[12] One's skepticism is encouraged by the ease with which an owner of personal property, including a debt or other intangible, can circumvent the requirement by a mere oral declaration of trust naming the recipient as trustee.[13]

Consider the case of Ethel Yahuda, a widow who wished to give to Hebrew University in Jerusalem the library that her late husband, a distinguished Hebrew scholar, had collected. She announced her gift of the "Yahuda Library" at a public luncheon in Israel, attended by such notables as the president of Israel, and gave the university a memorandum listing the contents of the library. But after returning to the United States, she died before she had finished cataloguing and crating the library. When her estate refused to turn the library over to the university, the university sued and prevailed in the trial court on the reasoning that Ethel had orally constituted herself a trustee of the manuscripts.

The trial court's decision turned on a doctrine developed during the nineteenth century that permits a donor to create a self-declared trust of property by a simple declaration that the donor, as trustee, holds the property in trust for a beneficiary, the donee.[14] Unlike a gift, no delivery of the property is required, since the donor is both the creator of the trust and the trustee. And unlike a promise of a gift, the declaration of trust need not even be communicated to the donee or to anyone else, though it must be manifested by some external expression.[15] In this sense, the declaration is more like a resolution than a promise. The trust that is created is commonly revocable, though it may be irrevocable, but even if revocable it can no longer be revoked after the donor's death.

However, Connecticut's highest court held that it was error to find a self-declared trust in Ethel's case because there were "no facts even intimating that Ethel ever regarded herself as trustee of any trust whatsoever."[16] If Ethel had only said, "I give the *beneficial interest* in the manuscripts to Hebrew University," the court's decision would have been different and the University would have prevailed as beneficiary of a trust. But saying, "I give *all my interest* in the manuscripts to Hebrew University" could give it nothing without delivery.

On the one hand, the liberality of the law of trusts, in requiring no formality at all, seems extreme. On the other hand, the rigor of the law of gifts, in insisting that delivery is the only formality, seems unjustifiable. It is difficult to justify the anomaly on the ground that in the case of a trust the donor must assume a fiduciary relationship to the donee. An authority on trusts has written that it "is at least a matter for argument whether the requirement of delivery is a survival of a more primitive system of law in which symbolism is more important than intention."[17]

The impact of the "unfortunate" liberality of the law of trusts is said to be mitigated by the circumstance that few non-lawyers are likely to be aware of this device for avoiding the requirement imposed by the law of gifts.[18] (Jack Tallas may well have been a case in point.) But it is with the rigor of the law of gifts and not the liberality of the law of trusts that we are concerned.

If, as appears both appropriate and likely, some sort of formality is to be required for a gift, why should not a signed writing suffice, as was earlier suggested for a promise to make a gift (Chapter 8)?[19] From an early time it came to be recognized that as to land, where no true delivery was possible, a deed under seal would suffice.[20] And at least as early as the nineteenth century there was similar authority with respect to gifts of personal property, even though delivery was possible. The abolition of the seal left in doubt the efficacy of a writing as a substitute for the delivery of personal property. By now, however, a solid body of authority has accumulated to support the efficacy of a signed writing,[21] witness the happy ending for the Hebrew University of its attempt to acquire the Yahuda Library.

Connecticut's highest court remanded the case for a second trial, and after that trial an intermediate appellate court held that a "constructive" delivery "is sufficient if manual delivery is impractical or inconvenient," and that the delivery of the memorandum coupled with [Ethel's] acts and declarations, which clearly show an intention to give and to divest herself of any ownership of the library, was sufficient to complete the gift. If the itemized memorandum . . . had been incorporated in a formal document, no one would question the validity of the gift. But formalism is not an end in itself. . . . The circumstances . . . —a public announcement at a luncheon attended by a head of state, accompanied by a document which identified in itemized form what was being given—are a sufficient substitute for a formal instrument purporting to pass title.[22]

Although Ethel had not met the requirements for a trust, she had met the requirements for a gift—at least as the court had stretched them to fit the facts. As a member of the Supreme Court of New Jersey wrote in a dissent, though, "the artificial requirement of delivery is still widely entrenched . . . , where, as here, the donor's wishes were freely and clearly expressed in a written instrument and the donee's ensuing possession was admittedly bona fide . . . every consideration of public policy would seem to point toward upholding the gift."[23]

Gone, then, is the self-executing aspect of a gift. If Edgar Degas can make an effective gift by delivering a signed writing instead of the painting to Henri Rouart, a court will have to devise a remedy if the artist refuses to deliver the painting and his friend hauls him into court. But the erosion of the requirement of delivery does not affect the two salient characteristics of relinquishments. First, a gift, even if accomplished by the delivery of a signed writing, is still completed in the present, although it can be argued that the cautionary effect of the delivery of a writing is not as great as that of delivery of the painting itself. (It can also be argued that delivery of the painting avoids the possible ambiguity of a writing, which might be unclear as to whether a present transfer or merely an undertaking to make a future transfer was intended.) Second, the erosion of the requirement of delivery does not weaken the restriction that one cannot give what one does not have. As long as the law clings to the restraint of nemo dat, one cannot, by writing any more than by delivery, make a gift of something that one does not already own.[24] Thus a profligate artist would be as powerless to squander his future by means of a writing as by means of delivery—even if the writing were to recite that Edgar was giving Henri his entire output of paintings for the rest of Edgar's life.

Therefore, even a paternalistic judge might grudgingly give effect to a signed writing in this context. In contrast to my earlier suggestion that by promising to make a gift, accompanied by some such formality, you ought to be able to make a *commitment,* here I suggest only that you be able, by using such a formality, to make a *relinquishment.* Under the Restatement (Second) rule already discussed in that connection, Edgar could by an oral promise commit himself to give his lifetime's output of paintings to the Guggenheim Museum. All that I suggest here is that Edgar should have the power, by using a formality, to relinquish his right to such paintings as he has at the time without delivering them.

You might want to make a gift of something that you could not deliver, such as a contract right. Suppose, for example, that I owed you $1,000 and you wanted to give your right to the $1,000 to a friend. Could you do so by writing out an assignment of your right, signing it, and delivering the writing to your friend? You could, of course, have done so in the days of the seal simply by delivering a sealed writing, but after the seal was deprived of its effect it was far from clear that you could do so by using a signed writing instead of a sealed one. Fortunately, the Restatement (Second) of Contracts states that you can do this, though not all courts may choose to follow this rule.[25] Even if a court were to follow the Restatement rule, it could nevertheless conclude that when you could have delivered the subject of the gift itself, as Edgar could deliver his painting to Henri, your delivery of a signed writing instead was not a suitable substitute. Nevertheless, as has already been pointed out, a solid

body of authority supports your power to make a gift by delivery of a signed writing even in that case.

It would, however, be a mistake to suppose that, because
your gift is a present transfer of your ownership rights, it is
inevitably beyond recall in the event of your regret. A notorious example involved Yale University's return of billionaire
Lee M. Bass's $20 million gift when it concluded that it could
not meet his conditions of expanding its Western civiliza-
tion curriculum.[26] Such conditions need not be express, and
courts have occasionally taken account of regret by attaching a condition by inference. They have done so in the case
of the gift of an engagement ring, which is regarded as conditional on the engagement not being broken, so that if the
donor's intended breaks it off, the gift can be retaken.[27]

A brief comparative excursus reveals that both French
and German law go beyond this in taking account of the
donor's right. The applicable codes impose implied conditions that allow a donor to revoke a gift in specified circumstances of ingratitude or changed circumstances.[28] No
common law court has gone this far. If courts were to fashion such conditions for promises to make gifts, it would not
be difficult to adapt those conditions to completed gifts, but
courts have thrown up their hands at this task.

In view of the common law's reluctance to supply conditions, it behooves a donor to give thought to attaching
explicit conditions to the gift. It is true that a transfer conditioned on the occurrence of some future event will not
suffice as a gift. Thus if Edgar Degas delivered the painting to Henri Rouart, Henri to become the owner if Edgar
should predecease Henri, there would be no present transfer
of ownership, no effective gift, and the painting would not
become Henri's on Edgar's death. But this does not prevent
a donor from subjecting the gift to a condition that will deprive the donee of ownership and give the donor the right
to retake the property should a specified event occur. Edgar
might, for example, give Henri the painting with a right to

retake it if Henri should predecease Edgar. Under the prevailing view, a donor may so condition a gift to take account of the possibility of regret. The donor may, for example, reserve the right to retake a gift should the donee fail to support the donor, or should the donor be in need of support.[29]

In the next chapter we examine in more detail the restriction that a gift is limited to what one has—the restraint of nemo dat.

CHAPTER FOURTEEN

What Can Be Given

The difficulty of drawing a line between what one has and what one has not under the restraint of nemo dat. Occasional failures of courts to indulge their paternalistic inclinations by applying the restriction. Despite the restriction, Gabriel Pascal succeeds in giving a piece of My Fair Lady *to his mistress. General observance of the restriction. Its significance for promises to make gifts.*

We have seen the paternalistic effect of the restraint of nemo dat, which prevents you from giving what you do not have. To appreciate the extent of the paternalism it becomes important to know what you *have* and what you *do not have* within the meaning of this restraint. Drawing the line between the two has sometimes pushed judicial creativity to its limit. To begin with, take the heir apparent, whose interest is what the law calls an "expectancy" of inheritance, or the wage earner, whose interest is the anticipation of payment under employment terminable "at will" by either party.

Courts have been unanimous in holding that the expectancy of the heir apparent is not something that the heir *has* and so is not something that the heir can give. Because wills can be made and changed until death, the possibility that the heir will finally inherit is too ephemeral to be given.[1] In the words of the Supreme Court of North Carolina more than a century ago, "The expectancy of . . . one who . . . is an heir apparent of his father cannot be assigned, for he has nothing to assign."[2] Indeed, out of paternalistic concern for the heir apparent, a court that usually shows no concern for the fairness of a swap will deny effect to an heir apparent's attempt to swap a promise to make a transfer if the expectancy is realized, unless the heir's promise is supported by consideration that the court regards as "fair." A court today would not allow a modern Esau to swap his birthright for a single meal. Even in the heyday of the seal, not even a seal would have sufficed.[3]

Courts have, however, come to a different conclusion with respect to the interest of the wage earner to earn future wages under an at-will employment, even though the wage earner has no enforceable contract right to earn such wages. As long as the employment is an existing one, the wage earner's anticipation of future wages is seen as something that the wage earner *has* and so can give. But here paternalistic courts have drawn the line, for the rule is otherwise as to an employment that has not yet begun. In the century-old words of the Supreme Court of Iowa, in that case "an attempt is made to assign something which exists in expectancy only," and "it is apparent that there is nothing to assign" because the "expectancy may never become a reality."[4]

You may, however, have more than you think, because courts have not always indulged their paternalistic inclinations with respect to anticipated earnings. Consider the gift made by Gabriel Pascal, the noted movie producer whom George Bernard Shaw called a genius and entrusted to bring his plays to the screen. Under an agreement with the playwright's estate, Gabriel had the exclusive rights to make a musical version of *Pygmalion*. At the end of divorce proceedings and shortly before his death, Gabriel gave to his mistress, Marianne Speelman,[5] a signed writing stating: "I give you from my shares of profits of the Pygmalion Musical stage version five per cent (5%) in England, and two per cent (2%) of my shares of profits in the United States. From the film version, five per cent (5%) from my profit shares all over the world." At the time, Gabriel had no right to any such profits, for it was not until nearly a year after his death that the Chase Manhattan Bank, acting for his estate, was able to capitalize on his exclusive rights by making a contract under which Alan Jay Lerner and Frederick Loewe were to write "the Pygmalion Musical" under the name of *My Fair Lady*. But that contract, which *did* give Gabriel's estate a right to profits, did not exist at the time of Gabriel's gift to Marianne.[6]

After Gabriel's death, Valerie, his estranged wife and the administrator of his estate, contested Marianne's right to a share of profits. How, asked Valerie, could Gabriel have given Marianne a right to profits at a time when he did not yet have such a right? Nevertheless, the trial court held for Marianne. "The seed which Pascal had painstakingly planted has flowered, and [Valerie] may not be heard to deny [Marianne] its bloom."[7] Valerie appealed twice but lost twice more, New York's highest court concluding that Gabriel, "who owned and was conducting negotiations to realize on the stage and film rights, could grant another a share of the moneys to accrue from the use of those rights by others."[8]

The courts that upheld Gabriel's gift gave no more than lip service to the restraint of nemo dat. What Gabriel gave—a right "to profits of the Pygmalion Musical"—he did not have. What Gabriel had—an exclusive right to make the Pygmalion Musical—he did not give. True, what he gave was *derived* from what he had, for his exclusive right was part of his capital that later yielded the right to profits. But this reasoning, if not somehow limited, would have enabled Edgar Degas to have made a gift to Henri Rouart of all the artist's *future* paintings. Those paintings were, after all, derived from the artist's *human* capital—his productive capacity based on his skill and training—which Edgar had as surely as Gabriel had the exclusive rights.[9]

But the restraint of nemo dat is deeply rooted in the law of gratuitous transfers. Although it was often justified on the ground of the supposed logic of the maxim itself, the impact was undeniably paternalistic in restraining party autonomy where it might be exercised in an ill-considered manner.[10] Hesitation in allowing people to give away more than is theirs at the time once extended even to the making of wills, for "our ancestors, in times not very remote from our own, found great difficulty in conceiving that a man can give by his will what does not belong to him when he makes that will."[11] The same reluctance can still be detected in the field of trusts, as can be seen from the example of the self-declared trust. Ethel Yahuda could have circumvented the requirement of delivery for a gift simply by declaring that she held the manuscripts collected by her husband in trust for Hebrew University, but she could have done so only as to manuscripts that were hers at the time of her declaration. Under the restraint of nemo dat, one who gratuitously creates a trust can include in the trust property only what the donor owns at the time of the declaration of trust, not what the donor may later acquire.[12]

Thus, though the law of trusts relaxes the requirements for making a gift, it does not disturb the restraint of nemo dat imposed on making a commitment of a future gift.[13] By a self-declared trust the donor can dispose of no more than the donor has, for, even by a trust, a donor cannot commit assets to be acquired in the future. Edgar Degas could use a self-declared trust to make Henri Rouart the beneficiary of his existing paintings, but not of his future works.

Contrast the hypothetical case of an Edgar Degas who seeks to dispose of all future paintings to be realized from his human capital with the actual case of a Gabriel Pascal who seeks to dispose of a share of the profits to be derived from a single item of capital. The contrast is not unlike that between the wage earner who seeks to dispose of future earnings under all employments, existing and future, and the wage earner who seeks to dispose of future earnings under an existing employment. Surely a court would find Edgar's situation the more appealing one in which to indulge its paternalistic urges.

Before the abolition of the seal, however, you could dispose of future assets by a promise to make a gift of those assets. Even today courts have not been inattentive to the presence or absence of a writing in marginal cases,[14] and the notion that a mere signed writing should make an otherwise unenforceable promise binding is not without appeal.[15] But in a variety of contexts, courts remain reluctant to confer on a potentially profligate donor the power to give away future assets. One may question whether a distinction rooted in paternalism between the power to commit present and future assets was influential or even explicitly recognized during the patchwork evolution of the law governing gratuitous transactions. Nonetheless, it stands as the only apparent justification of the law's stubborn refusal to afford promisors a substitute for the seal.

We next look at another remarkable—indeed notorious—example of the law's paternalism.

CHAPTER FIFTEEN

Relinquishment by Renunciation

*Julia Beer recovers interest from John Weston Foakes, giving rise
to the rule that a debt cannot be discharged by payment of
a lesser sum. How the rule is much maligned and often circumvented. Salient characteristics of such transactions and the
illogic of applying the doctrine of consideration to them. Discharge analogized to gift. A few inroads into the law of discharge
and some possible questions were the rule discarded.*

Suppose that I owe you $1,000 and you are minded to
make me a gift of that debt. It would be more difficult to do
this than you might suppose because of the success of Julia
Beer. In August 1875, Julia got a £2,090 judgment in a London court against John Weston Foakes. Sixteen months later,
when he asked her for time to pay, the parties signed a writing under which "in consideration of" his paying her £500
on signing and "on condition of his paying" the balance in
installments over five years, she undertook not to "take any
proceedings whatever on the said judgment." (John made no
promise to pay the installments.) In June 1882, after he had
paid the £2,090 in full, she sought to enforce the judgment
to recover £360 in interest.[1]

The House of Lords held that Julia could recover. It ad-
hered to the rule, laid down by Lord Coke nearly three centuries before, that "payment of a less sum on the [due] day
in satisfaction of a greater, cannot be any satisfaction for the
whole."[2] As the Earl of Selborne saw matters, because the
writing was not under seal, "it cannot be legally enforced
against the respondent, unless she received consideration for
it."[3] Although Lord Blackburn reluctantly went along with
the decision because he thought the law already settled, he
observed that "all men of business, whether merchants or

tradesmen, do every day recognize and act on the ground that prompt payment of a part of their demand may be more beneficial to them than it would be to insist on their rights and enforce payment of the whole."[4] Thus, my $1,000 debt to you cannot be discharged by the payment of a lesser sum, even if that is what we intend. Nor can you make me a gift of my $1,000 debt simply by saying so. If a present-day St. Anthony desired to forgive his debtors their debts (Chapter 7), he would have to contend with the rule of *Foakes* v. *Beer.*

This application of the doctrine of consideration to the discharge of a debt has been subjected to much criticism on the ground that it shows, in the words of a distinguished judge of the Supreme Court of Minnesota, the "capacity of lawyers and judges to make the requirement of consideration an overworked shibboleth."[5] As Lord Blackburn remarked, the rule departs from commercial understanding,[6] and it frustrates both the creditor's intention and the debtor's expectation. It may seem curious that the requirement of consideration, relegated to a mere technicality in its proper domain (Chapter 5), should retain enough vigor to infect the law of discharge. Nevertheless, the rule took firm root in the United States and is applied to the discharge not only of money debts but of contract duties of all kinds.[7]

The rule is often circumvented. Since even a peppercorn can serve as consideration, the great Lord Coke himself had allowed that, though the mere payment of a lesser sum cannot discharge a greater debt, "the gift of a horse, hawk, or robe, &c. in satisfaction is good."[8] So, for example, payment at an earlier time or at a different place would suffice, as would the debtor's surrender of an honestly asserted defense.[9] Furthermore, the rule can be circumvented by the use of a negotiable promissory note, for if I give you such a note to secure my antecedent debt to you, you can then discharge the debt simply by canceling or destroying the note or by surrendering it to me with the intention to discharge the debt.[10] But in spite of all circumvention, the rule of *Foakes* v. *Beer* still casts a pall over the law governing discharge and stands in stark contradiction to the intention principle.

No logic compelled the House of Lords to subject this branch of the law to the requirement of consideration, a requirement that had evolved to deal with persons who make promises and then change their minds and renege on them. The question there is: Are their promises irrevocable? Here there is no promise. Rather, as in the case of gifts, we are concerned not with commitments but with relinquishments—with persons who consent to give up rights against others (for example, Julia's right against John to interest) and who then change their minds and assert those rights. The question here is: Are their surrenders irreversible? If I owe you $1,000 but you tell me that I need not pay you, has your renunciation relinquished your right to be paid $1,000?

In general, such gifts by renunciation of rights have the same salient characteristics as do other gifts. First, your renunciation of your right is completed in the present.[11] I renunciation precludes reassertion of the right, there is nothing more for you to do. Had the Lords decided that Julia's renunciation barred her from asserting her right to interest there would have been nothing more for her to do. Second, your renunciation of your right is limited to the right that you have. You cannot renounce more. Julia could have renounced her right to the principal of £2,090 as well as her right to the interest, but that would have been the limit. She could not renounce her right to future debts that John might owe her.[12] Furthermore, renunciation of a right is self-executing. To give effect to a renunciation of a right, a court need only deny relief. Had the Lords seen matters differently, it would have sufficed to deny relief to Julia.

These characteristics are, of course, the same as those singled out earlier to distinguish gifts from promises.[13] And renunciations have another similarity to gifts, for altruism is a common motive for renouncing a right just as it is for making a gift. It therefore makes sense to suppose that i would be "easier to give up a right than to create one."[14] The law applicable to the renunciation of rights would then resemble the law applicable to gifts, and the irreversibility of your surrender of my $1,000 debt would be determined by rules similar to those that determine the irreversibility of a $1,000 gift that you might make to another person. However, the development of the law in this area has not, to put it mildly, been marked by inexorable logic, and it has taken scant account of the kinds of characteristics just mentioned.

For this, *Foakes* v. *Beer* is largely to blame for failing to distinguish relinquishments from commitments and so importing into the law applicable to discharge by renunciation all of the baggage of consideration carried by the law applicable to commitment by promise. During the nineteenth century the propensity of English judges for finding promises was conspicuous (Prologue). Less than a decade before the decision in *Foakes* v. *Beer,* English judges had characterized an offeror's indication that his offer was irrevocable not as a relinquishment of the power to revoke but as a promise not to revoke that was subject to the requirement of consideration.[15] The paternalistic consequences of this unfortunate characterization have still not been eradicated.[16] It should therefore come as no surprise that nineteenth-century English judges regarded a renunciation as a promise, though it would have been far more logical to have treated it as a gift. A creditor can, on good authority, make a gift of a $1,000 debt to another person by delivering to that person a signed writing assigning the debt. Why can the creditor not make a gift of the $1,000 debt to the debtor in the same way?

This analogy to a gift has been accepted in civil law systems.[17] It has also received halting recognition in the Restatement (Second) of Contracts. If, for example, you contract to sell me for $1,000 a machine that I have already borrowed from you, but you then tell me I can keep the machine as a gift, my duty to pay the $1,000 is discharged. The discharge results from an effective gift of the machine under cases holding that the requirement of delivery to me is met because I am already in possession of the machine.[18] In this situation the law shows greater willingness to give effect to renunciation of a right than to enforce a promise.[19] Unfortunately, however, there is no generally accepted rule that empowers you irreversibly to renounce your right and thereby discharge my debt to you by delivering to me a signed writing. This is so even though you might be able to make a gift of your right to someone else by delivering to them a signed writing.

Fortunately, a few significant steps have been taken in this direction. The Uniform Commercial Code gives effect to written and signed releases of claims for breach,[20] and a few states have gone all the way and enacted statutes giving effect to written and signed releases.[21] In addition, the Code abolishes the requirement of consideration for a modification of a contract for the sale of goods.[22] As a federal judge observed, relinquishment of a claim for breach of contract rests "on an idea no more complicated than that any competent adult can abandon a legal right and if he does so then he has lost it forever."[23] In all of these situations, the renunciation is subject not only to the restraints imposed in cases of unfairly influenced and uninformed decisions, but to the additional restraint of a requirement of good faith and fair dealing that applies whenever parties are already bound by contract.[24] If the doctrine of *Foakes* v. *Beer* is discarded, you would be similarly protected by a requirement of good faith and fair dealing on my part in obtaining the discharge of my $1,000 debt. Nevertheless, in spite of some inroads, the residual rule persists as laid down in *Foakes* v. *Beer,* and still today not even a writing signed by Julia would prevent her from once again besting John.

Discarding the rule of *Foakes* v. *Beer* and empowering you to discharge my debt to you by delivering to me a signed writing might seem to raise questions of interpretation. What if your writing leaves it unclear whether you intend a renunciation of your right or merely a commitment not to assert that right? (As has already been observed, if what is involved is, say, a painting rather than a contract right, this question is unlikely to arise because delivery of the painting ordinarily makes it clear that what is intended is a relinquishment.) But the question is chimerical because a commitment of this sort, commonly called a "covenant not to sue," is held to have the same legal effect as a discharge.[25] So substance prevails over form, and what appears as a commitment is treated instead as a relinquishment. In any case, for present purposes it would make no difference how your language was interpreted if, as I urge, the same formality were to suffice for both an irrevocable promise to make a gift and an irreversible discharge made as a gift.

There is an inevitable relationship between the rules for relinquishments and those for commitments because the making of a bilateral contract followed by one party's relinquishment of all rights under the contract may have the same result as a promise to make a gift. Suppose that Jack Tallas, wishing to commit himself to give $50,000 to his friend Peter Dementas, had made a contract with Peter under which Peter promised to sell an icon that he owned and in return Jack promised to pay $50,000, after which Jack gave Peter a signed writing that read, "I renounce my right to the icon and make you a gift of it." Would Peter have had the right to enforce the promise to pay $50,000? If so, this would seem to be a scheme by which Jack could in effect make a commitment to make a gift of that sum to Peter, an apparently anomalous result. If, however, as I have urged, the same formality would have sufficed for a gratuitous promise in the first place, the anomaly disappears.

In the three chapters that follow, we consider whether this reluctance to give effect to renunciations carries over into other situations.

CHAPTER SIXTEEN

Relinquishment by Waiver

*The condition that treatise writer William L. Clark not drink in
order to be paid $6 a page is waived by West, his publisher. How
loose use of "waiver" leads to confusion and why use of the
term should be limited to conditions as distinguished from discharge. The difference between discharge and waiver, and three
explanations for it. How further confusion has resulted from the
description of waiver as based on a new promise. Promissory
waiver distinguished from true waiver.*

Suppose that you make a contract under which your duty
to perform is subject to a condition. If you later consent to
give up the advantage of asserting that condition, have you
irreversibly relinquished that advantage? Consider the case
of William L. Clark, a prolific writer of legal treatises at the
beginning of the twentieth century, who made a contract
with his publisher, West, for a three-volume work on corporations. The contract required West to pay William $6 per
page, rather than a mere $2 per page, on condition that he
"totally abstain from the use of intoxicating liquors during
the continuance of the contract."

When William sued for the full $6, West answered that,
by William's own admission, "he did not totally abstain."
William's answer was that West had waived the condition
by accepting his manuscript and representing that William
would be paid in full, while having full knowledge of William's "nonobservance of that stipulation." The New York
Court of Appeals agreed with William, wryly observing that
this was "not a contract to write books in order that the
plaintiff shall keep sober, but a contract containing a stipulation that he shall keep sober so that he may write satisfactory books."[1] West had relinquished its advantage of assert-

ing the condition that William abstain though William had given nothing in exchange and did not claim to have relied on West's conduct.

Lawyers call such a relinquishment a "waiver," a term condemned by no less a scholar than Arthur Linton Corbin as a slippery word of "infinite connotations" that "like a cloak, covers a multitude of sins."[2] Sometimes the term is used to describe provisions in contracts by which one party gives up some right, for example a right to notice, that the law would otherwise require.[3] Sometimes the term is confused with discharge, the sort of relinquishment of a right involved in *Foakes* v. *Beer*,[4] a confusion that courts encourage by mindlessly repeating that waiver is the intentional relinquishment of a "known right."[5]

Since loose use of "waiver" can result only in confusion, it is best, following Corbin, to confine the word to relinquishments of *conditions*.[6] Waiver is then properly described as consent to give up a condition of one's duty, and when one gives such consent one can be said to waive the condition. West's consent to relinquish the condition of William's abstinence would thus be described as a waiver. But Julia's consent to relinquish the right that John pay her interest would be described as a discharge of that right and not as an attempted waiver.

This distinction between waiver and discharge is particularly important when the other party has promised that the condition will occur. Suppose that your duty under a contract is subject to such a condition. Your consent to give up the advantage of the condition may bar you from asserting it, thereby making your own duty unconditional, but it will not discharge the other party from its duty that the condition occur. Had William *promised* West to abstain, West's waiver of the condition that he abstain would not have affected William's duty. Though William would still have been entitled to the full $6 per page, West could have recovered any damages that it could have proved were caused by William's failure to perform his duty to abstain. West's waiver of the condition would not have resulted in a discharge of that duty.

Although waiver, like discharge, results in a relinquishment, the doctrine of *Foakes* v. *Beer* has never been applied to cases of waiver. What explains this difference between waiver and discharge? Three possible explanations come to mind.

The first is that there is a limit to the magnitude of the advantage that can be relinquished by waiver. Courts have confined the doctrine to relatively minor conditions, regarding some conditions as too substantial to be relinquished by waiver. "Otherwise," mused a leading jurist, "why would someone give it up in exchange for nothing?"[7] According to the Restatement (Second) of Contracts, a condition cannot be waived if its occurrence was a *material* part of the exchange agreed on by the parties.[8] The condition of William's abstaining could be waived because it was not a material part of his deal with West—witness the court's observation that it was "not a contract to write books in order that the plaintiff shall keep sober." But some of the other conditions of William's deal with West could not have been waived. It was, for example, a condition of William's right to be paid anything at all that he submit a manuscript of the three-volume work that he had promised, and submitting the manuscript *was* a material part of the exchange. Therefore, no matter how clearly West expressed its intention to waive that condition, which would leave it only its action for damages against William, it could not do so. A court will characterize an attempt to surrender so substantial a condition as a "modification," irreversible only if it is part of a swap and so supported by consideration.[9]

Because of this limit on the magnitude of the advantage that can be relinquished by waiver, it is scarcely surprising that courts have not been tempted to extend to cases of waiver the doctrine of *Foakes* v. *Beer,* questionable as that doctrine is even in cases of discharge. If, as I urge, the doctrine is discarded in favor of a rule requiring a formality for discharge, this would therefore have no impact on cases like William's. But it should then be open to a party, by whatever means would suffice for discharge, to relinquish the advantage of a condition that cannot be waived because its occurrence *is* a material part of the agreed exchange.[10] The Uniform Commercial Code has already moved in this direction by giving effect to a modification of a contract for the sale of goods even though it is not supported by consideration.[11]

The second explanation of the difference between waiver and discharge is that conditions characteristically have a draconian effect, often suggested by the word "forfeiture." Under the terms of his contract with West, William would forfeit two-thirds of the price per page if he failed to abstain, entirely without regard to whether his failure affected the quality of his manuscript. This effect is especially evident under contracts of insurance, which commonly contain provisions making the insurance company's duty to pay subject to the condition that the insured give notice of loss within a specified time. If the insured delays in giving the required notice, the insured cannot recover under the policy entirely without regard to whether the delay harmed the insurance company.[12] Courts have often resorted to waiver as a means of avoiding the draconian effect of such conditions, under which an insured may forfeit the premiums paid under a contract of insurance. In such cases, as in William's, the intention principle is buttressed by a desire to avoid the impact of a harsh term imposed by a party that appears to have had the better of the bargaining.

The third explanation of the difference is that, aside from the insurance cases, claims of waiver most often arise in the course of a continuing relationship. Perhaps circumstances have changed so that the advantage of the condition no longer seems as important as it once did. Perhaps giving up that advantage will preserve the relationship or make the other party more cooperative. Claims of waiver are often based on a course of conduct that manifests continuing disregard of a condition, and a court may discern the requisite intention in conduct that borders on the inadvertent or inattentive, such as carelessly failing to object to defects when accepting performance.[13] In these situations, as in William's case, the intention principle is shored up by a desire to preserve continuing relationships and to protect likely though unproved reliance.

Scholarly analysis of waiver has taken an odd turn by concocting yet a fourth explanation for the distinction between waiver and discharge. Otherwise respectable sources assert that a waiver is not a relinquishment at all but rather a commitment—that waiver should be viewed not as assent to the elimination of a condition to an existing promise but as an entirely new promise to perform that promise without the condition.[14] This is yet another example of the propensity of common law judges for finding a promise where what is involved is a relinquishment (Prologue).

Once a promise is found, it would seem necessary to embark on the usual search for consideration or reliance to make it binding, but plainly West was not free to renege as long as William had not either given consideration or relied. The Restatement (Second) adopts the odd strategy of simply cutting this Gordian knot: it rechristens the topic of waiver as Promise to Perform a Duty in Spite of the Non-occurrence of a Condition, and then neatly tucks it away under the general heading Contracts Without Consideration.[15] West's waiver is thus made irreversible. This wrongheaded analysis confuses two different situations, to both of which the term "waiver" is commonly applied, and results in an odd turnabout.

Suppose that West had told William, before he had done any work on the book, that it would pay him $6 per page even if he drank. This, of course, would be a promise, and because it is a promise to perform a duty in spite of the non-occurrence of a condition, it would seem that under the Restatement (Second) it would be binding without either consideration or reliance. But now comes the turnabout, for the Restatement (Second) goes on to say that if the promisee can still cause the condition to occur, the promisor can reinstate it by notifying the promisee, unless this is "unjust because of a material change of position by the promisee."[16] Thus, in the hypothetical just posed, West could change its mind and reinstate the condition if William had not yet relied on West's promise not to insist on the condition. In brief, there is nothing special about that promise, and it is subject to the rules applicable to any other promise not supported by consideration—the reliance principle determines whether it is binding.

It would have been far simpler to distinguish the actual case from the hypothetical one by treating the actual case as one of a relinquishment, irreversible under the intention principle. There would then be no need to characterize West's conduct as a promise and to place it among Contracts Without Consideration. I will confine my use of the term "waiver" to such expressions of relinquishment. The hypothetical case could be treated as one of commitment, governed by the ordinary rules applicable to promises, and West's promise would be binding only if the reliance principle made it so. In order not to do too much violence to traditional terminology, I will call such an expression of commitment a "promissory waiver" to distinguish it from an expression of relinquishment—a true waiver. West's hypothetical promise is an example of promissory waiver that would be binding only if the reliance principle made it so. Finding a promise in the actual case in order to treat the two cases together obscures the fact that one involves a relinquishment and the other a commitment.

At this point a quarrelsome reader might object that the two cases could be treated together not by treating both as involving expressions of commitment, as the Restatement does, but by treating both as involving expressions of relinquishment. In the hypothetical case, when West told William that it would pay him $6 per page even if he drank, could this not be regarded as a present surrender by West of the advantage of the condition, a surrender just as irreversible under the intention principle as the one in the actual case? This raises a broader question that we can no longer avoid: If the words are unclear, how is an expression of relinquishment to be distinguished from one of commitment? It should be noted that an expression of relinquishment such as "I give you my ship *Argo*" is as much a performative as an expression of commitment such as "I promise to give you my ship *Argo*" (Chapter 3). The question of how to tell the difference arises in several contexts: gift, renunciation, and waiver.

In the cases of relinquishment by gift, the question is ordinarily one of interpretation only, turning on intention. A court distinguishes a present gift from a commitment to make a gift by looking at the donor's intention. If the question arises in connection with tangible property, such as Edgar Degas's painting, Edgar's delivery to Henri will go far toward proving that Edgar's intention was to make a present gift. If, however, the gift arises in connection with intangible property such as a contract right, it may be less clear whether the donor meant to say "I hereby give you my contract right" or only "I hereby promise to give you my contract right."[17] In that case the requirement of the formality of a signed writing has the distinct advantage of providing a reliable basis for deciding which the donor intended.

Cases of relinquishment by renunciation, however, involve more than mere interpretation. As we have seen, for present purposes it makes no difference whether what is intended is the renunciation of a right or a commitment not to assert that right—commonly called a "covenant not to sue"—for courts have held that, in order to avoid unnecessary circuity of action, such a promise has the same legal consequence as does a discharge (Chapter 15). Furthermore, if, as I urge, the same formality were to suffice for both an irrevocable promise to make a gift and an irreversible discharge made as a gift, it would make no difference which was intended.

The distinction between true waiver and promissory waiver can be seen by distinguishing between cases in which the event on which the duty is conditioned has already occurred and cases in which it has not yet occurred. In cases in the first category, a waiver can be only a true waiver. In cases in the second category, a waiver can be either a true waiver or a promissory waiver.

If the event has occurred, as where William had already begun to drink, West's waiver can be only a true waiver. It would therefore make no difference whether West said "We promise not to assert the condition" or "We surrender the right to assert the condition," for the result would be the same whichever it said. Once William had begun to drink, even an explicit promise by West not to assert the condition would be treated in the same way as an expression of relinquishment in order to avoid unnecessary circuity of action. The result would be a relinquishment under the intention principle.

If the event on which the duty is conditioned has not yet occurred, as in the hypothetical situation in which William had not yet begun to drink, it becomes important to determine which West has said in order to know whether what is involved is a true waiver or a promissory waiver. A promise by West not to assert the condition would be binding as a promissory waiver only under the reliance principle, but a statement surrendering the right to assert the condition would seem to be irreversible without more as true waiver under the intention principle. If West could relinquish the advantage of asserting the condition by true waiver in the case in which William had already begun to drink, it is difficult to see why it could not do the same in a case in which he had not begun to drink as long as West made it clear that this was its intention. A court called on to give a meaning to ambiguous conduct like that of West might, however, leave open to West a chance to change its mind by assuming that what is involved is a promissory waiver binding only on William's reliance.

Having covered three types of relinquishment—by gift, by renunciation, and by waiver, we look now at preclusions.

CHAPTER SEVENTEEN

Preclusion by Equitable Estoppel and Laches

David Horn's lie to Caleb Cole comes back to haunt David under the doctrine of equitable estoppel. Equitable estoppel as one kind of preclusion. How, though it turns not on the intention principle but on the reliance principle, it shares with relinquishments the salient characteristics that distinguish them from commitments. Ostensible ownership and laches as related kinds of preclusion. How the government benefits from a no-estoppel rule, along with some criticism of that rule. Equitable estoppel distinguished from promissory estoppel and from estoppel to assert the statute of frauds.

As we turn from relinquishments to preclusions, David Horn's case is illuminating. During the Civil War, David, who was planning to move to Illinois, took a box of his household goods to the freight depot in East Milan, New Hampshire, for shipment to his son Charles, who had already moved to Illinois. On the way to the depot, David passed the shop of Caleb Cole, who asked, "Are you going to leave us, Horn?" David, fearing that his creditors might find out that he was sending his goods outside the state and attach them, decided to deny ownership of the box. He lied, "No, but Charles had some things at my house and I am sending them to Charles." Although Caleb was not one of David's creditors, he was, unbeknownst to David, a creditor of Charles and, believing David, had the box attached as belonging to Charles. When David sued Caleb for wrongful interference with his property, Caleb defended on the ground that David should be precluded from denying the truth of his false representation because Caleb had relied on it. David responded that, since he did not know that Caleb was a creditor of Charles, he could not have intended to deceive *Caleb;* he intended to deceive only his *own* creditors. But David's lie came back to haunt him, for the Supreme Court of New Hampshire rejected his argument and held that he was precluded from denying that the box was Charles's.[1]

I characterized preclusions earlier as "voluntary but not intentional" (Interlude). In contrast to relinquishments, which are based on an intention to surrender the advantage in question, preclusions require no such intention. When David lied to Caleb, he surely did not intend to surrender any rights as owner of the box. On the contrary, David lied in the hope of shielding the box from his creditors. His initial decision was not to surrender ownership of the box but to deny ownership as a means of retaining it. When David changed his mind, he regretted having denied ownership because under a rule of law he was precluded from later claiming ownership and therefore had—at least against Caleb—irreversibly surrendered ownership of the box. While relinquishment results in a surrender that you once intended, preclusion results in a surrender that you never intended. So preclusions must have a basis other than the intention principle, and in David's case that basis is, of course, the reliance principle.

To reach its decision the Supreme Court of New Hampshire applied the doctrine of equitable estoppel, sometimes called estoppel *in pais.* (The term is a quaint anglicization of the old French *estoupail,* the stopper in the bunghole of a cask, modified by *en pays* to indicate that the representation was not made "in court" but instead "in the country.") Under this doctrine, one who has made, as David did, a false representation of fact on which another has relied, as Caleb did, may be precluded (estopped) from taking a position that involves denial of that statement. David was precluded from claiming that he owned the box because Caleb had relied on David's representation that it was Charles's by attaching it, presumably passing up the opportunity to attach other goods that actually were Charles's.[2]

No matter that David did not intend to cause Caleb to rely on what David said about the box, much less to surrender ownership of the box. Whatever David may have intended as the effect of what he said, he did intend to say it, and Caleb was protected if he relied on it.[3] Indeed, the doctrine of equitable estoppel does not even require actual knowledge that the representation is false. As a Lord Chancellor said over a century ago, "I think it is not necessary that the party making the representation should know that it was false . . . [b]ut if the party has unwittingly misled another, you must add that he has misled another under such circumstances that he had reasonable ground for supposing that the person whom he was misleading was to act upon what he was saying."[4] On this view, David might have been precluded on the basis of "imputed" knowledge, even though he thought that the box actually belonged to Charles and, not knowing that he himself was really its owner, had never made an initial decision to deny ownership.

That preclusion, unlike relinquishment, does not rest on intention was made clear by the Supreme Court of Washington when it distinguished waiver and equitable estoppel in the face of the contention that an independent insurance adjustor had dispensed with the condition that the insured furnish a proof of loss. For the adjustor, engaged by the insurer to adjust a claim, "to effect a waiver of a policy provision, *i.e.,* a voluntary and intentional relinquishment of the provision," the adjustor would have to have *actual* authority to do so. But for the adjustor's acts to give rise to an estoppel, it would be enough if the adjustor had *apparent* authority, for "it would be somewhat anomalous" to require the insured "to establish that the adjustor was vested by his principal with *actual* authority to consciously or inadvertently mislead the assured."[5] The court recognized true waiver, as I have called it, as a relinquishment based on the intention principle (Chapter 16), and equitable estoppel as a preclusion based on the reliance principle.

Although equitable estoppel does not rest on intention, it shares with relinquishments the two salient characteristics identified earlier. First, equitable estoppel, like relinquishments and unlike commitments, speaks to the present, not the future. David's lie resulted in an immediate surrender, though it became irreversible only when Caleb relied. Second, equitable estoppel, like relinquishments and unlike commitments, surrenders only what one has. By even the most extravagant lie, David could surrender no more goods than were his. Furthermore, as is true of relinquishments but not of commitments, equitable estoppel does not usually require a court to devise a remedy.[6]

The principle that underlies equitable estoppel is found in other contexts under other names. Two of the most important examples are the doctrines of ostensible ownership and that of laches.

Under the doctrine of ostensible ownership, an owner of goods may be precluded from claiming ownership because of misleading conduct (see Chapter 6). A striking illustration is the "entrusting" rule of Uniform Commercial Code 2–403(3), under which an owner who entrusts "possession of goods to a merchant who deals in goods of that kind gives him power to transfer all rights of the entruster to a buyer in ordinary course of business." In effect, if you entrust your goods to one who is a merchant you are treated as having represented that the merchant is the owner of the goods, or at least has the power to sell them. If someone relies on your representation by buying them, you are precluded from denying that representation, just as David was precluded from denying his, and you cannot claim ownership as against the buyer.

The doctrine of laches, like its close cousin equitable estoppel, grew up in courts of equity. There it was commonly linked with the maxim that equity aids the vigilant and not those who slumber on their rights. A court will invoke it to preclude a party from asserting a right against another when the former knew or should have known of the right and unreasonably delayed in asserting it. The delay is, in effect, treated as a representation that the right will not be asserted. Since delay may be caused by inattention or sloth and not by a decision at all, you may be precluded by laches even though you have not made an initial decision—without any change of mind—though our concern is with not with such cases.[7] But your slumber alone will not cause a court to invoke the concept of laches, for your delay must have caused harm to the other party, as by loss of evidence or a change in value of property. Thus laches, like its more important cousin equitable estoppel, turns on the reliance principle. This distinguishes laches from a statute of limitations, under which your mere delay without resulting prejudice will bar you from asserting an advantage (Chapter 20).[8]

Even the reliance principle may be trumped by a weightier policy, however, and up to now the United States Supreme Court has been unwilling to apply the doctrine of equitable estoppel against the federal government. A dramatic instance of its hostility to that doctrine came in 1947 in a case involving an Idaho farmer who had purchased crop insurance from the Federal Crop Insurance Corporation, after having been assured by its agent that his crop of reseeded winter wheat was insurable. When a drought destroyed his crop he learned that under the applicable regulation his reseeded wheat was not insurable. He took his case to the Supreme Court, where Justice Frankfurter admitted that the "case no doubt presents phases of hardship" but, speaking for a five-justice majority, concluded that "anyone entering into an arrangement with the Government takes the risk of having accurately ascertained that he who purports to act for the Government stays within the bounds of his authority."[9] Four justices dissented, with Justice Jackson—whose role in the *Allegheny College* case will be recalled—protesting that were the farmer "to peruse this voluminous and dull publication [containing the regulations], he would never need crop insurance for he would never get time to plant any crops."[10]

In 1990, the Supreme Court brought to the fore the appropriations clause of the Constitution as a basis for the no-estoppel rule. In that year, a plurality of the justices pointed out that "we have reversed every finding of estoppel that we have reviewed."[11] Nevertheless, the plurality concluded that "we need not embrace a rule that no estoppel will lie against the Government in any case in order to decide this case," because "narrower ground of decision is sufficient to address the type of suit presented here, a claim for payment of money from the Public Treasury contrary to a statutory appropriation."[12] This is because the appropriation clause provides that "No Money shall be drawn from the Treasury, but in Consequence of Appropriations Made by Law."[13] According to the plurality, "Extended to its logical conclusion, operation of estoppel against the Government in the context of payment of money from the Treasury could in fact render the Appropriations Clause a nullity."[14] Still, the door remains open at least a crack to the possibility that in an appropriate case the federal government might be precluded on the ground of equitable estoppel.

There are some sound practical reasons for the Supreme Court's position. Estopping the government might have serious adverse effects on administrative efficiency and flexibility and would, for example, severely limit the availability of information and advice from government employees. As scholars have argued, "The federal government implements hundreds of extraordinarily complicated regulatory and benefit programs. . . . If the government began to lose much money as a result of estoppel cases, agencies would respond by limiting severely the availability of information and advice from government employees."[15] To return to the metaphor of planners and doers (Chapter 10), the doctrine would hamstring the doers in implementing the policies of the planners. Of course the same objections could be raised to the application of the doctrine of equitable estoppel to private corporations that are called upon to dispense information and advice, but their activities are not supported by our taxes.

In some contexts, however, the no-estoppel rule seems distinctly out of place. When the government descends into the marketplace, for example, there is authority that it risks preclusion on the ground of ostensible ownership in the same way as do other players.[16] Furthermore, lower federal courts have held that the conduct of government lawyers in their cases can result in judicial estoppel just as the conduct of other lawyers can.[17] And there is authority that when the government makes a promise, as distinguished from a misrepresentation, it is subject to the doctrine of promissory estoppel (Chapter 8).[18]

At the other end of the spectrum are cases involving public lands. In 1947 the Supreme Court held that the federal government was not precluded by its delay from asserting its rights to submerged off-shore oil lands. "The Government, which holds its interest here as elsewhere in trust for all the people, is not to be deprived of those interests by the ordinary court rules designed particularly for private disputes over individually owned pieces of property."[19] More than a century earlier, Justice Joseph Story had based this rule on the "great public policy of preserving the public rights, revenues, and property from injury and loss, by the negligence of public officers."[20] As already noted, there was once a time when the doctrine of sovereign immunity prevented the federal government from being bound by its promises, but the federal government was forced to give up this immunity during the latter half of the nineteenth century as the price of getting others to swap their own promises (Chapter 1). As we have seen, there are good reasons why you might want to be able to make both commitments and relinquishments. Since it is more difficult to think of why you would want to be precluded, it is not surprising that the federal government has clung tenaciously to the no-estoppel rule.

While there are sound reasons for hesitancy in finding that the federal government is precluded because of the action or inaction of its agents, adamant refusal to apply the rules to which others are subject is not easy to justify. It is scarcely convincing to repeat the metaphor of Oliver Wendell Holmes that "Men must turn square corners when they deal with the Government."[21] Now that the immunities that government once had against tort claims have been widely abolished or at least curtailed—producing what is said to be the "most striking feature of the tort law of governmental entities today"[22]—it seems anomalous to continue to insulate the government against estoppel. As a leading critic of the no-estoppel rule has written, "Repudiation of representations is dirty business, no less at the hands of the government than of its citizens."[23] As the federal Court of Appeals for the Ninth Circuit exclaimed, "To say to these appellants, 'The joke is on you. You shouldn't have trusted us,' is hardly worthy of our great government."[24]

The word "estoppel" has gained currency in a variety contexts that have no connection with the principle that underlies equitable estoppel. Loose use of the term has come to rival that of "waiver." For an instance of this, reconsider the use of "estoppel" in connection with the enforcement of promises under the doctrine known as "promissory estoppel" (Chapter 8). The names are similar because equitable estoppel is the etymological ancestor of promissory estoppel (much as estoppel "in court" was the progenitor of estoppel "in the country" or equitable estoppel). The first courts to apply the then novel doctrine of promissory estoppel sought to mask their creativity by purporting to apply the established doctrine of equitable estoppel.[25] But preclusions, like relinquishments, are fundamentally different from commitments, and equitable estoppel, which results in preclusion, is fundamentally different from promissory estoppel, which results in commitment.[26]

An example of more recent origin involves the availability of the statute of frauds. Despite the evident differ-

ences between the two sorts of estoppel, their relationship
became tangled in a series of cases decided in the middle of
the twentieth century, resulting in a kind of false estoppel.
The cases involved the statute of frauds, which requires that
specified kinds of contracts be evidenced by a signed writing in order to be enforceable. The statute of frauds found
in American states is the descendant of the seventeenth-
century English statute. It reflects the same sort of paternalism that underlies the formality of the seal, though in
contrast to the seal, which was a means of making a promise *binding,* the writing required by the statute of frauds is
an additional requirement, needed to make a binding promise *enforceable.* Although the statute was intended to bar
fraudulent claims, over the centuries many courts came to
share the view of a distinguished English judge who concluded in the middle of the nineteenth century that the statute "promotes fraud rather than prevents it."[27] Early on,
claimants successfully avoided the statute by arguing that
equitable estoppel precluded the other party from insisting
on it if the claimant had relied on a false representation by
the other party. The representation might be that a writing
was not necessary, that the other party had executed a writing or intended to execute one, or that the other party did
not intend to rely on the statute. But equitable estoppel was
not available if there was no representation and the claimant had simply relied on the very promise by the other party
that came within the statute of frauds in the first place.

So it was at least until 1950, when a landmark decision
by the Supreme Court of California rejected the contention
that "an estoppel to plead the statute of frauds can only
arise when there have been . . . representations going to the
requirements of the statute itself," and concluded that an
estoppel might also arise when a party relies on the "promise that the contract will be performed."[28] This decision did
not make clear what it was that was being relied on, but
four years later a federal appeals court filled this gap by
concluding that promissory estoppel could preclude a party

from asserting the statute of frauds "if the additional factor of a promise to reduce the contract to writing is present."[29] Implicit in such a promise, as we have seen, would be a representation that the promisor intended to execute a writing, and a false representation of that intention was a traditional ground of equitable estoppel.

The idea that such an additional promise was necessary did not take hold, however, and somewhat more than a decade later, when the drafters of the Restatement (Second) faced this question, they formulated a rule that said nothing about an additional promise.[30] The upshot is a curiously circular rule. The other party is barred from claiming the advantage of the statute of frauds. But there is no preclusion as that term is used here since there is no voluntary surrender of that advantage. There is not even a voluntary undertaking not to assert that advantage. The promisor, indeed, does nothing whatsoever to lose that advantage. The promisor does not lose it by making the promise in the first place, since the promise is then subject to the requirement imposed by the statute. And the promisor does nothing else—makes no representation or other promise. It is the promisee that does something—by relying. But on what does the promisee rely? If no additional promise is required, the argument must be the circular one that the reliance is on the very promise that the statute declares to be unenforceable, an unreliable promise indeed. More than one court has concluded that if "mere pleading of reliance on the contract [were] sufficient to permit a party to assert rights and defenses based on a contract barred by the statute of frauds . . . the statute of frauds would be rendered meaningless and nugatory."[31]

In sum, the Restatement (Second) rule is not one of preclusion at all, and it is misleading to represent it to be a rule of estoppel.[32] The promisor never voluntarily surrenders the advantage of asserting the statute, as in cases of equitable estoppel. Nor is there a voluntary undertaking that could be the basis of promissory estoppel—unless one disregards the very promise that the statute makes unenforceable. Rather, it is as if an exception had been written into the statute itself, saying that specified promises were unenforceable except where evidenced by a signed writing and *except where* relied upon. Reliance would then be just another way of satisfying the statute of frauds. The rule reflects a growing judicial hostility to the statute of frauds. But for judges to have openly written an exception into the statute of frauds would have subjected them to the accusation that they were infringing on the province of legislators by rewriting the statute. So, having concluded—sensibly it well may be—that the statute imposed too great a hardship on relying promisees, they rewrote the statute in the guise of finding preclusions. Courts might, in the end, have reached the same result by directly confronting the issue instead of circumventing it by concocting a false estoppel—one that is neither equitable nor promissory. In doing so, they might have avoided at least some of the confusion that attends use of the word estoppel.

Having seen how, in cases of equitable estoppel, ostensible ownership, and laches, preclusion may result where there is actual reliance, we next consider how preclusion may result when there is only the likelihood of reliance. There we will find yet another estoppel.

CHAPTER EIGHTEEN

Preclusion by Rejection

How an offeree's rejection of the offer surrenders the offeree's power of acceptance and precludes the offeree, on a change of mind, from accepting. How irrelevance of actual reliance under this rule can be justified. A comparison with the rule under which the offeree's assent results in commitment and an analogy to the balk rule in baseball. Analysis of a decision applying the rule to dealings between prisoners and Washington state in a case on the margins of contract law.

Consider once again the position of the Zehmers when W. O. Lucy offered to buy their farm for $50,000. The Zehmers had a power—the power to accept the offer by giving their return promise. As we saw earlier in discussing commitments, once they exercised that power by accepting W. O.'s offer, they were bound by their promise, and it was too late, even an instant later, to change their minds. The Zehmers were committed to sell their farm. But they could also have rejected the offer. What if they had done so and then, only an instant later, after a change of mind tried to accept? Would they still have had the power to accept? Now the question is not one of commitment. The question is whether by rejecting W. O.'s offer the Zehmers would have surrendered their power to accept that offer.

Contract law says yes: by rejecting an offer the offeree surrenders the power to accept it. As the Restatement (Second) puts it, the "offeree's power of acceptance is terminated by his rejection of the offer."[1] This rule cannot be rooted in the intention principle, for it would be a rare offeree that would, when rejecting an offer, harbor any intention with respect to the possibility of accepting it on a change of mind. It is a rule not of relinquishment but of preclusion, and its roots are not in the intention principle but in the reliance principle. An offeror is likely to do something in reliance on the offeree's rejection, and it would then be unfair to allow the offeree, on a change of mind, to accept.[2]

The rule, however, is a bright-line rule that does not require the offeror to prove any reliance. The Zehmers would have been precluded by their rejection even if they had changed their minds only an instant later and tried to accept before there had been any chance for W. O. to rely. Why a bright-line rule?

Its justification turns on the probability of reliance, not on actual reliance. The reasoning parallels that which we saw before in the case of an offeror's reliance when the offeree accepts rather than rejects. Just as a bright-line rule under which the Zehmers' acceptance without more results in their commitment spares W. O. the task of proving reliance on the acceptance, so too a bright-line rule under which the Zehmers' rejection without more precludes acceptance spares W. O. the task of proving reliance on the rejection. This is so even though an offeror's reliance in response to a rejection is not likely to be as difficult to prove as the offeror's reliance in response to an acceptance. It will not consist of forbearance from arranging a substitute, though it might still be negative, as by failing to get ready to perform the contract. But it is more likely to be affirmative as by arranging for a substitute contract or, perhaps, by eliminating the need for any contract.[3] The argument for a bright-line rule therefore seems weaker here than it was in the case of an acceptance. There is, however, the countervailing consideration that the impact of the rule on the rejecting offeree is softened in three ways. The difficulty in justifying a bright-line rule is not unlike that when a party has repudiated a contract and then seeks to retract the repudiation (Chapter 6) or when a party with a power to avoid a contract has made a statement of disaffirmance and then seeks to affirm (Chapter 19).[4]

First, the regret that comes from rejection tends to be less acute than the regret that comes from acceptance. Admittedly, an offeree can no more avoid regret by rejecting the offer than by accepting it. And from a purely monetary point of view, it can be argued that if it turned out that the Zehmers' farm was worth only $30,000, their regret at having passed up W. O.'s offer was no different from the regret that would have resulted from their acceptance if it turned out that the farm was worth $70,000. But if, as was suggested earlier, we tend to undervalue lost opportunities, the Zehmers would feel the regret less acutely if it resulted from passing up a desirable opportunity than if it resulted from seizing an undesirable one. There is more drama in the tears of the Esau who seized the opportunity to sell his birthright for a single meal than in the remorse of an Esau who passed up a sumptuous meal to keep a worthless birthright.

Second, the power of acceptance that is surrendered on rejection could have been destroyed by the offeror simply by revoking the offer at any time before the rejection. The power that the Zehmers would have surrendered by rejection was a power weakened by its vulnerability to revocation by W. O. It is worth noting that if the offeree values the power of acceptance enough to purchase an "option," a rejection of such an irrevocable offer does not surrender the offeree's power of acceptance.[5]

Third, the offeree can avoid the impact of the rejection rule by indicating an intention not to accept together with "an intention to take it under further advisement," to use the Restatement's words. An offeree who has no interest in an offer has, after all, no reason to reject it and can simply let it lapse, retaining the power of acceptance until it does. The offeree who wishes to keep the offer under consideration while making a counteroffer can, by using the Restatement's formulation, do so without being precluded from accepting the initial offer.

If, for these reasons, the offeree is less prejudiced by the rejection rule than might first appear, it may be of less concern that proof of the offeror's reliance might not be difficult. Although the rule may rest on a somewhat unstable foundation, it has advantages for administration of the legal system. First, opportunities seized are of more concern to the legal system than are opportunities passed up, for it is the former that give rise to lawsuits. Second, bright-line rules make it easier to resolve the common sorts of disputes that involve contract formation. The rejection rule presumably extends to the case of a purported principal, who can decide whether to ratify the act of an unauthorized agent. The situation of the purported principal has been likened to that of an offeree,[6] an apt simile in that the purported principal is subject to the third party's power of withdrawal in the same way that the offeree is subject to the offeror's power of revocation. Pursuing the simile, it would seem that disaffirmance by the purported principal would be irreversible for the same reason that an offeree's rejection is.

The bright-line rules of the law on contract formation give this subject its gamelike quality.[7] Compare, for example, the rejection rule with baseball's balk rule. When a baserunner takes a long lead off first base, he dares the pitcher to throw him out. The pitcher has the choice of accepting this dare, by trying to pick the runner off first, or rejecting it by pitching to the plate. What the balk rule says is that once having rejected the dare by beginning the pitching motion, it is too late for the pitcher to change his mind and try to pick the runner off first. To interrupt the pitching motion once it has begun is therefore a balk, and the sanction is that runner advances to second base.[8] The pitcher should not try to "deceive" the runner, as the explanation often runs, by interrupting the pitching motion in order to throw the runner out or to bluff the runner back to first. The runner may have run to a more vulnerable position in reliance on the beginning of the pitching motion, but the rule does not require that any such reliance be shown. A balk is a balk even if, as often happens, the pitcher does not try to throw the runner out and even if the runner does not notice the motion.[9] As in the case of contract law's rejection rule, the possibility of reliance is sufficient.

There are, however, limits to the advantages of bright-line rules in such situations. Consider the case of the inmates of a Washington state prison who had sued the state, claiming overcrowding. The parties appeared to have reached a settlement before trial, and the state submitted to the judge a proposed consent decree providing for reduction of the prison's population by stated dates. The state then discovered that one of the dates was mistakenly listed as earlier than agreed and filed a revised decree, offering to go forward with the later date. The prisoners sought approval of the original version with the earlier date. When the judge refused approval, the prisoners, hoping for second best, tried to accept the state's offer to go forward with the later date. But the state refused to perform, contending that, under the rejection rule, it was too late for the prisoners to accept its offer because they had rejected it by seeking approval of the original version. Was the state free to renege? A federal appeals court upheld a lower court's decision that it was not, conceding the applicability of the rejection rule but sidestepping it by concluding that the prisoner's request for approval of the original version "would not clearly indicate to a reasonable person that the prisoners were rejecting" the state's offer.[10]

Surely the appeals court reached the correct result. But did it make sense to concede the applicability of the rejection rule, resting as it does on an unstable foundation, to this situation on the margins of contract law? In the situation for which the rejection rule is designed, the offeror has a variety of potential parties with whom to contract. On rejection by the offeree, the offeror is likely to rely by taking steps to arrange a contract with another one of those potential parties.

If the Zehmers had rejected W. O.'s offer of $50,000 for their farm, it is possible that he might have relied on their rejection by attempting to find another farm to buy. But in the case of the state's offer to the prisoners there were no other potential parties with whom the state could contract. Even if the prisoners had rejected the state's offer, there was no one else to whom the state could have turned in reliance on the rejection. While the state might have relied in other ways, there was no possibility of the particularly compelling type of reliance that justifies the rule. If the principle underlying the rejection rule is the reliance principle and the reasoning is that an offeror should be free to rely on a rejection without having to prove reliance where there is a strong likelihood of actual reliance, it is at best doubtful whether this principle applied to the state. The state's offer was, after all, revocable, and if the state had desired protection in the event of its unprovable reliance, it could simply have revoked its offer.

This analysis finds support in the rules applied to collective bargaining, where an analogous situation arises. There both employer and union are obliged to deal exclusively with the other, and there are no other potential parties with whom they can contract. And there courts have departed from contract law's bright-line rule, finding that the "common law rule that a rejection or counter proposal necessarily terminates the offer has little relevance in the collective bargaining setting."[11] Instead, the rule is that "an offer will remain on the table unless the offeror explicitly withdraws it or unless circumstances arise that would lead the parties to reasonably believe that the offeror has withdrawn the offer."[12]

Here courts have sensibly declined to defer to the contract rule because the principle that underlies does not apply. It would have been wise to have done the same in the case of the inmates of the Washington state prison. The case of the prisoners gives cause to lament the tendency of courts in marginal cases to apply contract rules mechanically, without regard to the underlying general principles, a tendency that is particularly marked when the rules are the kinds of bright-line rules discussed here.

Preclusion by rejection is a different matter from preclusion by election, which we consider now.

CHAPTER NINETEEN

Preclusion by Election

The concept of election as an irreversible choice between two alternatives. Election restricted to situations in which one party to a relationship has a right against another party and can choose to end that relationship, resulting in the other's vulnerability. Irreversibility in cases of affirmance based on an assent rule. Irreversibility in cases of disaffirmance justified by an anti-speculation principle. Some examples of election, including the case of Karl's obligation to support Nora's child, who was conceived by artificial insemination. The discredited doctrine of election of remedies distinguished. The role of a public interest principle in connection with litigation and to wills.

The Romans fixed the concept in a maxim: *Quod semel placuit in electione, amplius displicere non potest* (If a man once determines his election it shall be determined forever).[1] Longfellow gave the concept meter:

> Decide not rashly. The decision made
> Can never be recalled. The Gods implore not,
> Plead not, solicit not; they only offer
> Choice and occasion, which once being passed
> Return no more.[2]

The concept, of course, is that of *election*—an irreversible choice between two alternatives.[3]

But do you not make such a choice every time you make up your mind? You can choose to give up sweets or not, to sell your jet plane or not, to give away your painting or not, and so on. What is special about situations in which the judges and lawyers use the term "election"?

A convincing answer can be given if the term "election" is restricted to situations in which one party to a relationship has a right of some kind against another party and can, by timely action, choose to end their relationship.[4] The other party, having no control over the choice, is therefore vulnerable to the party having the power of election. (I will not address situations in which one party can assert a right against either of two different parties and must at some point choose between them.[5])

Take, for example, the situation in which the other party has committed a serious breach of contract. You can choose to insist on performance. Or you can instead choose to terminate the contract and claim damages for its total breach, if you act within a reasonable time. You are properly said to have a right of election. You can maintain your contractual relationship with the other party or you can, by timely action, end it, and the other party, having no control over your choice, is therefore vulnerable to you.

Or take the situation in which the other party has induced you to make a contract by fraud. You can choose to insist on performance by "ratifying" the contract. Or you can choose to "rescind" or "avoid" the contract and seek restitution, if you act within a reasonable time. Again, you can maintain your contractual relationship with the other party or you can, by timely action, end your relationship. And again, the other party is vulnerable to you in a way characteristic of election.

It follows from the nature of an election—by whatever name—that it cannot be partial. To put it as the high court of Massachusetts did a century and a half ago: "If a party would rescind a contract, he must do it *in toto*. He cannot disclaim it in part and enforce it in part."[6]

If the term is restricted as suggested here, it has nothing to do with your resolving to give up sweets, promising to sell your jet plane, or making a gift of your painting. In those situations you have no right against anyone; no one is vulnerable to you in the way characteristic of election. Preclusion by election is therefore a very different matter than preclusion by rejection. After W. O. Lucy had made his offer

to buy the farm from the Zehmers, he was still free to revoke it at any time. He was not vulnerable to the Zehmers,
for they had no right of any kind against him—only a power
of acceptance that was itself vulnerable to his revocation of
his offer. The case for preclusion is thus more compelling in
cases of election than in cases of rejection.

As was signaled at the outset, election is characterized
by irreversibility—reliance plays no role, and no signed writing or other formality is required. A clear indication of intention is enough. In Longfellow's words, "The choice once
made can never be recalled." Thus if, after the other party to
your contract has committed a serious breach you indicate
your intention to stand by the contract, you have made an irreversible choice to continue the relationship, retaining the
possibility of claiming damages. Similarly if, on discovering the deception, you indicate your intention to affirm the
contract you made as a result of fraud, you have made an irreversible choice to continue the relationship. In these situations your power to end the relationship is lost without any
showing of reliance by the other party.[7]

It is not difficult to justify an assent rule under which
your ratification of the contract is irreversible without any
showing of reliance by the other party. The other party may
have relied on your ratification, and the reliance may have
consisted in lost opportunities, just as in the case of the assent rule that we discussed earlier in connection with your
promise. If you indicate your intention to stand by an existing contract, the other party may forgo other opportunities
just as that party may have done when the contract was
made in the first place.[8] As the possibility of such reliance
was a sufficient ground to impose liability in the case of unexecuted bilateral agreements, so too it is a sufficient ground
to preclude a party from reasserting a power of avoidance.[9]

Courts also apply the concept of election when a party
acts in the opposite sense—declining the benefits of the contract rather than taking advantage of them. Election is again

irreversible, with no requirement of any reliance or formality. If, in the face of a serious breach of contract by the other party, you terminate the contract, you have also made an irreversible choice. The same is true if on discovering the deception you avoid the contract you made as a result of fraud.[10] Irreversibility in these situations is harder to explain because, though the other party may have relied, the reliance will not have consisted of lost opportunities, and the assent rule does not apply. Analogous situations have already been encountered where a party has repudiated a contract and then seeks to retract the repudiation (Chapter 6) and where an offeree rejects an offer and then seeks to accept it (Chapter 18). Indeed, an observant scholar has pointed out that courts seem more hesitant to find an election in these situations than when there has been affirmance.[11]

Why should an election be irreversible absent a showing of actual reliance?[12] Irreversibility is bound up with the requirement of a prompt decision. If a party could reverse an election, the party would, in effect, have additional time before making a final decision. More than a century ago the Supreme Court of the United States stressed the importance of a prompt final decision, saying that one who has the power to avoid a contract on the ground, for example, of fraud "is not permitted to play fast and loose" where the contract involves "speculative property" with "large and constant fluctuations in value."[13] Similarly, a Texas appeals court explained that allowing a minor to procrastinate after reaching the age of majority before deciding whether to avoid a contract for the sale of real property would enable the minor "to speculate upon fluctuations in value, to affirm or disaffirm, as his subsequent interest might dictate; whereas, the other party would be helpless until the minor might see fit to act."[14]

Procrastination permits speculation, and there is a pronounced judicial distaste for allowing one party to speculate at the other's risk. This anti-speculation principle finds voice in the orthodox catechism that unless both parties are bound neither is bound, or, as an English court said three centuries ago, "Either all is a *nudum pactum,* or else the one promise is as good as the other." [15] The judicial distaste persists even if the other party has been guilty of fraud or duress. This skepticism about one-sided commitments would be perfectly appropriate if all commitments were motivated by a difference in risk aversion or by different beliefs about the future.

The anti-speculation principle is evident when there is a breach of an "aleatory" contract—a contract such as a gambling or insurance contract under which a duty to pay is conditioned on a fortuitous event. It would be unfair to allow the injured party to wait and see how things turned out— even if the other party has been guilty of fraud—and only then decide whether to put an end to the relationship. To prevent this kind of opportunistic behavior courts insist that an injured party that wishes to put an end to the relationship let the other party know an irreversible decision before the event occurs or becomes more probable. Otherwise the injured party will be held to the contract, with a right to any damages caused by the breach.[16]

Even if the contract is not aleatory, the injured party's power to elect whether to terminate the contract puts that party in a somewhat similar position. The pervasiveness of the assumption that parties make contracts in order to be able to shift market risks was noted earlier (Chapters 6 and 11). If shifts in a market or in other changing circumstances impose a significant risk that the contract will turn out to be advantageous or disadvantageous to the injured party, that party might await the outcome and then use the power to the other party's disadvantage. There would evidently be unfairness, then, in letting the injured party procrastinate and thereby prolong the time during which the other party is at the injured party's mercy. The anti-speculation principle is, however, harder to justify when the purpose of the contracting parties is to encourage one party's reliance in the form of investment in the relationship rather than to shift market risks.

Under the anti-speculation principle, the power of

avoidance is lost by inaction as well as by action, for it must be exercised within a reasonable time. Even the victim of fraud is expected to deal fairly in this way with the one who has perpetrated the fraud.[17] But the Texas court went on to hold that when a minor's obligation is merely one to pay a sum of money as a surety, there is "no reason why he should be required to do more than resist enforcement of the contract whenever attempted by the other party" because the creditor "could not possibly suffer any detriment or inconvenience by the minor's inaction."[18] You need not make an election unless the other party is at your mercy.

The concept of election has an appeal that is not limited to the examples given so far, and it is scarcely surprising that instances of election are found throughout the law, often under other names. For example, under the Uniform Commercial Code a buyer who is tendered defective goods can choose to accept or reject them,[19] and by doing nothing the buyer is taken to have accepted them—subject to a claim for damages.[20] The seller is thus vulnerable to the buyer's power of election; a buyer, once having exercised that power, is not free to make a different choice.[21] The same is true when a party has a power of approval like that of Peter Mattei (Chapter 5). Peter could choose to indicate satisfaction or dissatisfaction, and by doing nothing he would be taken to be satisfied. Amelia Hopper was thus vulnerable to Peter's power of election; Peter, once having exercised that power, would not have been free to make a different choice.[22]

For an unusual application of the doctrine of election, take the case of Karl and Nora, as I will call them, who were married in 1977.[23] Unable to have children because Karl had undergone an irreversible vasectomy, they resorted to artificial insemination by a third-party donor. Karl participated in child-birth classes, became enthusiastic about the pregnancy as it progressed, and, when a baby boy was born in 1982, Karl named him Junior, was listed as father on the birth certificate, and spoke of "our baby." Some years later, however, when divorce proceedings began, Karl denied paternity and resisted paying child support. At common law, Karl would not have been liable for child support because the boy would not have been regarded as Karl's legitimate child. Under a Texas statute, however, if a husband consents to the artificial insemination, the resulting child is the legitimate child of both husband and wife. But the statute requires that to be valid the consent must be in writing and acknowledged. Though Karl's consent to the procedure was oral only, the trial judge ordered child support, and, when Karl appealed, a Texas intermediate appellate court affirmed. That court concluded that Karl's consent was irreversible despite the failure to observe the required formality because, by his conduct, Karl had "ratified the parent-child relationship." [24]

Even if the court had read a promise or a representation into Karl's conduct, he would not have been estopped to renege because the procedure, having preceded the conduct, could not have been carried out in reliance on it. And had the court viewed the statute as a mini-statute of frauds, as it might have seemed to be, Karl would not have been precluded from asserting it because there had been no reliance (Chapter 17). But instead the court treated the statute as making Karl's oral consent voidable, raising the possibility of election. Karl thus had a choice of either standing by the relationship or not, a power that made Nora vulnerable to him in the way characteristic of election. When he indicated by his conduct that he chose the former, he "ratified" and by this election was precluded from making the other choice when divorce proceedings began. (It would seem to follow that since Karl had for years done nothing to *avoid,* he would have been precluded by the mere passage of time, but the court did not have to face this issue.)

What conduct will amount to an election? This question has plagued litigants under a doctrine of "election of remedies." [25] If a plaintiff has two inconsistent remedies for a single wrong, should the commencement of a lawsuit to obtain one of the remedies amount to an election?[26] Since the plaintiff cannot have both remedies, a time must come when an election must be made. But when is that time? Should the victim of fraud be held to have manifested an intention to affirm by claiming damages for breach of contract and to have manifested an intention to disaffirm by claiming restitution?

Graphic illustrations of an affirmative answer can be found in Arkansas, where the Supreme Court has held that a plaintiff who, on breach of contract, commences a suit to enforce a contract by specific performance makes a binding election that bars a subsequent claim for damages for total breach of contract instead,[27] and conversely that a plaintiff who commences a suit to recover damages for total breach makes a binding election that bars a subsequent request for specific performance instead.[28] Although this doctrine of election of remedies is sometimes justified as preventing duplication of remedies, this can be accomplished by allowing a plaintiff to pursue inconsistent remedies until a verdict is rendered and only then requiring the plaintiff to make an election.[29]

The increasingly maligned doctrine has now fallen into disrepute. Even though a party has a power of election, that party's mere recourse to a court to get relief in an adversary proceeding is not regarded as such an indication of intention as will amount to an election. The plaintiff that seeks damages for breach of contract can be seen as indicating an intention to affirm the contract only if damages are paid.[30] And the plaintiff that seeks restitution can be seen as indicating an attention to disaffirm the contract only if restitution is made.[31]

Despite the disrepute into which the doctrine of election of remedies has fallen, courts have at their disposal a formidable array of rules to confront litigants who have changed their minds in the course of litigation. While these rules may benefit the other party, their justification rests primarily on the interest of the public at large. In allocating precious judicial resources, it is in the public interest to encourage parties to make their peace by ensuring that litigants receive one, but only one, fair opportunity to present their cases in court. Preclusion here rests on a *public interest* principle.[32] Although these rules do not require actual reliance, they do not involve election and are not based on a distaste for speculation.

Some of these rules apply as soon as litigation has begun. Others apply only after the trial is over. All of them stand in sharp contrast to the rules applicable before litigation has begun when, for example, a party that has had a change of mind after terminating a contract on a stated ground is free to abandon that ground as a justification for termination and assert a completely different ground.[33]

Once litigation has begun, a party is restricted in a number of ways from changing grounds. In addition to serving the public interest, these restrictions enable the other party to prepare its case. Rules of civil procedure commonly limit a party's freedom in amending pleadings and in asserting new defenses.[34] In some jurisdictions there is also a doctrine picturesquely styled "mend the hold," a name, taken from nineteenth-century wrestling jargon, meant to suggest that as a wrestler should not be permitted to get a better grip on an opponent, a defendant should not be permitted to change defenses or add new ones once the match has begun. As the United States Supreme Court stated in the same century, a party "cannot, after litigation has begun, change his ground, and put his conduct upon another and a different consideration,"[35] even though the party can do just that before litigation has begun.[36] The doctrine, which gives a defendant a reasonable opportunity to formulate its defenses, "can be seen as a corollary of the duty of good faith," as a prominent federal judge has written. "A party who hokes up a phony defense to the performance of his contractual duties and then when that defense fails (at some expense to the other party) tries on another defense for size can properly be said to be acting in bad faith."[37] In addition, when during trial a party gives testimony adverse to that party's case, that testimony may be binding on the party as a "judicial admission." The party will be precluded from later contradicting it if the admission is within the party's personal knowledge, there is no reasonable chance for mistake, and the admission is "clear and unequivocal."[38]

Once the litigation ends, the arguments in favor of preclusion are even greater because the public also has an even stronger interest in finality. The Romans had a phrase for that too: *Interest reipublicae ut sit finis litium* (It is in the state's interest that there be an end to lawsuits). This is the thought behind the doctrine of *res judicata* (a matter adjudicated).[39] Under this doctrine, now commonly called "claim preclusion," a party is precluded from advancing in a second proceeding claims that were or could have been litigated in a prior proceeding.[40] This has, the United States Supreme Court has said, "the dual purpose of protecting litigants . . . and of promoting judicial economy."[41] The claims need not be inconsistent, and what is involved is not election. Similar reasoning explains the principle of the "law of the case," which prevents relitigation on a settled issue in the same case and requires that courts follow decisions in prior proceedings, including the mandates of higher courts when the case is remanded after appeal. This, according to a federal appeals court, is in the interest of "judicial economy."[42]

The same justification underlies what in many jurisdictions is known as judicial estoppel, which precludes a party from taking a factual position in a judicial proceeding that is inconsistent with a position successfully asserted by the same party in a different judicial proceeding, even if the party asserting the preclusion was not a party to that proceeding. The rationale most often cited for the doctrine is, in the words of one federal appeals court, "to prevent the party from 'playing fast and loose' with the courts, and to protect the essential integrity of the judicial process"[43] from abuse by what another court called "cynical gamesmanship."[44] The word "estoppel" is of course misleading, for as in the case of "estoppel by deed" (Chapter 8) no showing of reliance is required. The Supreme Court of Oregon has explained: "Because judicial estoppel is primarily concerned with the integrity of the *judicial* process and not with the relationship of the parties, it does not depend for its application on a showing that the party raising judicial estoppel as an affirmative defense detrimentally relied on the other party's prior inconsistent position."[45] As in the other examples given, reliance by the other party is not the key under the public interest principle.

Although these illustrations of the public interest principle do not involve election, that principle may play a role in cases involving election. A person who is provided for in a will and who has an alternative and inconsistent claim has a power of election. For example, a surviving spouse may have a claim under the will of the deceased spouse and an alternative and inconsistent claim under a statutory provision that guarantees the surviving spouse a minimum share. The surviving spouse can choose between the two claims, and failure to take timely action is treated as a choice to proceed under the will and to surrender the claim under the statutory provision. But whichever choice is made, it has generally been held to irreversibly surrender the other, even if there has been no reliance on that choice. The surviving spouse is therefore precluded by election.[46]

The irreversibility has been explained by one authority on the ground that the provision in the will "is considered to be the equivalent of an offer, the acceptance of which requires the surrender of the other right . . . [while] an election by the devisee to take against the will . . . could be viewed as analogous to the rejection of an offer."[47] But this explanation misses the mark because the position of the spouse is not analogous to that of an offeree. An offeree, as we have seen, is subject to the offeror's power of revocation, so that the offeror is not vulnerable to the offeree in the way characteristic of election. But the decedent's estate is vulnerable in just such a way. In contrast to the decision of a purported principal as to whether to ratify the act of an unauthorized agent, which has misleadingly been termed an election,[48] the decision of the surviving spouse as to whether to take under the will is properly viewed as an election. Furthermore, the arguments in favor of preclusion are shored up by a public interest in finality in the settlement of estates.

In this chapter we have seen that there may be a public interest in preclusion. That interest will reappear in the following chapter.

CHAPTER TWENTY

Preclusion by Prescription

How the doctrine of prescription may result in preclusion, as it did when Chicago Metallic Ceilings tried to bar Eugene Warsaw from its land. The origins of the doctrine. Its requirements and why it is not consensual but based on the repose principle and the public interest principle. Justifications of the doctrine and its relation to the reliance principle. How government lands are not subject to the doctrine, with an exception based on the lost grant fiction.

In most of the situations discussed so far, preclusion results from your having done something, though not with the intention of surrendering any advantage. Sometimes, however, you can be precluded by doing nothing. Had Eugene V. Klein waited seven years before going to court to seek relief for PepsiCo's refusal to deliver the G-II jet that it had promised (Chapter 11), no one would have been surprised to find that he was precluded from both specific performance and damages by his delay. The statute of limitations in the Uniform Commercial Code would have barred Eugene after four years. But why? In an earlier chapter we saw that the doctrine of laches might preclude a party from obtaining equitable relief, but that it did so only if the delay caused harm to the other party. Laches, like its more important sibling equitable estoppel, is squarely based on the reliance principle and may bar a party even before the statute of limitations has run.[1] A statute of limitations is, by contrast, a bright-line rule that requires no showing that the delay caused harm. Such a rule can be justified on two grounds.

First, it spares the potential defendant the burden of making out a case when evidence has grown stale.[2] After a fixed period of years one is entitled to repose, to be able to plan with greater certainty. A statute of limitations can thus be justified under a *repose* principle, what Oliver Wendell Holmes, writing to William James, called "one of the most sacred and indubitable principles that we have."[3] Such statutes, sometimes referred to as "statutes of repose," protect, as the Supreme Court put it, "defendants and the courts from having to deal with cases in which the search for truth may be seriously impaired by the loss of evidence, whether by . . . fading memories . . . or otherwise."[4]

Second, as the reference to "courts" in this quotation suggests, it is in the interest of the public as well as the individual to bring an end to controversy. "Peace is certainly worth more than all law," proclaimed Martin Luther long before the litigation explosion.[5] Society, as well as the parties, is entitled to have stale claims laid to rest. Therefore both the repose principle and the public interest principle support preclusion based on the passage of time.

It is unlikely, however, that Chicago Metallic Ceilings imagined that either principle would result in its being precluded from ousting Eugene Warsaw from its land. Chicago Metallic and Eugene had acquired adjacent tracts of land from a common owner in 1972. Eugene had built a large commercial building on his tract, leaving only a 40-foot-wide driveway along one side of Chicago Metallic's tract to provide access to his loading docks. Chicago Metallic had built a smaller building on its tract, leaving vacant a 150-foot-wide strip along Eugene's driveway. From the beginning it had been apparent that Eugene's driveway was inadequate to let the large trucks that used his loading docks turn and position themselves without going into Chicago Metallic's property. For seven years Chicago Metallic said nothing while trucks used a part of its vacant land to service Eugene's loading dock. Eugene tried, at least twice during that period, to get Chicago Metallic to grant him an easement, but Chicago Metallic refused. Then, in 1979, Chicago Metallic decided to build a warehouse, which would have blocked Eugene's use of Chicago Metallic's land. Eugene went to court and obtained an injunction on the ground that he had obtained a 25-foot-wide easement on Chicago Metallic's land by virtue of the doctrine of prescription. On appeal, the Supreme Court of California affirmed.[6]

Chicago Metallic, which knew of Eugene's use of its land, must have made a decision not to complain for seven years. But it had done nothing further except to refuse to grant Eugene an easement. Chicago Metallic had not taken the second step of consenting to Eugene's use of its driveway. And even if Chicago Metallic had consented, its consent would have been regarded as having granted Eugene only a revocable "license," and Chicago Metallic could still have changed its mind and reneged on that decision as long as Eugene had done nothing in reliance on it. The license would, however, have become irrevocable (Chicago Metallic would have been estopped to revoke its consent) if Eugene had substantially relied on Chicago Metallic's consent by, for example, investing in large trucks that could not be used without going on Chicago Metallic's property.[7] But why was Chicago Metallic precluded from excluding Eugene from its land when it had not consented and had at most made a decision not to complain?

The explanation, as anyone familiar with the seemingly magical doctrine of prescription will recognize, is that the doctrine is not based on consent—it is a doctrine of preclusion. One who acquires a prescriptive right from an owner does so not by virtue of the owner's consent but by virtue of the owner's inaction. That inaction may be voluntary, but its effect is not based on the premise that consent is to be implied from it. It was Chicago Metallic's very failure to act, not some consent inferred from that failure, that resulted in its being precluded from excluding Eugene from its land. This is then a situation in which an owner's decision to take no action may result in a preclusion, but, as in cases of estoppel and laches, the decision itself is not essential for it is not necessary that the owner have any intention to surrender the advantage in question. The result would be the same even if the failure to act resulted from inattention or sloth and not from a decision at all. As we shall see, prescriptive rights can be acquired by the use of an owner's land even if the owner has no actual knowledge of the use. Eugene's rights would have been no less clear had Chicago Metallic been an absentee owner, unaware of Eugene's use of its land—witness the graphic description of the doctrine of prescription as working against those who "sleep" on their rights.

The Restatement (Third) of Property explains that prescription is a doctrine "whereby a pattern of conduct can have the result of establishing a property interest having the same characteristics as one created by contract."[8] Under the doctrine, Eugene's use of the driveway gave him a property right good against Chicago Metallic.[9] What rationale underlies this doctrine under which, by sleeping on your property rights, you can lose them simply by the passage of time?

There was a time when the doctrine of prescription might have been thought to be based on consent, for it was inspired by the notion that long-continued use is evidence of an entitlement consented to in the past. This notion was embodied in the quaint if implausible fiction that the use was based on a grant given by the owner at the time of the coronation of Richard I in 1189 but subsequently lost.[10] The appeal of this fiction of the "lost grant" as an explanation of the doctrine of prescription, which applied to the *use* of another's land and resulted in an easement, seemed not to extend to its cousin, the doctrine of adverse possession, which applied to the *occupation* of another's land and resulted in outright ownership. But now that diligent scholarly effort has largely extirpated the lost-grant fiction from American property law,[11] the two doctrines of prescription and adverse possession have been "twinned" by conforming the elements of the former to those of the latter, leaving, of course, the distinction between use in the case of the former and occupation in the case of the latter.

The doctrine of prescription is now commonly rested on the same principles that underlie statutes of limitations.[12] The idea is that an owner, such as Chicago Metallic, has a right to prevent adverse use, such as Eugene's, by an action such as trespass for interference with its ownership interest and, indeed, would ordinarily be expected to take steps to bar the continuing invasion. If the owner fails to do this while the use continues for a statutory prescriptive period, the adverse user is at last entitled to the repose that the doctrine of prescription affords by conferring the legal right to continue the use. (The period is commonly ten to twenty years, though in California it is only five.[13])

Because the doctrine is premised on the failure of the owner to bring an action such as trespass, the use must be "open or notorious."[14] The purpose of this requirement of a use of which the owner should have been aware is to give the owner ample opportunity to act. The test is a combined objective and subjective one: actual knowledge of the use is not required if the use is such that the owner should have been aware of it; and use of which the owner should have been aware is not required if the owner had actual knowledge of it. The owner's loss is therefore voluntary, in the sense in which I have used that word in connection with the term "preclusion." The owner's inaction must have been voluntary in the sense that it was open to the owner to take legal action to bar the use. If one is to be barred for sleeping on one's rights, one must at least intend to sleep. If, for example, the owner is under age at the beginning of the use, the statutory period will not begin to run.[15]

Even more important for our purposes, the use must be "adverse to the owner of the land or the interest in land against which the easement is claimed."[16] This requirement, borrowed from the doctrine of adverse possession, rejects as "a remnant from the lost-grant fiction" the notion that prescriptive rights are based on the owner's "acquiescence."[17] But, though the use must be without the owner's consent, it is misleading to say, as it often is, that the use must be hostile. Not only is deliberate wrongdoing not required,[18] but the use may even be in an honest but mistaken belief that the user is entitled to make the use.[19] In addition, most courts indulge in a presumption that an unexplained use is adverse. The user must not, however, behave in such a way as to lead the owner to believe that no prescriptive right is asserted. On this reasoning, Chicago Metallic's refusal to grant Eugene an easement strengthened Eugene's claim of a prescriptive right,[20] while "thrusting" permission on Eugene would have defeated that claim.[21]

In sum, if Eugene had said while using the driveway, "I know it is wrong to use it, but I'll do it anyway," he would have prevailed. If he had said, "I know it is wrong to use it, but I don't think Chicago Metallic will object," he would also have prevailed. And if he had said, mistakenly, "I do not think it is wrong to use it because I believe that I have an easement to use it," he would still have prevailed. But if he had said, "I do not think it is wrong to use it because I believe that I have Chicago Metallic's consent to use it," he would have lost. (If, however, his belief was reasonable and he relied, he could prevail under the doctrine of estoppel though not under the doctrine of prescription.) Under the accepted view, then, the doctrine of prescription cannot be said to be consensual—indeed quite the opposite is the case.

The doctrine of prescription is often defended by focusing on the cost of resolving disputes and stressing that the doctrine provides a desirable degree of certainty with respect to rights in land. By cutting off stale claims the doctrine encourages timely assertion of rights before the quality of evidence has deteriorated, and by conforming rights to actual use, the doctrine gives assurance to those that openly and consistently assert rights. It should be considered, however, that the costs of on-site inspection may outweigh the savings in avoiding the search of old records. And as Eugene Warsaw's case shows, it will almost always be more efficient to rely on the records of title to establish rights than to resort to a lawsuit to determine whether all of the requirements of the doctrine of prescription have been met.

The doctrine is also defended by focusing on the maximum utilization of land and stressing that the doctrine prevents valuable resources from being left idle for long periods of time by allowing the productive user to acquire rights from an unproductive owner. By thus rewarding the longtime adverse user's productive use, the doctrine tends to increase the value of the land served by that use. It is also argued that the adverse possessor, if deprived of the land, would experience a diminution in wealth that would be felt more acutely than the original owner would feel the lost increase in wealth —just as, we have already seen, we tend to feel out-of-pocket losses more acutely than lost opportunities (Chapter 2).[22] It might be asked, however, why even a productive user, such as Eugene, should not be required to buy an easement from the original owner.[23] And since Eugene had been unable to come to terms with Chicago Metallic on an easement, he evidently did not value the use of the driveway more than Chicago Metallic valued the right to its exclusive use.

There is yet another type of justification—in terms of the justice of the particular case. Advocates of this approach speak, on the one hand, of protecting the expectations of the adverse user and, on the other hand, of punishing an original owner for sleeping on rights. And they often speak in terms of the adverse user's reliance.[24] Allusion is made to the simile of Oliver Wendell Holmes, who argued "that man, like a tree in a cleft of a rock, gradually shapes his roots to his surroundings, and when the roots have grown to a certain size, can't be displaced without cutting at his life." [25]

Such appeals to reliance are strangely silent as to what it is that is being relied on. We have already seen that if Chicago Metallic had given Eugene a revocable license, it could not have revoked the license if Eugene had significantly relied on it. But in that event it would have been the consent that was relied on. When, as in the actual case, there is not only consent but refusal, an argument in terms of reliance is puzzling. Indeed, if the requirement of adversity is to be taken seriously, there can be nothing consensual to be relied on if the doctrine of prescription is to be applied.

Instead of reliance, what takes place is adaptation—Holmes's tree does not rely on anything in shaping its roots to its surroundings, it just adapts itself to its surroundings. If we find the simile of the tree compelling in justifying the doctrine of prescription, it seems likely that we do so out of a sense that after many long years without disturbance by the owner the tree has acquired the right to be left alone—a right based on the repose principle.

As might be expected from the discussion of the government's immunity to the doctrine of equitable estoppel (Chapter 17), courts have also refused to apply the doctrines of adverse possession and prescription against government lands. *Nullum tempus occurrit regi* (time does not run against the king) was the historical explanation, though the real justification must be the same as in the case of estoppel. Where the government is concerned, the repose principle can be overridden just as the reliance principle can be overridden. The argument against allowing the acquisition of prescriptive rights in government land, particularly in extensive tracts of undeveloped land, is especially compelling given the burden that would fall on government officials, whose incentives and competence may be questionable, to detect and interrupt adverse uses.[26] Roughly a third of the states, however, have enacted statutes relaxing the common law barrier to such claims against state lands—an indication that this argument may be wearing thin.[27]

Furthermore, when faced with unusually appealing claims by adverse users, courts have resorted to the otherwise defunct fiction of a lost grant to give results that cannot otherwise be reached.[28] In the leading case, the Supreme Court of the United States upheld against the federal government a claim based on more than seventy years of adverse possession of Palmyra Island in the Pacific. Justice Reed ascended into the realm of fiction, explaining that the "presumption of a lost grant . . . recognizes that lapse of time may cure the neglect or failure to secure the proper muniments of title, even though the lost grant may not have been in fact executed," and the doctrine "applies to claims to land held adversely to the sovereign." [29] But this is a minor inroad into the government's immunity. As the reliance principle yields to competing considerations in the case of estoppel against the government, so too the repose and public interest principles yield to competing considerations in the case of prescription against the government.

Having identified an assortment of general principles that apply when you change your mind and feel regret, what conclusions can we draw?

Epilogue

At the outset of this book I described how the state of Illinois had a change of mind and reneged on its promise to Enricho Navarroli. In the intervening chapters I have surveyed many other situations in which someone has had a change of mind and reneged. Because one feels regret only if one has taken a step beyond that of making up one's mind in the first place, I arranged these situations according to whether that second step was what I have called a commitment, a relinquishment, or a preclusion.

The legal rules that govern the irrevocability of a commitment and the irreversibility of a relinquishment or a preclusion in these situations have been drawn from such fields as contracts, torts, property, trusts, wills, agency, family law, and procedure. I have identified six principles that underlie these legal rules. Much of my attention has been devoted to two, a reliance principle and an intention principle. But four others have been identified. I have suggested that a dependence principle may explain the commitment without promise by one who starts to rescue a drowning swimmer (Chapter 9), that an anti-speculation principle underlies the preclusion by election when an adult ratifies a contract made as a teenager (Chapter 19), that a public interest principle is the basis of the preclusions that put an end to judicial strife (Chapter 19), and that a repose principle supports the preclusion by prescription risked by an inattentive landowner (Chapter 20).

I hope that the identification and discussion of these rules will encourage courts to apply them more widely. Enricho's case is illustrative, for on appeal by the state, the Supreme Court of Illinois reversed the decision of the trial court, refusing to apply the reliance principle, holding that the state was not committed, and denying Enricho any relief.[1] No matter that Enricho had given his return promise or even that he had partly performed it. The controlling issue was "whether the State's repudiation of the asserted plea agreement constituted a denial of due process which can be rendered only by allowing the defendant specific enforcement of the agreement." Because the prosecutor's "refusal to carry out the claimed bargain did not deprive the defendant of due process . . . the defendant was not entitled to have the agreement enforced."[2] Enricho had only those rights that the Constitution granted; notions of fairness found in general principles added nothing. But even if Enricho had no constitutional right, the reliance principle surely justified the relief granted by the trial court.[3] In finding it, with Rousseau, "absurd that the will should put itself in chains for the future," and in allowing the state to change its mind to what Papinian would have called Enricho's "disadvantage," the Supreme Court of Illinois disregarded this widely recognized general principle of contract law.

I also hope that an understanding of these principles will help to expose the inconsistencies and other shortcomings of the rules themselves. Consider, for example, the related matters of the ascendancy of the reliance principle, the neglect of the intention principle, the propensity for finding a promise, and the impact of latent paternalism.

The ascendancy of the reliance principle, though spurned in Enricho's case, can be seen in the expansion of the doctrine of promissory estoppel as a basis for the en-

forcement of commitments (Chapter 8). As a basis for the
irreversibility of preclusions, the reliance principle remains
entrenched, as David Horn learned to his chagrin, in connec
tion with equitable estoppel and laches (Chapter 17).

The neglect of the intention principle is the obverse of
the ascendancy of the reliance principle. Not only is the
reliance principle now seen as a compelling reason for en
forcing promises (Chapter 4) and a basis in its own right for
doing so (Chapter 8), but it is also recognized as the chief
justification for the assent rule, which serves as its surrogate
(Chapter 6). The intention principle, by way of contrast, has
fallen into desuetude as far as commitments are concerned
The abolition of the seal as a means of making a promise
enforceable left promisors like Jack Tallas with no means of
effecting their intention (Chapter 7). I think it regrettable that
our legal system has not created an appropriate formality for
the enforcement of even the most plainly serious promises.

The neglect of the intention principle as far as commit
ments are concerned has been compounded by the propen
sity for finding a promise. This has the effect of negating the
intention principle with respect to some kinds of relinquish
ments by treating them as commitments. The most infamous
example involves relinquishment by renunciation, for this
was the technique used by the House of Lords when it trans
formed Julia Beer's renunciation of her claim against John
Weston Foakes into a promise and then refused to enforce
the promise (Chapter 15). But the same technique has been
used in connection with relinquishment by waiver (Chapter
16). Nevertheless, the intention principle continues to play
a significant role in connection with relinquishment by gift,
as Ethel Yahuda's estate learned in the case of her gift to He
brew University, where her intention was effectively mani
fested by delivery and she could have done the same by a
simple declaration of trust (Chapter 13). The inconsistency
highlights the fallacy of the rule as to renunciation.

Application of the intention principle is also hampered
by the same latent paternalism noted in connection with

romises to make gifts. That paternalism, narrowly escaped
by Marianne Speelman, is particularly notable in the limita-
ions on what can be given (Chapter 14).

And I hope that an understanding of the general principles underlying the legal rules discussed here will aid
courts in reaching decisions in marginal situations without
he kind of mechanical application of those rules exempli-
ied in the dispute between Washington state and its prisoners (Chapter 18). This is particuarly so when the rules
are the kinds of bright-line rules so favored by courts in the
situations described in this book.

Finally, I hope that at the very least the reader will agree
that there are many principles on which the law is right to
reject Rousseau's assertion that "It is absurd that the will
should put itself in chains for the future."

Notes

Prologue

1. Advertisement for *Crossing the Bridge,* New York Times, September 13, 1992.

2. Jean-Jacques Rousseau, Du contrat social (1792), reprinted in Oeuvres complètes 368–369 (Bernard Gagrebin ed. 1964).

3. Papinian in 4 The Digest of Justinian 50.17.75 (Theodor Mommsen & Alan Watson trans. 1985).

4. People v. Navarroli, 521 N.E.2d 891, 897, 899 (Ill. 1988) (Clark, J., dissenting). The argument that all such agreements should be unenforceable as against public policy has not been accepted by courts and is beyond the scope of this discussion.

5. I use the term "paternalism" broadly to include limitations that the law imposes on a person's control over the future for that person's own good, usually in the context of the extent of a person's freedom to make a commitment that will be irrevocable or a relinquishment or preclusion that will be irreversible. This is consistent with Mill's use of the term in his example of selling oneself into slavery (Chapter 7).

Chapter 1. Wanting to Make a Commitment

1. Homer, The Odyssey, book 12, lines 56–60, 210–213 (R. Fagles tr. 1996), discussed in the present context in Jon Elster, Ulysses and the Sirens chap. 2 (1979).

2. Richard P. Feynman, "Surely You're Joking, Mr. Feynman" 23 (1985).

3. *See* Erskine May's Treatise on the Law, Privileges, Proceeding and Usage of Parliament 379 (C. Gordon 20th ed. 1983).

4. On the extralegal aspects of such precommitment strategies *see* Thomas C. Schelling, Choice and Consequence (1984).

5. Time, May 14, 1984, at 67.

6. *See* 2 Austin W. Scott & William F. Fratcher, The Law of Trust §123 (4th ed. 1987), discussing also the controversy over whether th trustee should be permitted to carry out the trust even though it is un enforceable.

7. I use the term "renege" loosely, as in common speech. In car games "renege," originally a pinochle term, means to play a card o another suit when you can follow suit.

8. Henry Swinburne, A Briefe Treatise of Testaments and Las Willes 263 (1590). The common understanding that a will is revoked b a later will is reflected in the expression "*last* will and testament."

9. Another common instance of the use of legal rules to restrai changes of mind is the Christmas Club—a voluntary system of enforce savings in which your legal relationship with your bank penalizes yo if you do not keep your resolution to save. In any such two-part scheme, of course, the other party can release you, just as your frien can give you back your sweets.

10. Vynior's Case, 77 Eng. Rep. 597, 600 (1610).

11. I will not take up situations, addressed by philosophers, i which there is no one to complain if a promisor reneges. An example i the case of the deathbed promise, in which a promise is made in con fidence on the deathbed of the promisee, who then predictably die leaving the promisor the only person who knows of the promise.

12. 3 Seneca, Moral Essays (On Benefits) 313 (John W. Basore trans 1935).

13. Schaefer v. Williams, 19 Cal. Rptr. 2d 212, 214 (Ct. App. 1993) quoting Restatement (Second) of Contracts §9 (1981), which require "at least two parties to a contract." If a resolution involves two person ("I resolve to help you"), it may be regarded as a promise.

14. Strangely, the word "swap" is not used in this context in lega discourse, though its origin goes back to the sound made by strikin hands when closing a business deal.

15. Karl N. Llewellyn, What Price Contract?—An Essay in Perspec tive, 40 Yale L.J. 704, 725 (1931).

16. People v. Navarroli, 521 N.E.2d 891, 897, 899 (Ill. 1988) (Clark, J., dissenting).

17. Layman v. Combs, 981 F.2d 1093, 1103 (9th Cir. 1992) (Kozinski, J., "dissenting for the most part").

18. In 1855 Congress created the Court of Claims and accepted limited contract liability, broadened by the Tucker Act in 1887.

19. Thomas Kuehn, Law, Family, & Women 220 (1991), quoting Baldo degli Ubaldi on the institution of the *mundualdus*.

20. J. Bishop, Commentaries on the Law of Married Women §39 at p. 22 (1873).

21. Cohen v. Cowles Media Co., 457 N.W.2d 199, 202, 203 (Minn. 1990), rev'd on other grounds, 111 S. Ct. 2513 (1991).

22. Johann Wolfgang von Goethe, Faust (Part One) p. 44 lines 1413–1415 (David Luke trans. 1987).

Chapter 2. Regretting Being Committed

1. Johann Wolfgang von Goethe, Faust (Part One) p. 52 lines 1722–1726 (David Luke trans. 1987).

2. Edward FitzGerald, The Rubaiyat of Omar Khayyam stanza 20.

3. The two-faced version of the icon, favored by Tiepolo, is that of Cesare Ripa's *Iconologia,* first published in 1593. *See* Cesare Ripa, Baroque and Rococo Pictorial Imagery 179 (Edward A. Maser ed. & trans. 1971). Titian, in his *Allegory of Prudence,* favored a three-faced version, the third face concerned with the ordering of the present. *See* Erwin Panofsky, Meaning in the Visual Arts 149 (1955).

4. Andrews v. Styrap, [1872] 26 L.T.R. 704, 706 (1872). For a similar thought, *see* Henslee v. United States, 335 U.S. 595, 600 1949) Frankfurter, J., dissenting: "Wisdom too often never comes, and so one ought not to reject it merely because it comes late.").

5. Of course not every failure to perform a promise is the result of a decision not to perform it. A promisor may try to perform and still fail.

6. *See* Patrick S. Atiyah, The Rise and Fall of Freedom of Contract 156 (1979).

7. As I use the term, "regret" does not encompass "disappointment," meaning that you need not have done anything to cause it. You could, for example, be disappointed at having been left a pittance in a rich relative's will. For a broad definition of regret, *see* Janet Landman, Regret: The Persistence of the Possible 4 (1993) ("regret is a more or less painful judgment and state of feeling sorry for misfortunes, limitations,

losses, shortcomings, transgressions, or mistakes"). For a narrower defi nition, *see* Anthony Kronman, Paternalism and the Law of Contracts 92 Yale L.J. 763, 780–781 (1983) (confining "regret" to the situation in which the promisor has "grounds for questioning the rationality of his initial decision"). *But see* Bernard Williams, Shame and Necessity 69 (1993) (regret may focus "on the outside circumstances that made the action go wrong" as well as on "the moments of deliberation"). For an argument that you can regret an earlier choice on the ground that it was irrational, even though you are not now dissatisfied with that choice, *see* Mark Kelman, Choice and Utility, 1979 Wis. L. Rev. 769, 785.

8. Division into two categories according to the role of time ac cords with economic decision theory, under which the chief ingredi ents of a procedurally rational decision are said to be "knowledge of one's preferences" and "knowledge of probabilities." Landman, note 7 *supra* at 190.

9. *See* Restatement (Third) of the Foreign Relations Law of the United States §331 (1987) (dealing with "fraudulent conduct" and "co ercion of the state's representative" or "threat or use of force against the state"), following Articles 49, 51, and 52 of the Vienna Convention on the Law of Treaties.

10. 2 Henry de Bracton, On the Laws and Customs of England 61 (S. Thorne trans. 1968).

11. *See* Farnsworth on Contracts §4.16.

12. *See* Farnsworth on Contracts §4.20.

13. For a rare exception, *see* Uniform Commercial Code 2A-108(2), which provides that a court may grant relief if a consumer lease con tract or any clause in it "has been induced by unconscionable conduct," even if the contract or clause is not itself unconscionable.

14. *See* Farnsworth on Contracts §4.28.

15. *See* Farnsworth on Contracts §9.4. There is less tolerance of such mistakes in other arenas. In bridge, a player "has no recourse if he has made a call [bid, double, redouble, pass] on the basis of his misunderstanding." Charles H. Goren, Goren's New Bridge Complete 662 (1985).

16. The problem described here has been attributed to "incomplete heuristics" (a term used to describe "tools that individuals employ in processing and assessing information"). For a seminal discussion, *see* Amos Tversky & Daniel Kahneman, Judgment Under Uncertainty: Heu ristics and Biases, 185 Science 1124 (1974). *See also* Melvin A. Eisen berg, The Limits of Cognition and the Limits of Contract, 47 Stan. L. Rev. 211 (1995).

17. *See* R. H. Strotz, Myopia and Inconsistency in Dynamic Utility Maximization, 23 Rev. Econ. Stud. 165, 177 (1956).

18. Richard A. Posner, Aging and Old Age 85 (1995).

19. This reluctance to part with something that one sees as part of one's endowment was dubbed the "endowment effect" in Richard Thaler, Toward a Positive Theory of Consumer Choice, 1 J. Econ. Behav. & Organ. 39, 43–47 (1980).

20. *See* Timothy D. Wilson & Jonathan W. Schooler, Thinking Too Much: Introspection Can Reduce the Quality of Preferences and Decisions, 60 J. Personality & Soc. Psychol. 181, 181, 191 (1991).

21. For discussion of impulsive behavior in the context of discharge in bankruptcy, *see* Thomas Jackson, The Fresh-Start Policy in Bankruptcy Law, 98 Harv. L. Rev. 1393 (1985).

22. On the role of emotions related to such desires as that to preserve self-esteem, *see* Antonio R. Damasio, Descartes' Error: Emotion, Reason, and the Human Brain 191 (1994).

23. *See* Paul Gray, What Price Camelot? Time, May 6, 1997, at 66, reporting that the humidor went for $574,500, some two hundred times its estimated value, at the auction of the estate of Jacqueline Kennedy Onassis,

24. Such a decision may, of course, be unfairly influenced as well as ill considered.

25. This is a common reason for what are often termed "default" rules. It is not the only reason. Sometimes such a rule is designed to provoke the parties to insert a different rule to fit their particular circumstances. *See* Farnsworth on Contracts §7.16.

26. *See* Restatement (Third) of the Foreign Relations Law of the United States §336 (1987), adopting Article 62 of the Vienna Convention of the Law of Treaties, which Comment *a* suggests is somewhat more restrictive. On how this doctrine is more generous than the comparable doctrine in contract law and how it would have a "devastating effect" on contract law, *see* Arnold D. McNair, So-Called State Servitudes, 6 Brit. Y.B. of Int'l L. 111, 122 (1925).

27. Uniform Commercial Code 2–615.

28. The classic illustration is the "coronation case," Krell v. Henry, [1903] 2 K.B. 740 (C.A.).

29. If it seems odd to say that the aggrieved party reneges in this situation, it should be remembered that until the latter part of the eighteenth century contract law did not excuse the aggrieved party from

performing in this situation. *See* Kingston v. Preston, 99 Eng. Rep. 43 (K.B. 1773).

30. As to nations, *see* Restatement (Third) of the Foreign Relation Law of the United States §335 (1987) ("Material Breach of Internationa Agreement"), following Article 60 of the Vienna Convention on the Law of Treaties. As to prosecutors, *see* United States v. Ballis, 28 F.3d 139 1409 (5th Cir. 1994), holding that a material breach by the accused re leases the government.

31. *See* Farnsworth on Contracts §7.17.

32. An economist would say endogenous as distinguished from exogenous and that these endogenous changes in preferences alter th utility of earlier choices.

33. As to the extreme cases of lack of capacity on such grounds a immaturity or mental infirmity, *see* Farnsworth on Contracts §4.2.

34. For a classic description from a philosophical point of view, se Derek Parfit, Later Selves and Moral Principles, in Philosophy and Pe sonal Relations 137, 144 (A. Montefiore ed. 1973), elaborated in Dere Parfit, Reasons and Persons pt. 4 (1984). I do not refer to short-term predictable changes. You may, for example, prefer coffee with breakfa and wine with dinner, but you would be able to predict the former a dinner and the latter at breakfast.

35. Lewis Carroll, Alice in Wonderland ch. 5; The Maxims of L Rochefoucauld 57, maxim 135 (Louis Kronenberger trans. 1959).

36. *See* Posner, note 18 *supra* at 84–95, with citations to illustra tive discussions from various disciplines in fn. 24. For criticism of thi notion, *see* Jackson, note 21 *supra* at 1393, 1407; Glen O. Robinson, Ex plaining Contingent Rights, 91 Colum. L. Rev. 546, 566 (1991).

37. 60 Minutes, April 20, 1997 (CBS).

38. B's Co. v. B. P. Barber & Assocs., 391 F.2d 130, 137 (4th Ci 1968).

39. Posner, note 18 *supra* at 93.

40. If bankruptcy is included in the list of exceptions, it is th abrupt transition on the filing of a petition that is determinative, no the gradual slide into financial ruin that precedes it.

41. For a case in which the second prosecutor's failure was in advertent because staff lawyers failed to let "the left hand know wha the right hand" had done, *see* Santobello v. New York, 404 U.S. 257 262 (1971).

42. Of course the statutes that make unenforceable some promise by consumers, employees, franchisors, and others protect them from

their obsolete decisions as well as their ill-considered ones by allowing them to renege for no reason at all.

Chapter 3. How a Promise Expresses Commitment

1. Wisconsin & Michigan Railway Co. v. Powers, 191 U.S. 379 (1903).

2. Edgington v. Fitzmaurice, 29 Ch. Div. 459, 483 (C.A. 1885) (Lord Bowen).

3. Lazar v. Superior Court, 909 P.2d 981, 985 (Cal. 1996).

4. For an introduction with bibliography to performative utterances, *see* John R. Searle, How Performatives Work, 58 Tenn. L. Rev. 371 (1991). For the seminal treatment, *see* J. L. Austin, How to Do Things with Words 99, 151, 157–158 (J. O. Urmson & M. Sbisà eds, 2d ed. 1975). On verbal acts, *see* 2 McCormick on Evidence §249 (John W. Strong 4th ed. 1992).

5. *See* Restatement (Second) of Contracts §2(1) (1981), criticized as "Gertrude Steinian" in Ian R. Macneil, The New Social Contract 6 (1980). For a definition of a promise as a commitment communicated to an addressee "who acquires a right to demand the performance of the promise and the right to release the promisor from his obligation," *see* Joseph Raz, Promises and Obligations 210, 214, in Law, Morality, and Society (P. M. S. Hacker & J. Raz eds. 1977). According to Raz, a promise to do thus-and-so is not itself a reason for doing thus-and-so but rather an "exlusionary reason" excluding other possible reasons for *not* doing thus-and-do. *Id*. at 222. *See* Richard Craswell, Contract Law, Default Rules, and the Philosophy of Promising, 88 Mich. L. Rev. 489, 493–494 (1989).

6. Whether there are other commitments that limit future action is discussed in Chapter 9.

7. State of Indiana ex rel. Anderson v. Brand, 303 U.S. 95, 99, 105 (1938).

8. WKBW, Inc. v. Children's Bible Hour, 52 N.W.2d 219 (Mich. 1952).

9. For a contrary suggestion, *see* Adam Smith, Lectures on Jurisprudence 87 (Oxford ed. 1978), where it is said that words commonly used for promises are "I promise to do so and so, you may depend upon it." Yet it is possible to concoct a promise that does not meet this requirement, as where, knowing of my profligate proclivities, you say: "I promise to pay you a thousand dollars next month on condition that you do nothing in reliance on my promise." *See* Joseph Raz,

Voluntary Obligations and Normative Powers, 46 Aristotelian Soc'y 7
(Supp. vol. 1972).

10. Wickham & Burton Coal Co. v. Farmers' Lumber Co., 179 N.W
417, 419 (Iowa 1920). Though case law is lacking, it seems that th
maker of an illusory promise might be liable for promissory fraud i
the maker had no intention of performing in any circumstances. *Se*
W. Page Keeton, Fraud—Statements of Intention, 15 Texas L. Rev. 185
209 (1937) (suggesting the possibility of such liability in the case of
gratuitous promise).

11. Anderson v. Backlund, 199 N.W. 90, 91 (Minn. 1924).

12. Uniform Commercial Code §2–313.

13. John R. Searle & Daniel Vanderveken, Foundations of Illocu
tionary Logic 180 (1985).

14. Beatty v. Guggenheim Exploration Co., 122 N.E. 378, 381 (N.Y
1919).

15. *See* 1 Austin W. Scott, The Law of Trusts §24.2 (4th ed. 1987).

16. Matter of Brown's Will, 169 N.E. 612, 614 (N.Y. 1930).

17. *See* Charles Fried, Contract as Promise 41–43 (1981).

18. Seaver v. Ransom, 120 N.E. 639 (N.Y. 1918). Note that Albert'
commitment to Marion was *in addition* to his commitment to Nettie
the promisee, at whom it was directed.

Chapter 4. Why a Promise Should Commit

1. See Patrick S. Atiyah, The Rise and Fall of Freedom of Con
tract 654 (1979); Charles Fried, Contract as Promise 12, 13 (1981); Joh
Rawls, Two Concepts of Rules, 64 Phil. Rev. 3, 26 (1955).

2. Examples given are usually of constitutive conventions tha
define the game itself (e.g., three strikes and you're out), while my con
cern is more with regulatory rules that govern the conduct of the game

3. *See* Rawls, note 1 *supra* at 3, 14, 16, 18; Charles Goetz & Rober
Scott, Enforcing Promises: An Examination of the Basis of Contract, 8
Yale L.J. 1261, 1263 n. 15 (1980).

4. Thus the practice of promising gives the participants a latitud
in making their own rules that is not accorded to participants in games
Furthermore, the practice of promising goes on in the workaday world
though games may acknowledge the workaday world by rules designe
to prevent players from being injured (e.g., by clipping or charging) o
spending too much time at the game (e.g., by taking too many time-out

r too long between plays or moves). See generally A. Bartlett Giamatti, ake Time for Paradise: Americans and Their Games 60 (1989).

5. A long line of philosophers, including Hobbes, Locke, Kant, nd Rousseau, has built on the response of Socrates that "whoever of ou remains, when he sees how we conduct our trials and manage the ity in other ways, has in fact come to an agreement with us to obey our nstructions." Plato, Crito, in The Trial and Death of Socrates 52 (51d–) (G. M. A. Grube trans. 2d ed. 1984).

6. It is sometimes suggested that what is required is an intention o be legally bound. See Cohen v. Cowles Media Co., 457 N.W.2d 199, 03 (Minn. 1990), rev'd on other grounds, 111 S. Ct. 2513 (1991); Randy Barnett, A Consent Theory of Contract, 86 Colum. L. Rev. 269 (1986). or rejection of this view, see Restatement (Second) of Contracts §21 1981); Neil McCormick, Voluntary Obligations and Normative Powers, 16 Aristotelian Soc'y 59, 63 (Supp. vol. 1972). It is, to be sure, open to he parties to make a gentlemen's agreement by indicating their inten- ion not to be legally bound by their promises. For a suggestion that a vriting indicating an intention to be legally bound should be an inde- pendent basis for enforcing a promise, see Chapter 8.

7. Barnes v. Treece, 549 P.2d 1152, 1155 (1976).

8. See Morris R. Cohen, The Basis of Contract, 46 Harv. L. Rev. 553, 571–572 (1933).

9. See Fried, note 1 *supra* at 14–17; Atiyah, note 1 *supra* at 405, 407.

10. See Morris R. Cohen, The Basis of Contract, 46 Harv. L. Rev. 553, 575 (1933). Hume protested that there "could not naturally . . . arise any obligation from a promise, even supposing the mind could fall into the absurdity of willing that obligation." David Hume, A Trea- tise of Human Nature 518 (L. A. Selby-Bigge ed. 1888).

11. Adam Smith, Lectures on Jurisprudence 472 (Oxford ed. 1978).

12. Patrick S. Atiyah, Promises, Morals, and Law 36 (1981).

13. 5 Bowe-Parker: Page on Wills §5.17 at 207 (1960).

14. See Lon L. Fuller & William Perdue, The Reliance Interest in Contract Damages (pt. 1), 46 Yale L.J. 52, 59–60 (1936).

15. Thomas M. Cooley, A Treatise on the Law of Torts 365 (2d ed. 1888) (said with respect to revocable licenses). But the same author, when on the bench, said that the "injustice of a revocation" after sub- stantial reliance "is so serious that it seems a reproach to the law that it should fail to provide some adequate protection against it." Cooley, J., in Maxwell v. Bay City Bridge Co., 2 N.W. 639, 646 (Mich. 1879).

16. For "evidence . . . that the promisee relied because of business custom and usage and that this usage exists independently of legal sanctions," see Weintraub, A Survey of Contract Practice and Policy, 1992 Wis. L. Rev. 1, 28.

17. Cohen v. Cowles Media Co., 457 N.W.2d 199, 202 (Minn. 1990), rev'd on other grounds, 111 S. Ct. 2513 (1991).

18. Peter Westen & David Westin, A Constitutional Law of Remedies for Broken Plea Bargains, 66 Calif. L. Rev. 471, 526 (1978).

19. See Fuller & Perdue, note 14 *supra* at 57–58.

20. William Shakespeare, The Merchant of Venice act 1, scene 3, lines 17–18. That a lender is under no duty to refrain from making a secured loan because of a belief that the borrower cannot repay it, see Northern Trust Co. v. VIII South Michigan Assocs., 657 N.E.2d 1095, 1102 (Ill. App. 1995). And that "the fact that a contracting party is in some circumstances unlikely to extract his pound of flesh does not mean that he has no right to it," see Jones v. Padavatton, [1969] 2 All E.R. 616, 622 (1968). See also Thomas Scanlon, Promises and Practices, 19 Phil. & Pub. Aff. 199, 217 (1990), putting the case of a loan to a profligate friend whom you do not want to humiliate though you have no expectation of repayment. It might be also be asked whether there is reliance in these situations. See note 23 infra.

21. Arguing against expectation and for reliance, see Atiyah, note 1 *supra* at 762–763; Neil McCormick, Voluntary Obligations and Normative Powers, 46 Aristotelian Soc'y 46 (Supp. vol. 1972). Although reliance may help explain the power of a promise, a promise need not invite or solicit reliance; see note 10 to Chapter 3.

22. Restatement (Second) of Contracts §90 (1981) refines this statement by including reliance by third persons as well as by the promisee and by making the promise binding "if injustice can be avoided only by enforcement of the promise."

23. An interesting if improbable case of no reasonable reliance arises when the promisee does not believe, or has no reason to believe, that the promisor will perform the promise. See note 20 *supra;* Atiyah, note 12 *supra* at 56, 57.

Whether reliance is required for a warranty is controversial. That a buyer's claim for breach of warranty fails if the defendant proves that the buyer knew that the "affirmation of fact or promise was untrue" and so could not have relied, see Cipolone v. Liggett Group, Inc., 893 F.2d 541, 568 (3d Cir. 1990), modified, 112 S. Ct. 2608 (1992). For a contrary view, see Lutz Farms v. Asgrow Seed Co., 948 F.2d 638, 645 (10th Cir. 1991); CBS Inc. v. Ziff-Davis Publishing Co., 553 N.E.2d 997, 1000–1001 (N.Y. 1990); Sidney Kwestel, Freedom from Reliance: A Contract

Approach to Express Warranty, 26 Suffolk U.L. Rev. 959, 1029 (1993) ("both a promise and an affirmation of fact should be enforceable under contract principles" and "no reliance should be required to create such a warranty").

Chapter 5. When a Promise Does Commit

1. *See* Farnsworth on Contracts §2.16.

2. 1 Williston on Contracts §205 (1957). In addition, the defense of fraud was not allowed at common law, though an injunction was available in equity. 12 Williston on Contracts §1525 (1970).

3. John Dawson, Gifts and Promises 69 (1980).

4. The tripartite analysis by Lon Fuller, who described the evidentiary, cautionary, and channeling functions of formalities, has found favor with subsequent writers. Lon L. Fuller, Consideration and Form, 41 Colum. L. Rev. 799 (1941).

5. It was also said that it was sufficient if, in the alternative, it was a *benefit* to the promisor. *See* Farnsworth on Contracts §1.6. I do not dwell on this here because my focus is on reliance—and therefore on detriment.

6. A. W. Brian Simpson, A History of the Common Law of Contract 461 (1987). Simpson goes on, however, to explain that even "the sixteenth-century cases do not concern themselves with the question 'When is a promise binding?' [in the sense of not revocable] but only with the question 'When is a breach of promise actionable?' " *Id.* at 466.

7. Restatement of Contracts §75 (1932).

8. An exception is the preexisting duty rule, under which a promisee's performance of a preexisting duty or a promise of such performance is not consideration even though it is bargained for. The rule is sometimes justified on the ground that the promisee suffers no detriment. *See* Farnsworth on Contracts §4.21. Uniform Commercial Code §2–209(1) rejects the rule by dispensing with the requirement of consideration for the modification of a contract for the sale of goods, reaffirming the hegemony of the bargain test.

9. Pillans & Rose v. Van Mierop & Hopkins, 3 Burr. 1663, 97 Eng. Rep. 1035, 1038 (K.B. 1765), rejected by the House of Lords in Rann v. Hughes, 101 Eng. Rep. 1014n (1778).

10. On the fate of on proposed substitute, the Model Written Obligations Act, *see* Chapter 8.

11. That "legislators have an abiding faith in formality," *see* Farnsworth on Contracts §6.2.

12. Whitney v. Stearns, 16 Me. 394, 397 (1839).

13. Wood v. Lucy, Lady Duff-Gordon, 118 N.E. 214 (N.Y. 1917).

14. Mattei v. Hopper, 330 P.2d 625, (Cal. 1958).

15. United States v. Kahn, 920 F.2d 1100, 1105 (2d Cir. 1990).

16. Holt v. Ward Clarencieux, 2 Strange 937, 93 Eng. Rep. 954 (K.B 1732). Enricho's case involved a cooperation agreement in which the prosecutor sought a return promise by the accused. A proposal of a simple plea bargain commonly invites performance rather than a return promise and would, under contract law, be revocable until the accused began performance. *See* Restatement (Second) of Contracts §45 (1981). In plea bargain cases, however, the effect of even performance by the defendant can be undone by setting aside the plea, which blurs the usually distinct line between an unperformed promise and a performed promise.

17. Central Adjustment Bureau v. Ingram, 678 S.W.2d 28, 33, 35 (Tenn. 1984).

18. Krell v. Codman, 28 N.E. 578 (Mass. 1891).

19. This is especially so with the decline in importance of two vestigial aspects of the doctrine of consideration: the preexisting duty rule and the rule making even purportedly firm offers revocable.

Chapter 6. A Surrogate for an Enigma

1. The state would be bound if it did not renege until after he pled guilty. Santobello v. New York, 404 U.S. 257, 262 (1971). But a mere executory agreement "does not deprive an accused of liberty or any other constitutionally protected interest." Mabry v. Johnson, 467 U.S. 504, 507 (1984) (habeas corpus).

2. Plainly, assent is usually *necessary,* for an offeree who could accept an offer by assenting but relies without doing so is not protected. But this is not to say that assent should be *sufficient.*

3. Lucy v. Zehmer, 84 S.E.2d 516 (Va. 1954) (specific performance). So obvious was this point that the court simply assumed its correctness and devoted its opinion to rejecting the argument that the agreement was not binding because the Zehmers were joking.

4. Quick v. Quick, 1953 V.L.R. 224 (Austl. 1953) (action for divorce). So obvious was this point that the court simply assumed its correctness and devoted its opinion to rejecting the argument that the ceremony was not binding because the clergyman had not pronounced the couple "man and wife."

5. For support from a survey indicating "that by better than two to one, respondents would enforce a commercial contract once the bright line of commitment had been crossed," *see* Weintraub, A Survey of Contract Practice and Policy, 1992 Wis. L. Rev. 1, 32. *But see* Patrick S. Atiyah, The Rise and Fall of Freedom of Contract 759 (1979), asserting that "business men usually expect, and are usually conceded, the right to cancel orders for goods prior to any expenditure by the seller." Enforcement of unperformed bilateral agreements carries over to the law applicable to treaties, under which an exchange of promises between two nations enters into force "as soon as consent to be bound by the treaty has been established" for both. Vienna Convention on the Law of Treaties art. 24(2)(1969). Although the United States has not ratified this Convention, a similar rule is found in Restatement (Third) of the Foreign Relations Law of the United States §312(1) (1987).

6. *See* Lon Fuller & William Perdue, The Reliance Interest in Contract Damages (pt. 1), 46 Yale L.J. 52, 62 (1936).

7. It has even been argued that, because of the "value of assurance," the buyer—content at having the matter settled—may refrain from further bargaining with the seller to obtain, for example, some security for the seller's promise. *See* Thomas Scanlon, Promises and Practices, 19 Philos. & Pub. Affairs 199, 206 (1990).

8. Robert Frost, The Road Not Taken. Frost notes, however, that "the passing there [h]ad worn them really about the same." As a biographer of Frost observes, "The most important thing . . . is not the road itself, but the *decision* about which road to take." Jeffrey Meyers, Robert Frost: A Biography 141 (1996).

9. Carole Klein & Richard Gotti, Overcoming Regret: Lessons from the Road Not Taken 45 (1992). This may be so *ex post,* even though one tends to undervalue a lost opportunity *ex ante.*

10. This was certainly the case in the seminal article by Fuller and Perdue, in which the authors repeatedly call attention to lost opportunities to enter other contracts. Fuller & Perdue, note 6 *supra* at 52, 60, 62.

11. *See* note 2 *supra.* Enricho's cooperation as an undercover agent would surely have been misplaced reliance had he not first accepted the state's offer by giving his return promise.

12. *See* Patrick S. Atiyah, Promises, Morals, and Law 40 (1981).

13. For an extreme case, suppose an alpinist finds an accident victim at the top of Mont Blanc, pinned under a block of ice, and promises to free the victim in return for a promise of $100,000. Both know that no rescue party can come before the next day. The victim promises, but the alpinist reneges, and the victim suffers frostbite before rescue. Is

the alpinist committed? Was any reliance on the promise *possible* if the victim could do nothing to get free and had no opportunities to lose? Might the victim claim reliance on the alpinist's promise by not offering $1 million, which would have been more likely to have induced the alpinist to perform? *See* note 7 *supra* on the value of assurance.

14. The issue commonly raised by such cases is not whether the builder can enforce the owner's promise but whether the builder can recover damages based on "lost volume." *See* Farnsworth on Contracts §12.10. It seems paradoxical that the neophyte builder that later obtains another similar job can recover the profit on both jobs by showing that it could and would have undertaken both jobs, which suggests that it did *not* lose any opportunity by making the contract that was later broken. (Of course, in lost volume disputes the ability to take the other similar job in addition is determined at the time the second job is taken.)

15. Overstreet v. Norden Laboratories, Inc., 669 F.2d 1286 (6th Cir. 1982). In the court's hypothetical, the seller delivered the product and it failed to prevent baldness, so the claim was breach of warranty rather than total breach of contract. This distinction should not, however, make a difference on the court's reasoning. The court's suggested rationale was lack of causation. This is, however, unsound because the breach *is* the cause of the harm since, but for the seller's failure to perform its promise to deliver a product that would prevent the loss of hair, the continued balding would have stopped. The court also noted that if the balding man had thrown away his wigs, he could recover for this loss.

16. For a case rejecting a seller's argument that no alternative computer system with comparable capability was available for less than about four times the price, *see* Chatlos Systems, Inc. v. National Cash Register Corp., 670 F.2d 1304 (3d Cir.), cert. dismissed, 457 U.S. 1112 (1982).

17. *Cf.* Reeves v. Alyeska Pipeline Serv. Co., 926 P.2d 1130 (Alaska 1996) (though "forbearance may sometimes be considered an action that changes one's position, . . . [promisee's] failure to hire an attorney did not amount to a substantial change of position" for purposes of promissory estoppel).

18. For another example, *see* Restatement (Second) of Agency §88 (1958), under which assent by a purported principal to the act of an unauthorized agent results in ratification, binding the third party in much the same way as assent by an offeree binds the offeror. Comment *a* attributes this to the fact that the relation of third party to purported principal is "similar to that of an offeror to an offeree."

19. *See* Farnsworth on Contracts §8.22.

20. Restatement (Second) of Contracts §256 (1) cmt. *c* (1981).

21. Restatement (Second) of Contracts §311 (1981). On the history of this vesting rule, *see* Farnsworth on Contracts §10.8.

22. Restatement (Second) of Contracts §311 cmt. *h* (1981).

23. 44 American Law Institute Proceedings 324–325 (1967). It has been argued that the rule shows that the binding character of a promise arises from its moral force. Charles Fried, The Power of Promise 44–45 (1981). But the history of the Restatement (Second) rule shows that acceptance was added merely as surrogate for reliance.

24. 44 American Law Institute Proceedings 325 (1967).

25. The vesting rule leads to an apparent anomaly. As will be seen in Chapter 7, if you make a contract with me under which I agree to pay you $1,000 in return for a service and you then make a gratuitous promise to a mutual friend to pay our friend the $1,000, you are free to renege on your gratuitous promise. But if instead you make a contract with me under which I agree to pay the $1,000 *to our friend* in return for the same service by you, our friend's rights as an intended beneficiary vest on assent and you can do nothing to defeat them even if I agree.

26. It can be argued that even a buyer that has bought on credit has relied by forgoing the opportunity to buy another watch instead, and therefore the buyer's promise to pay is value. Uniform Commercial Code §1–201 (9) & (44).

27. Uniform Commercial Code §1–201(44).

28. Swift v. Tyson, 41 U.S. (16 Pet.) 1,20 (1842) (Story, J.).

29. The analogy to the situation of the creditor beneficiary is recognized in the Restatement (Second), where it is explained that protecting the creditor beneficiary once the beneficiary has assented, without regard to reliance, "is supported by the analogy of the rule that a creditor gives 'value' for rights acquired as security for a pre-existing claim." Restatement (Second) of Contracts §311 cmt. *h* (1981).

Chapter 7. Wanting to Make a Commitment (Reprise)

1. Allegheny College v. National Chautauqua County Bank of Jamestown, 159 N.E. 173 (N.Y. 1927).

2. As to whether there is such a thing as a "simply generous and unself-interested gift," *see* Carol M. Rose, Giving Some Back—A Reprise, 44 Fla. L. Rev. 365, 365–368 (1992). On the effects of altruism on organ donors, *see* Roberta G. Simmons, Susan K. Marine & Richard L. Simmons, Gift of Life xviii (1987).

3. The Golden Legend of Jacobus de Voraigne 99 (Granger Ryan & Helmut Ripperger trans. 1941).

4. Thomas R. Pezzullo & Barbara E. Brittingham, The Study of Money, 16 CASE Currents, July–August, 44, 46 (1990). A classic study of how, in archaic societies, exchange itself is sometimes driven by obligations to give, receive, and repay is Marcel Mauss, The Gift (Ian Cunnison trans. 1967).

5. Carol Vogel, Clash over Name Puts Museum Gift in Doubt, New York Times, December 17, 1994, at 13. The Guggenheim put LeFrak's name on its fifth-floor gallery.

6. Shortly before Christmas 1993, multimillionaire Victor Posner gave $2 million to the homeless in Florida so that he could avoid going to jail for tax evasion. Manny Garcia & David Hancock, Posner Doles Out $2 Million to Homeless, Miami Herald, December 22, 1993, at B1. It might, of course, be argued that his gift was part of a swap for a promise not to prosecute.

7. On the remarkable impact on donations of art of a 1986 change in the tax laws, see William D. Zabel, The Rich Die Richer 146 (1995).

8. As to the importance of peer pressure among wealthy philanthropists, see Francie Ostrower, Why The Wealthy Give: The Culture of Elite Philanthropy (1995).

9. For a suggestion by Nannerl O. Keohane, then president of Wellesley College, a leading institution in alumni donations, that women differ from men in making such donations since for women it is "the cause that matters, not the competition," see Fox Butterfield, As for that Myth About How Much Alumnae Give, New York Times, February 26, 1992.

10. See Steven Shavell, An Economic Analysis of Altruism and Deferred Gifts, 20 J. Legal Stud. 401, 402 (1991).

11. See Konefsky, How to Read, Or at Least Not Misread, Cardozo in the Allegheny College Case, 36 Buffalo L. Rev 645, 697 (1987) (reproducing excerpts from Jackson's brief). On the many ways of indicating intention short of promising, see Andrew Kull, Reconsidering Gratuitous Promises, 21 J. Legal Stud. 39, 63 (1992).

12. Eight years before, Cardozo himself had said as much in Dougherty v. Salt, 125 N.E. 94, 95 (N.Y. 1919), describing an aunt who promised her nephew $3,000 on hearing good reports about him, as merely "conferring a bounty." For a Canadian case taking the same position on facts similar to those in the Allegheny College case, see Governors of Dalhousie College v. Estate of Boutilier, [1934] S.C.R. 642 (Can. 1934).

13. When Mary made her pledge in 1921, a seal would have been

only presumptive evidence of consideration under New York law, and it could therefore have been shown that there was no consideration.

14. The term "sterile transmission" was adopted from the nineteenth-century French writer Claude Bufnoir by Lon Fuller, who thought that gratuitous promises "do not present an especially pressing case for the application of the principle of private autonomy." Lon L. Fuller, Consideration and Form, 41 Colum. L. Rev. 799, 815 (1941). For criticism of the term, *see* Kull, note 11 *supra* at 49.

15. Since 1993, charitable contributions from individuals have totaled more than $100 billion a year. Bureau of the Census, U.S. Department of Commerce, Statistical Abstract of the United States 388, tbl. 611 (1996).

16. Allegheny College, 159 N.E. at 174.

17. For an example of an old acquaintance who gets you to promise not to reveal an embarrassing incident but does not rely on the promise, *see* Thomas Scanlon, Promises and Practices, 19 Phil. & Pub. Aff. 199, 207 (1990).

18. Konefsky, note 11 *supra* at 645, 697.

19. *See* Konefsky, note 11 *supra* at 645, 698.

20. *See* Richard A. Posner, Gratuitous Promises in Economics and Law, 6 J. Legal Stud. 411, 412–414 (1977).

21. But for a report that many charitable organizations are moving away from legally binding pledge in the hope that donors will give more and that there will actually be less attrition, *see* Jerold Panas, Official Fundraising Almanac 33 (1989).

22. Shavell, note 10 *supra* at 406, 409.

23. As to how Dostoevsky made the deadline by dictating a 200-page novel, The Gambler, in less than a month, *see* Joseph Frank, Dostoevsky: The Miraculous Years, 1865–1871, 32, 58, 162–163 (1995); Leonid Grossman, Dostoevsky: A Biography 391–396 (Mary Mackler trans. 1975).

24. John Stuart Mill, On Liberty 95 (David Spitz ed. 1975).

25. Charles J. Goetz & Robert E. Scott, Enforcing Promises: An Examination of the Basis of Contract, 89 Yale L.J. 1261, 1304–1305 (1980).

26. That extralegal sanctions may be adequate, *see* Robert E. Scott, Error and Rationality in Individual Decisionmaking: An Essay on the Relationship Between Cognitive Illusions and the Management of Choices, 59 S. Cal. L. Rev. 329, 357–358 (1986); Posner, note 20 supra at 411, 417.

27. Mary Louise Fellows, Donative Promises Redux, in Property

Law and Legal Education 27, 32 (Peter Hay & Michael H. Hoeflich eds. 1988); Kull, note 11 *supra* at 58.

28. William D. Zabel, author and trusts and estates lawyer, as quoted in Geraldine Fabrikant & Shelby White, Noblesse Oblige . . . with Strings, New York Times, April 30, 1995.

29. Edward Resovsky, director of principal gifts at the University of Pennsylvania, as quoted in Karen W. Arenson, Alumni Generosity Has a Catch, New York Times, March 19, 1995.

30. Allegheny College, 159 N.E. at 175. *See* David W. Dunlap, $3 Million Zoo Gift Revoked Because Plaque Is too Small, New York Times, May 15, 1997 (donors received $750,000 installment back when the "Art Commission overturned our agreement by deciding that for our $3 million gift a plaque with two-inch letters" was sufficient acknowledgment).

31. John P. Dawson, Gifts and Promises 102–113, 165–185 (1980).

32. Oliver Wendell Holmes, The Common Law 293 (1881).

33. Zan Dubin, Arts Groups Still Taking Pledges on Faith, Los Angeles Times, November 25, 1994, at F1 (citing Pat House of the Bowers Museum of Cultural Art).

Chapter 8. Enforceable Promises to Make Gifts

1. Little v. Blunt, 26 Mass. (9 Pick.) 488 (1830); Restatement (Second) of Contracts §82 (1981).

2. Webb v. McGowin, 168 So. 196 (Ala. Ct. App. 1935), cert. denied, 168 So. 199 (Ala. 1936).

3. Restatement (Second) of Contracts §86 (1981).

4. *See* Patrick S. Atiyah, Promises, Morals, and Law 70 (1981); Lon L. Fuller, Consideration and Form, 41 Colum. L. Rev. 799, 822 (1941).

5. *See* Richard S. Posner, Gratuitous Promises in Economics and Law, 6 J. Legal Stud. 411, 418 (1977). That the promisee has "good reason to suppose that the promise is meant seriously," *see* Samuel Stoljar, Enforcing Benevolent Promises, 12 Sydney L. Rev. 17, 38 (1989).

6. *See* Charles J. Goetz & Robert E. Scott, Enforcing Promises: An Examination of the Basis of Contract, 89 Yale L.J. 1261, 1311 (1980). *See also* Melvin A. Eisenberg, The World of Contract and the World of Gift, 85 Cal. L. Rev. 821, 850–851 (1997) ("such promises are typically made between strangers or business associates").

7. For an argument that, at least in the case of a debt barred by the

statute of limitations, enforcement will be advantageous to the promisor in the future, *see* Posner, note 5 *supra* at 418.

8. Allegheny College v. National Chautauqua County Bank of Jamestown, 159 N.E. 173, 175 (N.Y. 1927).

9. For examples of the difficulty of satisfying the reliance requirement in the context of charitable subscriptions, *see* Mount Sinai Hosp. v. Jordan, 290 So.2d 484, 487 (Fla. 1974); Maryland Nat'l Bank v. United Jewish Appeal Fed'n, 407 A.2d 1130, 1138 (Md. 1979).

10. For a case applying this language in declining to enforce an oral charitable pledge against an estate absent reliance, *see* Congregation Kadimah Toras-Moshe v. DeLeo, 540 N.E.2d 691, 692–694 (Mass. 1989).

11. Restatement (Second) of Contracts §90(2) (1981). On the origins of this exception, *see* Farnsworth on Contracts §2.19.

12. *See* Barnes v. Perine, 12 N.Y. 18, 24 (1854) ("judges . . . have been willing, nay apparently anxious, to discover a consideration which would uphold the undertaking"). A common solution was to find that the promises of subscribers were consideration for each other, a solution that was especially inviting if one subscriber was the bellwether of the flock. *See* Congregation B'nai Sholom v. Martin, 173 N.W.2d 504 (Mich. 1969).

13. Jewish Fed'n v. Barondess, 560 A.2d 1353, 1354 (N.J. Super. 1989), quoting More Game Birds in America, Inc. v. Boettger, 14 A.2d 778, 780 (N.J. 1940).

14. Congregation Kadimah Toras-Moshe v. DeLeo, note 10 *supra* at 693, distinguishing earlier cases "because they involved written, as distinguished from oral, promises and also involved substantial consideration or reliance."

15. *Compare* Salsbury v. Northwestern Bell Tel. Co., 221 N.W.2d 609 (Iowa 1974) (favorable), *with* Maryland Nat'l Bank v. United Jewish Appeal, note 9 *supra* (unfavorable).

16. *See* Congregation Kadimah Toras-Moshe v. DeLeo, note 10 *supra*.

17. *See* Posner, note 5 *supra* at 420.

18. Goetz & Scott, note 6 *supra* at 1307–1308.

19. Handbook of the National Conference of Commissioners on Uniform State Laws 308 (1925).

20. Code Commissioners on Revision of the Utah Statutes, Report to the Governor and 19th Legislature 12, 35 (1933), as quoted in Donald B. Holbrook, Note, 3 Utah L. Rev. 73, 95 n. 166 (1952).

21. If promises to make gifts were enforceable on the basis of a for-

mality, the remedy of specific performance would not be available if the law that once applied to the seal were followed. Even in the heyday of the seal, a seal would not make a gratuitous promise specifically enforceable. *See* John N. Pomeroy, 4 Equity Jurisprudence §1293 (5th ed. by Spencer W. Symons 1941).

22. Dementas v. Estate of Tallas, 764 P.2d 628, 633 (Utah Ct. App. 1988). The court noted that the " 'moral obligation exception' has not been embraced in Utah," and that even under that exception Peter would lose because the services "were performed gratuitously." Of course, Jack could have changed his will.

23. Handbook of the National Conference of Commissioners on Uniform State Laws 194 (1925).

24. Rudolf B. Schlesinger in Rudolf B. Schlesinger, Hans W. Baade, Mirjan R. Damaska & Peter E. Herzog, Comparative Law: Cases — Text — Materials 22 (5th ed. 1988).

25. Ontario Law Reform Commission, Report on Amendment of the Law of Contract 292 (1987), proposing that the writing be executed "in the presence of a witness and signed by the witness in the presence of the executing party."

26. This is the reasoning used to impose an equitable lien on after-acquired personal property. For its application to real property, *see* R. G. Patton in 3 American Law of Property §15.21 (1952).

27. *See* Keel v. Bailey, 31 S.E.2d 362 (N.C. 1944); Robinson v. Douthit, 64 Tex. 101, 105 (1885), cited with approval in Ford v. Unity Church Society of St. Joseph, 25 S.W. 394, 397 (Mo. 1894). Case law is scarce because donors commonly use quitclaim rather than warranty deeds, and such cases as there are do not contain helpful discussions of the issue.

28. Van Rensselaer v. Kearney, 52 U.S. (11 How.) 297, 325 (1850).

29. Alfred T. Denning, The Discipline of Law 32 (1979).

30. 4 Page on Wills §30.1 (Bowe-Parker ed. 1961). Thus a deed conveying land as a gift to the donor's nieces was reformed on the basis of a mistake by the donor alone, under an exception to the rule requiring mutual mistake for reformation, since in the case of a donor's mistake it is "immaterial that the grantee was not cognizant thereof." Jonas v. Meyers, 101 N.E.2d 509, 515 (Ill. 1951).

31. Pappas v. Bever, 219 N.W.2d 720 (Iowa 1974) (quoting Corbin as defining a promise as an expression "in such a form as to invite reliance," which suggests that the court missed the point); *see* Pappas v. Hauser, 197 N.W.2d 607 (Iowa 1972).

32. John Murawski, Charities' Lawsuit Dilemma, The Chronicle of

Philanthropy, March 9, 1995, at 1; Richard B. Schmitt, Uncharitable Acts: If donors Fail to Give, More Nonprofit Groups Take Them to Court, Wall Street Journal, July 27, 1995, at 1.

33. For a case suggesting that the enforceability of a charitable pledge may turn on whether the pledge contains conditions, *see* Mount Sinai Hosp. v. Jordan, 290 So.2d 484, 486–487 (Fla. 1974), holding a pledge unenforceable against the pledgor's estate because the "donative intent as to the specific material plan . . . must be made an integral part of the pledge instrument, limiting the exercise of discretion by the donee." For a case suggesting the reluctance of courts to read in conditions when a donor has not been explicit, *see* Danby v. Osteopathic Hospital Ass'n, 104 A.2d 903, 906 (Del. 1954).

34. Alfred S. Konefsky, How to Read, Or at Least Not Misread, Cordozo in the *Allegheny College* case, 36 Buffalo L. Rev. 645, 699 (1987). For a description of a "well conceived plan to obtain large contributions," leading to a "high-pressure meeting," *see* Maryland Nat'l Bank v. United Jewish Appeal Fed'n, 407 A.2d 1130, 1132 (Md. 1979).

35. Konefsky, note 34 *supra* at 657.

36. For criticism of the "proposition that gratuitous promises in general are made without proper deliberation," *see* Andrew Kull, Reconsidering Gratuitous Promises, 21 J. Legal Stud. 39, 53–54 (1992). That swaps may not always be made with "proper deliberation," consider the example of the half-million-dollar humidor in Chapter 2.

37. For an example of a decision in which the court enfor ed the promise, *see* Woodmere Academy v. Steinberg, 385 N.Y.S.2d 549 (App. Div. 1976), aff'd, 363 N.E.2d 1169 (N.Y. 1977). Having made a signed pledge to a private school, the promisor changed his mind after moving, putting his children in a different school, and making a very large contribution to Israel following the Yom Kippur war. The recalcitrant promisor has since given $36 million to his alma mater, the University of Pennsylvania, which named two buildings after him. Geraldine Fabrikant & Shelby White, Noblesse Oblige . . . with Strings, New York Times, April 30, 1995.

38. Dig. 50.17.28 (Various Rules of Early Law 28), as translated in 4 The Digest of Justinian 958a (Theodor Mommsen, Paul Krueger & Alan Watson eds. 1985). For a suggestion that the phrase "if injustice can be avoided" in §90 "might have served a useful purpose if it directed the attention of the courts to the issues of improvidence and ingratitude," *see* Melvin A. Eisenberg, Donative Promises, 47 U. Chi. L. Rev. 1, 23 (1979).

39. *See* Ray A. Brown, The Law of Personal Property §7.15 (Wal-

ter B. Raushenbush ed., 3d ed. 1975). The analogy is imperfect because such a gift is considered revocable on recovery rather than conditional.

40. 22 Laws of the State of Israel 113 (1967/68). (While similar French and German statutes, mentioned in note 23 to Chapter 13, apply to gifts as well as to promises, the Israeli statute applies only to promises.)

41. For examples of charitable pledgers who were bound nevertheless, *see* Danby v. Osteopathic Hosp. Ass'n, 104 A.2d 903 (Del. 1954) (hospital changed plans for construction); Salsbury v. Northwestern Bell Tel. Co., 221 N.W.2d 609 (Iowa 1974) (pledgee's attempt to establish college collapsed); Congregation B'nai Sholom v. Martin, 173 N.W.2d 504 (Mich. 1969) (pledger had disputes with other members of congregation).

42. *See* Jerold Panas, Official Fundraising Almanac 163 (1989) (After H. Ross Perot gave $2 million and pledged $6 million more for a Dallas arboretum, few bonds were sold to raise additional money. Then "Perot decided that the arboretum would never become a world-class facility" and "wanted to withdraw his gift.")

43. *See* Ray A. Brown, The Law of Personal Property §7.13 (Walter B. Raushenbush 3d ed. 1975).

44. That an attempt to develop such rules might not be "worth the candle," *see* Melvin A. Eisenberg, Donative Promises, 47 U. Chi. L. Rev. 1, 15 (1979).

Chapter 9. Commitment Without Promise

1. *See* Ian R. Macneil, The New Social Contract: An Inquiry into Modern Contractual Relations 10 (1980).

2. Overlock v. Central Vermont Public Service Corp., 237 A.2d 356 (Vt. 1967).

3. The concerned citizens' abandonment of the collection was not consideration for the PSC's promise because William did not even contend that the PSC had bargained for it.

4. It has usually assumed that the reliance must be detrimental, though the Restatement formulations do not explicitly require this.

5. Usually conduct amounts to acceptance of an offer made in words, so that conduct does not define the content of the promise. Occasionally, the promisor's conduct also defines the content of the promise. *See* Smith-Scharff Paper Co. v. P. N. Hirsch & Co. Stores, 754 S.W.2d 928 (Mo. App. 1988).

6. F. H. Buckley, Paradox Lost, 72 Minn. L. Rev. 775, 806 (1988).

7. Cates v. Morgan Portable Building Corp., 780 F.2d 683, 687 (7th Cir. 1985) (Posner, J.).

8. H. R. Moch Co. v. Rensselaer Water Co., 159 N.E. 896, 898 (N.Y. 1928).

9. Erie R.R. Co. v. Stewart, 40 F.2d 855 (6th Cir. 1930).

10. Indian Towing Co. v. United States, 350 U.S. 61 (1955).

11. Florence v. Goldberg, 375 N.E.2d 763 (N.Y. 1978). In all three of the cited cases the defendant negligently furnished the service instead of withdrawing it.

12. Restatement (Second) of Torts §323 (1965).

13. Caveat to Restatement (Second) of Torts §323 (1965). For a suggestion that liability should be "imposed outright for breach of the promise alone when it is relied on to the plaintiff's detriment," *see* W. Page Keeton (gen. ed.), Prosser & Keeton on the Law of Torts §56 at p. 380 (5th ed. 1984).

14. It is not clear why, in the three cases cited, no claim was made for breach of contract as an alternative basis of recovery. Perhaps it was incorrectly assumed that a contract duty would be absolute rather than merely one to use reasonable care. Perhaps the damage rules for tort cases seemed more attractive than those for contract cases.

15. Percy H. Winfield, A Text-Book of the Law of Tort 404 (4th ed. 1948).

16. That reliance by others might reenforce the drowning swimmer's claim; *see* Restatement (Second) of Contracts §90 cmt. *c* (1981). For variations on the drowning swimmer hypothetical, *see* William C. Powers, Jr., Book Review, 57 Tex. L. Rev. 523 531–533 (1977).

17. The reliance would not trigger liability under Restatement (Second) of Torts §323 because that section requires "the other's reliance," meaning reliance by the recipient of the performance.

18. Restatement (Second) of Torts §324 (1965). *See* 3 Fowler Harper, Fleming James & Oscar Gray, The Law of Torts §18.6 at p. 722 (2d ed. 1986). A duty to do the same may also result from a promise implicit in a preexisting relationship. *See* Farwell v. Keaton, 240 N.W.2d 217, 222 (Mich. 1976).

19. The American Law Institute expressed no opinion on whether there may be situations in which an actor may be subject to liability where by discontinuance "he leaves the other in no worse position than when the actor took charge of him." Restatement (Second) of Torts

caveat to §324 (1965). *See* United States v. DeVane, 306 F.2d 182 (5th Cir. 1962); Fochtman v. Honolulu Police & Fire Depts., 649 P.2d 1114, 1117 (Hawaii 1982).

20. The fact that third persons happened to be on the beach would not, as discussed in Chapter 3, make them promisees.

21. Section 323 has a caveat concerning the section's application to a mere promise, not accompanied by other conduct, and Comment *d* states that "the question is left open." Comment *a* to §323 speaks of §324 as a "special application" of §323, and the discussion and illustrations to §324 str ngly suggest that it does not apply to a mere promise— for example, by using "assistance" to describe what is required.

22. Even if the conduct happened to consist of a promise, the scope of the commitment would not be defined by the promise—which might impose strict liability—but would be to use only reasonable care.

23. For some inexplicable reason, §324 covers only "bodily harm," while §323 covers persons and things. It is also odd that §324 requires that the other be "helpless."

24. Miller v. Miller, 478 A.2d 351, 353, 354, 359 (N.J. 1984). *Miller* was approved in Wiese v. Wiese, 699 P.2d 700, 702 (Utah 1985), where it was said that the New Jersey court "held that there must be evidence that the child will suffer because his stepparent's representation or conduct causes him to be cut off from his noncustodial natural parent's support." These cases are discussed in David L. Chambers, Stepparents, Biologic Parents, and the Law's Perceptions of "Family" after Divorce, in Divorce Reform at the Crossroads 102, 116 (Stephen D. Sugarman & Herma H. Kay eds. 1990).

25. The court in *Miller* muddied the waters by speaking of an "equitable estoppel," which would have sprung from the children's supposed reliance to their detriment on some representation of fact by Jay, but it is unclear what that representation was. The suggested rationale is more convincing.

26. *See* Marshall S. Shapo, The Duty to Act 69 (1977).

27. In re Certified Question (Bankey v. Storer Broadcasting Co.), 443 N.W.2d 112, 119 (Mich. 1989). For a suggestion that such a right is not contractual so as to come under the Constitution's contract clause, *see* Montana Public Employees' Ass'n v. Office of Governor, 898 P.2d 675 (Mont. 1995).

28. The court later analyzed handbook language in terms of "promise," but the employees in that case were aware of the contract language, so "promise" was not inappropriate. Rood v. General Dynamics Corp. 507 N.W.2d 591, 606 (Mich. 1993).

29. Restatement (Second) of Contracts §23 cmt. *c* (1981). *See* Farnsworth on Contracts §2.10. For a case perceiving the analogy to the reward cases, but assuming that knowledge of the offer would be required in such cases, *see* Anderson v. Douglas & Lomason Co., 540 N.W.2d 277, 284 (Iowa 1995), declining "to follow the traditional requirement that knowledge of the offer is a prerequisite to acceptance *in the limited context of employee handbook cases.*"

30. It might even be argued that if you announce to your bridge club your resolution to give up smoking, rather than your resolution to give up sweets (Chapter 1), you are, in the words of the happy-campers court, "seeking to promote an environment conducive to collective productivity" and making a commitment that could be enforced by your fellow members.

Chapter 10. The Reach of a Commitment

1. The term "best efforts" is sometimes used to mean reasonable efforts in this context.

2. Miami Coca-Cola Bottling Co. v. Orange Crush Co., 296 F. 693, 694 (5th Cir. 1924).

3. In re Certified Question (Bankey v. Storer Broadcasting Co., 443 N.W.2d 112 [Mich. 1989]).

4. Bankey, note 3 *supra* at 120. *See* Farnsworth on Contracts §2.10a.

5. If your change of mind is due to some deficiency on my part, my interest may also be that I would like an opportunity to "cure" that deficiency.

6. *See* Ricks v. Budge, 64 P.2d 208 (Utah 1937).

7. *See* American Bar Association's Model Rules of Professional Conduct Rule 1.16(d) (1983).

8. Uniform Commercial Code §2–309(3).

9. Comment 8 to Uniform Commercial Code §2–309(3).

10. Pharo Distrib. Co. v. Stahl, 782 S.W.2d 635, 638 (Ky. App. 1989).

11. K. M. C. Co. v. Irving Trust Co. 757 F.2d 752, 759 (6th Cir. 1985). *See* Farnsworth on Contracts §7.17a.

12. *Bankey,* note 3 *supra* at 120. *See* Alaska Marine Pilots vs. Hendsch, 950 P.2nd 98 (Alaska 1997) (duty of good faith and fair dealing requires employers to "treat like employees alike").

13. Clarke v. White, 37 U.S. (12 Pet.) 178, 200 (1838). In Williams v. Brown, 4 Johns. Ch. Rep. 682, 685 (1820), Chancellor Kent said, "Courts

of equity, as well as Courts of law, allow a debtor to give a preference to one creditor over another."

14. *See* Bankruptcy Code §547. On "the ideal of Even-handedness toward creditors" in such situations, *see* Robert C. Clark, The Duties of the Corporate Debtor to Its Creditors, 90 Harv. L. Rev. 505, 511–515 (1977).

15. Uniform Commercial Code §2–615, which goes on to say that the seller may, nevertheless, "at his option include regular customers not then under contract as well as his own requirements for further manufacture."

16. Restatement (Second) of Contracts §211(2) & cmt. *e* (1981).

17. The sovereign acts doctrine is not to be confused with the doctrine of sovereign immunity, which generally shields governments from suit (Chapter 1).

18. Horowitz v. United States, 267 U.S. 458, 461 (1925), quoting Johns v. United States, 1 Ct. Cl. 383, 384 (1865). The sovereign acts doctrine is judicially created and is not a constitutional doctrine. Even if the government avoids it, the government may run afoul of the due process clause.

19. United States v. Winstar Corp., 116 S. Ct. 2432, 2465 (1996) (Souter, J., joined by Stevens & Breyer, JJ., as to this part of the opinion, in which O'Connor did not join. Scalia, Kennedy, & Thomas, JJ., concurred in a separate opinion and Rehnquist, C. J., and Ginsburg, J., dissented.)

20. Id. at 2466 n.42 (quoting Deming v. United States, 1 Ct. Cl. 190, 191 [1865]). The plurality rejected the government's contention that "a regulatory object is proof against treating the legislature as having acted to avoid the Government's contractual obligations." Id. at 2464.

21. Richard H. Thaler & H. M. Shefrin, An Economic Theory of Self-Control, 89 J. Pol. Econ. 392, 294 (1981), described in Robert E. Scott, Error and Rationality in Individual Decisionmaking: An Essay on the Relationship Between Cognitive Illusions and the Management of Choices, 59 S. Cal. L. Rev. 329, 344–345 (1986). *See* Thomas C. Schelling, Choice and Consequence 93–94 (1984).

Chapter 11. The Strength of a Commitment

1. Of course, you might decide that it would be better to perform, in which case the measure of your regret would not be the cost of reneging.

2. This statement simplifies the facts. Eugene had engaged Patrick

Janas to act in his behalf, and Patrick agreed with PepsiCo to buy the G-II for $4.6 million and then sell it to Eugene for $4.75 million. Eugene sued as an intended beneficiary of Patrick's agreement with PepsiCo.

3. *See* Barry Nicholas, The French Law of Contract 217 (2d ed. 1992).

4. Klein v. PepsiCo, 845 F.2d 76 (4th Cir. 1988). Eugene seems to have made a tactical error in arguing that he wanted the plane for resale.

5. United States Trust Co. of New York v. New Jersey, 431 U.S. 1 (1977).

6. Fed. R. Civ. P. 70 (allowing a federal district court to grant such relief if real or personal property is within the district).

7. *See* Wasdworth v. Hannah, 431 So.2d 1186, 1189 (Ala. 1983).

8. Convention on Contracts for the International Sale of Goods art. 46(1). However, a court in this country need not order specific performance unless it would do so under its own domestic law in the case of a similar contract. Id. art. 28.

9. Karl N. Llewellyn, What Price Contract?—An Essay in Perspective, 40 Yale L.J. 704, 724 (1931).

10. Oliver Wendell Holmes, The Path of the Law, 10 Harv. L. Rev. 457, 462 (1887). For a dissenting view, *see* Douglas Laycock, The Death of the Irreparable Injury Rule, 103 Harv. L. Rev. 688 (1990).

11. *See* Restatement (Second) of Contracts §344(a) (1981); Uniform Commercial Code §1–106.

12. *See* Janet Landman, Regret: The Persistence of the Possible 47 (1993), explaining that *regret* is understood in economic decision theory as "the difference between the outcomes of a chosen versus an unchosen option." Nor does it measure *disappointment* in the sense of "the difference between actual versus expected outcomes." Id.

13. *See* Farnsworth on Contracts §12.15.

14. For an assertion that "one can hardly conceive of a term that is less appropriate than . . . 'expectation,'" *see* Daniel Friedmann, The Performance Interest in Contract Damages, 11 L.Q. Rev. 628, 634 (1995).

15. Richard A. Posner, Economic Analysis of Law 119 (4th ed. 1992). This analysis takes no acount of the possibility that an efficient breach may leave the injured party with a loss that is not recoverable in an action for damages for breach of contract. *See* Farnsworth on Contracts §12.20c. Nor does it take account of an "altruistic" breach, as where one breaks a contract to give a swimming lesson in order to rescue a drowning child.

16. *See* Farnsworth on Contracts §12.12.

17. If the choice that Eugene did not make and is therefore regretted was to buy such a G-II jet, this gives him in effect damages measured by his regret. *See* note 17 *supra*.

18. *See* Melvin A. Eisenberg, The Bargain Principle and Its Limits, 95 Harv. L. Rev. 741, 787 (1982). On the problems of proof, *see* Charles J. Goetz & Robert E. Scott, Enforcing Promises: An Examination of the Basis of Contract, 89 Yale L.J. 1261, 1288 (1980).

19. *See* Robert Cooter & Melvin A. Eisenberg, Damages for Breach of Contract, 73 Calif. L. Rev. 1432, 1463 (1985).

20. Melvin A. Eisenberg, Donative Promises, 47 U. Chi. L. Rev. 1, 32 (1979), criticizing §90 for wrongly implying that "expectation, not reliance, is the normal measure of damages in cases in which enforcement is based on the reliance principle." *But see* Edward Yorio & Steve Thel, The Promissory Basis of Section 90, 101 Yale L.J. 111, 131, 137, 150 (1991), stating that all the leading cases of the kind cited by reliance theorists are "commercial in nature."

21. For a suggestion that the recovery of a donee beneficiary should be limited to the reliance measure, *see* Melvin A. Eisenberg, Third Party Beneficiaries, 92 Colum. L. Rev. 1358, 1419 (1992). But this seems unjustified because the promisee has *paid* for the donee beneficiary's right just as under any swap. It is arguable that the donee's recovery should be limited in this way if the promisor and the promisee attempt mutually to rescind their contract after the promisee's right has vested. *See* Chapter 6.

22. For a suggestion that "expectation damages can be viewed as a penalty default rule designed to induce promisors to communicate to promisees the precise contingencies in which they wish to reserve the right to revoke a promise," *see* Michael J. Trebilcock, The Limits of Freedom of Contract 187 (1993).

23. Pomponius in 4 The Digest of Justinian 50.17.206 (Theodor Mommsen ed. & Alan Watson trans. 1985).

24. *See* Farnsworth on Contracts §12.19.

25. Snepp v. United States, 444 U.S. 507, 514 (1980) (per curiam).

26. *See generally* E. Allan Farnsworth, Your Loss or My Gain? The Dilemma of the Disgorgement Principle in Breach of Contract, 94 Yale L.J. 1339 (1985).

27. *See* Peter Westen & David Westin, A Constitutional Law of Remedies for Broken Plea Bargains, 66 Calif. L. Rev. 471, 526 (1978).

28. Nor could damages be recovered against the prosecutor. Taylor
v. Kavanagh, 640 F.2d 450, 451–452 (2d Cir. 1981).

29. In plea bargain cases, the effect of even performance by the accused can be undone by allowing the accused to withdraw the plea,
which blurs the usually distinct line between an unperformed promise and a performed one. Once withdrawn by leave of court, a plea of
guilty is not admissible on the trial of the issue arising on the substi-
tuted plea of not guilty. Kercheval v. United States, 274 U.S. 220 (1927).

30. Under contract law, a party that has made a losing bargain is
entitled to restitution as an alternative remedy for total breach. *See* 3
Farnsworth on Contracts §12.20. Judges and commentators, apparently
oblivious to this, have sometimes thought it necessary to concoct a misrepresentation even though the prosecution did no more than change
its mind. Thus Douglas, concurring in Santobello v. New York, 404 U.S.
257, 266 (1971) (mentioned in fn. 1 to ch. 6 *supra* at 266, stated that
"most jurisdictions [prefer] vacation of the plea on the ground of 'in-
voluntariness.'" *See* Westen & Westin, note 27 *supra* at 509, 511–512.

31. State v. Miller, 756 P.2d 122, 126 (Wash. 1988).

32. State v. Tourtellotte, 564 P.2d 799, 803 (Wash. 1977). *Accord:*
People v. Macrander, 756 P.2d 356, 362 (Colo. 1988); *see* Westen &
Westin, note 27 *supra* at 518–519 (1978). *But see* People v. Calloway,
631 P.2d 30, 33 (Cal. 1981). As to what amounts to specific performance,
see Yarber v. State, 437 S.2d 1330, 1336 (Ala. 1983).

33. On remand after the *Santobello* decision, note 30 *supra,* the
New York court refused to allow the accused to withdraw his plea and
ordered specific performance. People v. Santobello, 331 N.Y.S.2d 776,
777 (App. Div. 1972). *See* United States v. Johnson, 132 F.3rd 628, 631
11th Cir. 1998).(to allow withdrawal of plea "would be unwarranted");
People v. Tindle, 460 N.E.2d 1354, 1355 (N.Y. 1984) ("vacatur of appel-
lant's guilty plea more than six years after the crime would be unduly
prejudicial to the People").

34. *Cf.* Restatement (Second) of Contracts §381 (1981); Link Associates v. Jefferson Standard Life Insurance Co., 291 S.E.2d 212 (Va. 1982).

35. *Santobello,* note 30 *supra* at 263; United States v. Moscahlaidis,
868 F.2d 1357, 1363 (3d Cir. 1989).

Interlude

1. In Chapter 3 it was noted that philosophers refer to a promise
as a kind of "performative act." For discussion of a different kind of

performative act, called a "declaration," that in contrast to a promise actually "brings about the correspondence between the propositional content and reality," *see* John R. Searle, A Classification of Illocutionary Acts, 5 Language in Soc'y 1, 13 (1976). Examples are "I appoint you chairman" and "I discharge you."

2. Patrick S. Atiyah, The Rise and Fall of Freedom of Contract 754–756 (1979).

3. The New English Bible: The New Testament, Hebrews, 12:16–17 (2d ed. 1970).

4. Stephen W. Hawking, A Brief History of Time 143 (1988).

5. Easterbrook, J., dissenting in Wisconsin Knife Works v. National Metal Crafters, 781 F.2d 1280, 1290 (7th Cir. 1986).

Chapter 12. Relinquishment by Performance

1. *See* Barry Nicholas, The French Law of Contract 241–246 (2d ed. 1992).

2. UCC 2–702(2) affords the seller very limited relief in this situation.

3. In this situation the aggrieved seller cannot even recover as restitution a sum of money equal to what the goods are worth, which may seem odd since in the reverse situation, when a contract turns out to be a losing one for an aggrieved buyer who has not received the goods, the buyer can have restitution of anything paid (Chapter 11). *See* 1 George E. Palmer, Law of Restitution §4.3 at 379 (1978). The Restatement (Second) of Contracts attributes this discrepancy to the greater difficulty of measuring the amount to be recovered as restitution in the case of the aggrieved seller. Restatement (Second) of Contracts §373, cmt. *b* (1981).

4. As to leases, *see* Uniform Commercial Code §2A-525, which gives a lessor the right to take back possession of the goods on a significant breach by the lessee. In the case of a bailment for mutual benefit at common law, the bailee acquired a special property on delivery and resumption of possession by the bailor in the absence of a significant breach was actionable by the bailee as a tortious dispossession. *See* Joseph Story, Commentaries on the Law of Bailments §§385, 394 (5th ed. 1851).

5. Young v. Harris-Cortner Co., 268 S.W. 125, 126–127 (Tenn. 1924).

6. Uniform Commercial Code §2–507(2). *But see* §2–403(1)(c), cutting off the right of reclamation as against a good faith purchaser.

7. Uniform Commercial Code §9–503.

8. This is true if delivery was the result of such a decision even if the contract was not made as the result of such a decision. *But see* UCC 2–702(2), which modifies the common law power to retake goods based on a buyer's misrepresentation of solvency or intent to pay.

Chapter 13. Relinquishment by Gift

1. Paul Valéry, Degas, Manet, Morisot 92 (D. Paul trans. 1960). According to Rouart's son, the part about the padlock is "pure invention."

2. On the recognition in French law of delivery as a substitute for notarization in the case of gifts, *see* John P. Dawson, Gifts and Promises 70–74 (1980).

3. Restatement (Second) of Property: Donative Transfers, Introductory Note to Division III (1992).

4. In French law, however, delivery was recognized as a substitute for notarization. *See* note 2 *supra.*

5. Asaf A. A. Fyzee, Outlines of Muhammadan Law 230 (4th ed. 1974).

6. 2 Henry de Bracton, On the Laws and Customs of England 124 (S. Thorne translation 1968). This insistence on the delivery of personal property has been traced to the requirement of livery of seisin, developed in connection with transfers of land. For a description of how livery of seisin "was evidenced by handing over a stick, a hasp, a ring, a cross, or a knife, which was sometimes inscribed or curved or broken," *see* 3 William S. Holdsworth, A History of English Law 188–189 (1909).

7. Cochrane v. Moore, L.R. 25 Q.B.D. 57 (1890), following Irons v. Smallpiece, 106 Eng. Rep. 467, 468 (K.B. 1819). That a "true and proper gift . . . is always accompanied with delivery of possession," *see* 2 William Blackstone, Commentaries on the Laws of England 441 (1766).

8. *See* Restatement (Second) of Property (Donative Transfers) §31.1 (1992). The extent to which courts have, however, been inclined to bend the requirement of delivery to serve the ends of justice is suggested by the case of Ethel Yahuda.

9. *See* Philip Mechem, The Requirement of Delivery in Gifts of Chattels and of Choses in Action Evidenced by Commercial Instruments (pt. 1), 21 Ill. L. Rev. 341, 348–349 (1926). So strong was the common law's attachment to the requirement of delivery that it was even argued that delivery was not a mere formality evidencing the intention to give but a substantive element of the act of giving itself. Cochrane v. Moore, *supra* note 7, at 75 (Lord Esher concurring).

The effect of delivery by a donor to a donee differs from that of delivery by a seller to a buyer (Chapter 12). A seller is bound by a commitment to deliver, but a donor is not.

10. In Germany, notarization is required only for promises of gifts, while in France, where formalities were seen as preserving the donor's estate for the benefit of heirs by impeding its dissipation by gifts, notarization is also required for gifts. *See generally* John P. Dawson, Gifts and Promises 130, 226 (1980).

11. *See* Jacques Flour & Henri Souleau, Droit Civil: Les Liberalités §81 (1982), suggesting that delivery is a substitute formality that performs a cautionary function. *But see* Andrew Kull, Reconsidering Gratuitous Promises, 21 J. Legal Stud. 39, 59 (1992), arguing that because the civil-law impetus is protection of heirs, "civil-law formalities afford no analogy to the treatment of gift promises" in the common law.

12. *See, e.g.,* Cravens v. Holliday, 177 P.2d 495 (Okl. 1947).

13. Restatment (Third) of Trusts §10(c) (tent. draft no. 1, April 5, 1996).

14. Scott said that the rule that a gratuitous declaration of trust is valid is of "comparatively modern origin," citing for the "then novel doctrine" an 1811 English decision, *Ex parte Pye,* 18 Ves. 140, 34 Eng. Rep. 271 (1811), and adding that the rule is well established though it rests on a slender reed. 1 Austin W. Scott & William F. Fratcher, The Law of Trusts §28 (4th ed. 1987). Where the trust property is land, it is not as clear that this is so, though the trust has been held enforceable in equity. Id. at §28.1.

15. *See* Restatement (Second) of Trusts §24 cmt. *c* (1959); 1 Austin W. Scott & William F. Fratcher, The Law of Trusts §24.2 (4th ed. 1987).

16. Hebrew University Association v. Nye, 169 A.2d 641, 644 (Conn. 1961).

17. 1 Austin W. Scott & William F. Fratcher, The Law of Trusts §31 at 331 (4th ed. 1987). *See* John H. Langbein, The Contractarian Basis of the Law of Trusts, 105 Yale L.J. 625, 672 (1996), explaining that the "declaration functions as a curative doctrine to excuse noncompliance with the delivery requirement of the law of gifts."

18. For discussion of the anomaly and its possible explanations *see* Sarajane Love, Imperfect Gifts as Declarations of Trust: An Unapologetic Anomaly, 67 Ky. L.J. 309 (1978–79).

19. The efficacy of a written instrument of gift prepared by a donor should not be confused with the efficacy of the delivery of an already-existing writing that evidences an intangible right such as a contract right. Thus the Restatement (Second) of Contracts states that an irrevo-

cable gratuitous assignment can be made either by delivery of a signed writing, an example of the former, or "by delivery of a writing of a type customarily accepted as a symbol or as evidence of the right assigned," an example of the latter. Restatement (Second) of Contracts §332 (1981).

20. 3 William S. Holdsworth, A History of English Law 189–191 (1909).

21. *See* Restatement (Second) of Property (Donative Transfers) §§32.1, 32.2 (1992).

22. Hebrew University Association v. Nye, 223 A.2d 397, 399–400 (Conn. Super. Ct. 1961). The court went on to say that the university could also prevail on the ground that Ethel had made a promise enforceable because the university had relied on it. Id. at 400.

23. Foster v. Reiss, 112 A.2d 553, 562–563 (N.J. 1955) (Jacobs, J., dissenting in a 4–3 decision). For a leading example of a case in which the court diluted the delivery requirement, *see* Ferrell v. Stinson, 11 N.W.2d 701 (Iowa 1943), in which the grantor, an invalid, handed a deed to her houskeeper and asked her to put it in an unlocked box in her bedroom closet, where it remained until her death ten months later. The court held that this was a sufficient delivery to the grantees, who were the "principal natural objects of the grantor's bounty."

24. One can, of course, swap one's promise for a loan of money and then make a gift of the money. One's ability to do this is, however, limited by the extent of one's credit, and repetition is unlikely.

25. *See* note 15 *supra.*

26. Jacques Steinberg, Yale Returns $20 Million to an Unhappy Patron, New York Times, March 15, 1995.

27. *See* Restatement (Second) of Property (Donative Transfers) §31.2 lls. 5–9 (1992). For another example of a term implied in a gift, consider the gift *causa mortis. See* note 39 to Chapter 8.

It may seem odd that, though the donor can attach a condition to a gift, a "delivery of the personal property to the donee with no right of possession or use in the donee until some future date is not a delivery." Restatement (Second) of Property (Donative Transfers) §31.2 cmt. *l* (1992).

28. On French law, *see* John P. Dawson, Gifts and Promises 53 (1980), describing three grounds derived from Roman law: the donee's ingratitude (defined as an attempt on the donor's life, "cruelty and grave wrongs or injuries," and refusal of support), the donee's failure to perform an express condition, and a previously childless donor's acquisition of a child. *See also* Melvin A. Eisenberg, Donative Promises, 47

U. Chi. L. Rev. 1, 14 n.49 (1979), giving as examples of ingratitude "the infidelity of a spouse . . . and a serious libel in open court against the donor." On German law, *see* Dawson *supra* at 140–141, describing the grounds as the donee's gross ingratitude, the donor's subsequent impoverishment, and the donee's failure to perform a condition. *See also* Eisenberg, *supra*, at 15 n.50, noting as a ground the donee's not being in a position "to return the gift without endangering his own maintenance suitable to his station in life, or the fulfillment of the duties imposed upon him by law to furnish maintenance to others."

29. *See* Restatement (Second) of Property (Donative Transfers) §31.2 (1992) (gift of personal property); Restatement (Second) of Contracts §332 cmt *b* (1981) (gift assignment). *See also* John L. Garvey, Revocable Gifts of Personal Property: A Possible Will Substitute, 16 Cath. U.L. Rev. 119, 150 (1966). That, absent an express reservation, a donor has no standing to enforce the terms of a completed gift; *see* Herzog Foundation v. University of Bridgeport, 699 A.2nd 995 (Conn. 1997).

Chapter 14. What Can Be Given

1. Once a testator has died, a legatee has more than a mere expectancy and may make a gift of that interest even though the testator's estate has not been distributed and might be reduced by debts and expenses of administration. Chase National Bank v. Sayles, 11 F.2d 948 (1st Cir. 1926).

2. Martin v. Marlow, 65 N.C. 695, 703 (1871).

3. *See* 1A Austin W. Scott & William F. Fratcher, The Law of Trusts §86.1 (4th ed. 1987). As they point out, in some states the court's solicitude for the ancestor as well as the heir apparent is shown by holding that such a contract, even though made for a fair consideration, is not binding unless communicated to the ancestor, who will then have a chance to leave the property to someone else.

4. Metcalf v. Kincaid, 54 N.W. 867, 869 (Iowa 1893). *See* 1A Austin W. Scott & William F. Fratcher, The Law of Trusts §86.2 (4th ed. 1987).

5. Valerie Pascal's biography of her husband begins with a testimonial in which George Bernard Shaw says, "Gabriel Pascal is one of those extraordinary men who turn up occasionally—say once in a century—and may be called godsends in the arts to which they are devoted. . . . The man is a genius: that is all I have to say about him." Rather than refer to Marianne by name, Valerie calls her the "Woman of Shanghai." Valerie Pascal, The Disciple and His Devil 250 (1970).

6. That contract was, in fact, with a corporation of which Gabriel owned 98 percent.

7. In re Pascal's Will, 182 N.Y.S.2d 927, 929 (N.Y. Sup. Ct. 1959).

8. Speelman v. Pascal, 178 N.E.2d 723, 725 (N.Y. 1961). *But cf.* Brainard v. Commissioner of Internal Revenue, 91 F.2d 880 (7th Cir. 1937), in which the court concluded that an owner of stock could not make a present transfer of the profits to be earned from trading in his stock.

9. *See* Elkus v. Elkus, 572 N.Y.S.2d 901, 902 (N.Y. App. Div. 1991), holding that the career of the celebrated opera singer Frederica von Stade "and its accompanying celebrity status" constituted marital property subject to equitable distribution on divorce.

10. For a case suggesting this in the context of a charitable pledge, *see* Mount Sinai Hosp. v. Jordan, 290 So.2d 484, 486 (Fla. 1974), where the court said that while a charitable pledger "is alive, he undoubtedly has a viable income from which he has pledged funds" but on death "this income may stop."

11. 2 Frederick Pollock & Frederic W. Maitland, The History of English Law 313 (2d ed. 1898).

12. Restatement (Second) of Property (Donative Transfers) §32.4 cmt. *c* (1992). The final version dropped a sentence that said there is "no sound reason" why the donor "cannot include property the donor later acquires and owns at his death." Restatement (Second) of Property (Donative Transfers) §32.4 cmt. *a* (Tent. Draft No. 12, March 28, 1989).

13. It has been argued that the rule on self-declared trusts is inconsistent with the law's treatment of *promises* to make gifts. *See* Mary Louise Fellows, Donative Promises Redux in Property Law and Legal Education 27, 27 (Peter Hay and Michael H. Hoeflich eds. 1988). But because the restraint of nemo dat applies to self-declared trusts, it is more accurate to say that rule on self-declared trusts is inconsistent with the law's treatment of gifts rather than with the law's treatment of promises to make gifts.

14. *See* Congregation Kadimah Toras-Moshe v. DeLeo, 540 N.E.2d 691, 693–694 (Mass. 1989), where the court distinguished earlier cases because they involved written, as distinguished from oral, promises and also involved substantial consideration or reliance" and said that, absent consideration or reliance, "there is no injustice in declining to enforce . . . an oral promise . . . against an estate."

15. *See* Richard A. Posner, Gratuitous Promises in Economics and Law, 6 J. Legal Stud. 411, 420 (1977), describing the abolition of the seal as a "mysterious development from the standpoint of efficiency."

Chapter 15. Relinquishment by Renunciation

1. Foakes v. Beer, L.R. 9 A.C. 605 (H.L. 1884). The decision can be defended on the ground that, properly interpreted, the writing only gave Foakes time to pay and did not forgive interest.

2. Pinnel's Case, 77 Eng. Rep. 237, 237 (C.P. 1602). The rule is older than the doctrine of consideration, and Coke did not rest the decision on that doctrine. It was not until Lord Ellenborough's opinion in Fitch v. Sutton, 102 Eng. Rep. 1058 (K.B. 1804), that one finds judicial precedent for the view that there "must be some consideration for the relinquishment of the residue."

3. L.R. 9 A.C. at 611.

4. L.R. 9 A.C. at 617, 622. Blackburn, who had prepared a dissenting opinion, bowed to Ellenborough's expression, "however hasty or unnecessary," in Fitch v. Sutton.

5. Royal Stone, J., in Rye v. Phillips, 282 N.W. 459, 460 (Minn. 1938). *See also* James B. Ames, Lectures on Legal History 329, 333 (1913) (rule "has met with almost unparalleled animadversion"); John P. Dawson, Gifts and Promises 209–210 (1980) (rule is "misconceived aberration"); Merton L. Ferson, The Rule in Foakes v. Beer, 31 Yale L.J. 15, 23 (1921) ("rule lived because the discharge was mistaken for a contract").

6. *Foakes* v. *Beer* at 622.

7. *See* Restatement (Second) of Contracts §273 and cmt. *a* (1981). *See also* A. W. Brian Simpson, A History of the Common Law of Contract 470–475 (1987), stating that whether "it was right or wrong to reinterpret the doctrine of accord and satisfaction in terms of the doctrine of consideration . . . it is clear that the idea of doing so was current from Elizabethan times onward."

8. Pinnel's Case at 237.

9. Cochran v. Ernst & Young, 758 F. Supp. 1548 (E.D. Mich. 1991) holding that recital of payment of $1 was consideration for discharge of claims).

10. *See* Uniform Commercial Code §§3–604(a), 3–303(a)(3). The rules are not dissimilar to those for sealed documents (Chapter 5).

11. *See* Lon Fuller, Consideration and Form, 41 Colum. L. Rev. 799, 820–821 (1941), arguing that "release of a claim, even if made orally, carries with it normally a sense of deprivation which is lacking in the case of a promise," a "psychological wrench" that has a cautionary effect.

12. She could, however, renounce her right to debts incurred in the future under existing contracts.

13. It is, of course, possible to recast such a relinquishment to look like a commitment—to say that, by expressing her consent to discharge John's obligation to pay interest, Julia was in effect promising not to claim interest in the future. But this would be misleading, for an effective discharge would have disabled Julia from suing for interest but not made her liable for damages for breach of a promise had she tried to do so. *See* Patrick S. Atiyah, Promises, Morals & Law 177 (1981); Joseph Raz, Authority and Consent, 67 Va. L. Rev. 103, 121 (1981), reprinted in The Morality of Freedom 82–83 (1986).

14. Lon Fuller, Consideration and Form, 41 Colum. L. Rev. 799, 820 (1941).

15. Dickinson v. Dodds, 2 Ch. Div. 463 (1876). *See* John P. Dawson, Gifts and Promises 212–213 (1980), where the author would "eliminate this Victorian relic," noting that the "difficulties were all manufactured by treating offers as a subordinate form of promise" and that it "made the consideration test a still more prominent target of public ridicule."

16. *See* Farnsworth on Contracts §3.23.

17. Under French law, "where the one who 'renounced' has revealed a clear donative purpose, courts have been entirely ready to call such transactions gifts." John P. Dawson, Gifts and Promises 59 (1980). Since, under French law, a creditor's renunciation of a debt is regarded as a gift, the legal requirements for a gift must be met. If, however, the creditor delivers to the debtor the document evidencing the debt (*titre de créance*), the debt is discharged, and delivery of an untrue receipt may have the same result. J. Flour & H. Soleau, Droit Civil: Les Liberalités §120 (1982).

18. Restatement (Second) of Contracts §273 ill. 3 (1981). *See* Anderson v. Lord, 183 A. 269 (N.H. 1936), where it was said that the donor's statement that "those pictures are yours" effected a gift of paintings already in the donee's possession because the "right to a return of the property is relinquished." *See also* Restatement (Second) of Contracts §275 (1981), which extends to the furnishing of services as well as transfer of property the principle that one who is under a duty to render a performance in return for payment can discharge the other's duty to pay by agreeing to render the performance as a gift.

19. The result would be otherwise if you went about matters in a slightly different way and told me instead, while the sale was still on, that you would give up the advantage of the $1,000 debt I owed you. Although your intention might be the same in both cases, the result depends—without evident rationality—on the words you use in attempting to effectuate that intention.

20. Uniform Commercial Code §1–107.

21. *See* Farnsworth on Contracts §4,25. For a statement that this is the common law rule, *see* Ray A. Brown, The Law of Personal Property §8.5 at 172 (Walter B. Raushenbush 3d ed. 1975), citing Gray v. Barton, 55 N.Y. 68 (1873) (gift of debt by entry in account, delivery of receipt, and receipt of $1). *See* Tonkoff v. Coscia, 403 P.2d 668 (Wash. 1965) (gift of debt by informal writing).

22. Uniform Commercial Code §2–209(1).

23. McElroy v. B. F. Goodrich Co., 73 F.3d 722, 725 (7th Cir. 1996) (Posner, C. J., loosely characterizing the relinquishment of such a claim as a "waiver").

24. *See, e.g.,* Uniform Commercial Code §1–107 cmt., §2–209 cmt. 2.

25. The usual explanation is that to do otherwise would result in unnecessary circuity of action, for if you reneged on your promise and sued me for the debt I owed you, I could turn right around and sue you for damages in the same amount for my damages for your breach of your promise. *See* 5A Corbin on Contracts §1251 (1964). This is true, at least, in the case of a sole obligor.

Chapter 16. Relinquishment by Waiver

1. Clark v. West, 86 N.E. 5 (N.Y. 1908).

2. Arthur L. Corbin, Conditions in the Law of Contracts, 28 Yale L.J. 739, 754 (1919).

3. A common example is the waiver of notice of dishonor that is found in most promissory notes.

4. Even Uniform Commercial Code §1–107 uses "waiver" in the sense of discharge. For other contexts in which the term is used, *see* Edward L. Rubin, Toward a General Theory of Waiver, 28 UCLA L. Rev. 478, 478 (1981), discussing waiver of "the right to an indictment, the right to trial, the right to a jury, to counsel, to raise a specific defense to confront his accusers, and to appeal his conviction."

5. Johnson v. Zerbst, 304 U.S. 458, 464–465 (1938) (accused's waiver of constitutional right to counsel). As to what sort of intention is required, *see* John S. Ewart, Waiver Distributed 84 (1917), arguing that the intention required for waiver is the "intention to do the act or say the word," not the "intention to choose." *But see* Voest-Alpine International Corp. v. Chase Manhattan Bank, 707 F.2d 680, 685 (2d Cir. 1983), asserting that "one must show that the party charged with waiver relinquished a right with both knowledge of the existence of the right and an inten

tion to relinquish it." That the word "known" must be taken as going only to the facts and not to their legal effect and that "blameworthy ignorance" is enough, *see* 5 Williston on Contracts §685 (3d ed. 1961).

6. This is the sense in which the term is used in Restatement (Second) of Contracts §84 (1981). Corbin was influential in confining the use of "waiver" to "waiver of conditions." *See, e.g.,* 3A Corbin on Contracts §752 (1960).

7. Bank v. Truck Insurance Exchange, 51 F.3d 736, 739 (7th Cir. 1995) (Posner, C. J.).

8. Restatement (Second) of Contracts §84(1)(a). This is so, however, only if the promisee is under no duty that the condition occur.

9. This is subject to the exception for contracts for the sale of goods described in Chapter 15, text at note 22.

10. Undoubtedly it could be relinquished if there were consideration or reliance.

11. Uniform Commercial Code §2–209(1). The impact of the requirement of good faith and fair dealing in such situations is discussed in Chapter 15.

12. *See* Farnsworth on Contracts §8.5.

13. *See, e.g.,* Restatement (Second) of Contracts §246 (1981); Uniform Commercial Code §2–607.

14. The view that waiver is a new promise has widespread scholarly support. *See* 3A Arthur L. Corbin, Corbin on Contracts §753 at 484–485 (1960); 5 Williston on Contracts §693 at 322 (3d ed. by Walter H. E. Jaeger 1961). That the conception is the same in English law, *see* Michael P. Furmston, Cheshire, Fifoot and Furmston's Law of Contract 562 (12th ed. 1991); Guenter H. Treitel, The Law of Contract 110 (8th ed. 1991).

15. Restatement (Second) of Contracts §84 (1981) deals with the problem ordinarily described in terms of waiver in terms of a "promise to perform . . . a conditional duty," without using the word "waiver," but the comments to that section repeatedly use the word.

16. Restatement (Second) of Contracts §84(2)(b) (1981).

17. *See* Restatement (Second) of Contracts §317(1) (1981). The distinction between a relinquishment and a commitment may have important consequences as far as creditors of the donor and the donee are concerned.

Chapter 17. Preclusion by Equitable Estoppel and Laches

1. Horn v. Cole, 51 N.H. 287 (1868). The names "David" and "Caleb" have been invented because the report does not give the parties first names.

2. This is the idea behind Uniform Commercial Code §9–30 which subordinates the holder of an unfiled nonpossessory security interest in goods to a judgment creditor that has attached the goods presumably passing up the opportunity to attach other goods not subject to a security interest.

3. Alaska Trowel Trade Pension Fund v. Lopshire, 103 F.3d 88 884 (9th Cir. 1996) ("The intent element of estoppel can be established objectively through acts upon which the other party has a reasonable right to rely.").

4. Jorden v. Money, 10 Eng. Rep. 868, 881 (H.L. 1854). See Maze v. Jackson Insurance Agency, 340 So.2d 770, 773 (Ala. 1976) (knowledge of truth may be "imputed").

5. The court explained that this is because estoppel "need not be intentionally, voluntarily or purposely effected by or on the part of the insurer." Buchanan v. Switzerland General Insurance Co., 455 P.2d 344 349 (Wash. 1969). This is correct as to "intentionally" and "purposely," but surely the act could not be *in*voluntary.

6. Although, as in David's case, equitable estoppel is often asserted as the basis of a defense to a tort claim, it is sometimes asserted as the basis of the claim itself. Thus an owner of property who incorrectly states that the property is owned by another and later asserts rights as the owner may be tortiously liable in conversion to one who has, in the meantime, relied on the statement in attempting to acquire the property. See Restatement (Second) of Torts §872 (1965). But even here the action differs from one based on a commitment since it is not in any sense an attempt to enforce the statement, but rather to enforce rights that would have existed had the statement been true.

7. See Elvis Presley Enterprises v. Elvisly Yours, 936 F.2d 889 894 (6th Cir. 1991) (describing laches as a "negligent and unintentional failure to protect one's rights while acquiescence is intentional").

8. It has been said that laches requires the first party to be "actually or presumptively aware" of its rights. Diocese of Bismark Trust v Ramada, Inc., 553 N.W.2d 760, 767 (N.D. 1996). This, too, is not required for a statute of limitations.

9. Merrill v. Federal Crop. Ins. Corp., 332 U.S. 380 (1947). Addressing the possibility of an exception where the government acts in what might be regarded as a "proprietary" rather than a "governmental

capacity, the opinion rejected the notion that the government is "partly public or partly private," so that the rule applies "[w]hatever the form in which the government functions." Id. at 383–384. The opinion did not address the requirement of "affirmative misconduct" imposed by some courts as a prerequisite to application of the doctrine of estoppel to the federal government.

Courts have also been reluctant to apply the doctrine of estoppel against state governments. *Compare* State v. Superior Court of Placer County, 625 P.2d 256, 259 (Cal. 1981) (state not estopped from asserting rights to land because estoppel "will not be applied to the government if the result would be to nullify a strong rule of policy adopted for the benefit of the public"), *with* Mortvedt v. State, 858 P.2d 1140, 1142 (Alaska 1993) (state could be estopped from denying untimely application because "estoppel may be invoked against a public entity").

10. 332 U.S. at 387. The distinction rejected in *Merrill* may have some vitality in the prescription cases. According to the Restatement, "Government owned land that is held for sale to private parties, rather than for public uses, may be subject to the acquisition of prescriptive rights, so long as the acquisition does not frustrate . . . public policy interests. . . ." Restatement (Third) of Property (Servitudes) §2.16 cmt. e (Tent. Draft No. 3, April 5, 1993).

11. Office of Personnel Mgt. v. Richmond, 496 U.S. 414, 422 (1990). For a helpful discussion of this case, *see* 2 Kenneth C. Davis & Richard J. Pierce, Jr., Administrative Law Treatise §13.1 (3d ed. 1994).

12. Id. at 423–424.

13. U.S. Constitution, art. I, §9, cl. 7.

14. 496 U.S. at 428. In *Merrill,* Justice Frankfurter had, without citing the Clause, referred to the "duty of all courts to observe the conditions defined by Congress for charging the public treasury." 332 U.S. at 385.

It has also been argued that under the doctrine of separation of powers, the effect of estopping the government would be to impose on the government undertakings that would transgress the limits of authority granted by Congress, the legislative branch, to agencies of the executive branch—by planners to doers, it might be said. And it has been argued that estoppel is precluded by the doctrine of sovereign immunity, going back to the rationale that the King could not be estopped because "it cannot be presumed that the King would do wrong." 3 Matthew Bacon, A New Abridgment of the Law 442 (6th ed. 1793). For criticism of this argument, *see* Raol Berger, Estoppel Against the Government 21 U. Chi L. Rev. 680, 683 (1954).

15. Kenneth C. Davis & Richard J. Pierce, Administrative Law Treatise §13.1 at 229–230 (3d ed. 1994).

16. United States v. National Exchange Bank of Providence, 21 U.S. 302, 310 (1909) ("in a case coming within exceptional rule [for commercial paper] the laches of the authorized agents of the government can be imputed to it"); United States v. Bank of America, 4 F. Supp. 277, 281 (N.D. Cal. 1942) ("When the United States issues commercial paper it does so on the same basis as any individual and . . . like any other litigant it may be guilty of laches.").

17. United States v. Coast Wineries, Inc., 131 F.2d 643, 650 (9th Cir. 1942) (rejecting contention that government is not bound by its attorney where facts would establish estoppel between individuals in an ordinary case); First National Bank v. United States, 2 F. Supp. 107, 109–110 (E.D. Mo. 1932) ("when the United States once gets into court, its attorneys . . . may estop it of record"); Fleming v. Brownfield, 290 P.2d 993, 998 (Wash. 1955) (United States "cannot urge error on a ruling or judgment made with express or implied consent").

18. Ramallo v. Reno, 931 F. Supp. 884 (D.D.C. 1996) (promise not to deport plaintiff).

19. United States v. California, 332 U.S. 19, 39, 40 (1947), rejecting the argument that the federal government's rights to offshore lands had been "lost by reason of the conduct of its agents . . . by reason of principles similar to laches, estoppel or adverse possession." See Utah Power & Light Co. v. United States, 243 U.S. 389, 404, 409 (1917) holding that the Constitution gives "Congress the power 'to dispose of and make all needful rules and regulations respecting' the lands of the United States" and that "the United States is neither bound nor estopped by acts of its officers or agents in entering into an arrangement or agreement to do or cause to be done what the law does not sanction or permit." For lower court opinions to the contrary, see Tosco v. Hodel, 611 F. Supp. 1130, 1208 (D. Colo. 1985) ("it is wholly inequitable for the government to assert now, after the passage of forty to fifty years since the initial contest proceedings, that the plaintiffs have no claim to the land in question"); United States v. Eaton Shale Co., 433 F. Supp. 1256, 1273 (D. Colo. 1977) ("the passage of an entire generation has placed [the defendant] at a disadvantage in defending this suit, because of the . . . inability to reconstruct facts over the past quarter of a century").

20. United States v. Hoar, Fed. Cas. No. 15,373, p. 330, as quoted in Guaranty Trust Co. v. United States, 304 U.S. 126, 132 (1938), noting that though the rule that the sovereign is exempt from the consequences of its laches "appears to be a vestigial survival of the prerogative of the Crown . . . , the source of its continuing vitality where the royal privi-

lege no longer exists is to be found in the public policy [stated by Story] now underlying the rule even though it may in the beginning have had a different policy basis."

21. Rock Island, A. & L. R. Co. v. United States, 254 U.S. 141, 143 (1920), said in the context of "purely formal conditions" to the government's consent to be sued, but often repeated in connection with the no-estoppel rule.

22. Prosser & Keeton on the Law of Torts §131 (W. Page Keeton 5th ed. 1984).

23. Raol Berger, Estoppel Against the Government, 21 U. Chi. L. Rev. 680, 707 (1954). For more measured criticism, *see* Michael Asimow, Advice to the Public from Federal Administrative Agencies 68 (describing a body of case law that "presents an uninspiring picture of injustice, anachronism, and rampant confusion"); Joshua I. Schwartz, The Irresistible Force Meets the Immovable Object: Estoppel Remedies for an Agency's Violation of Its Own Regulations or Other Misconduct, 44 Admin. L. Rev. 653, 744 (1992) ("close examination of the cases and the applicable public law doctrines reveals that [the] impediments to estoppel have not in the past produced, and do not now warrant, an absolute bar to estoppel").

24. Brandt v. Hickel, 427 F.2d 53, 57 (9th Cir. 1970). *See* Menges v. Dentler, 33 Pa. 495, 500 (1859) ("Men naturally trust in their government, and ought to do so, and they ought not to suffer for it."); Pawlett v. Attorney General, 145 Eng. Rep. 550, 552 (1667) (Baron Atkyns: "it would derogate from the King's honour to imagine, that what is equity against a common person, should not be equity against him.").

25. *See, e.g.,* Ricketts v. Scothorn, 77 N.W. 365, 367 (Neb. 1898).

26. Furthermore, the doctrine of promissory estoppel requires a promise, which even under an objective standard must evidence an intention to undertake a commitment. The doctrine of equitable estoppel, as we have seen, requires no showing of an intention to surrender the advantage in question.

27. Marvin v. Wallis, 119 Eng. Rep. 1035, 1038 (1856) (Lord Campbell).

28. Monarco v. Lo Greco, 220 P.2d 737, 741 (Cal. 1950).

29. Alaska Airlines v. Stephenson, 217 F.2d 295, 298 (9th Cir. 1954).

30. Restatement (Second) of Contracts §139 (1981).

31. Farmland Service Cooperative v. Klein, 244 N.W.2d 86, 90 (Neb. 1976).

32. The Restatement (Second) of Contracts, to its credit, does not

label its rule as one of estoppel. But cases from Monarco on have used that term.

Chapter 18. Preclusion by Rejection

1. Restatement (Second) of Contracts §38(1) (1981), which adds "unless the offeror has manifested a contrary intention," a qualification that will be discussed shortly.

2. As Comment *a* to Restatement (Second) of Contracts §38 (1981) explains, "The legal consequences of a rejection rest on its probable effect on the offeror. . . . [I]t is highly probable that the offeror will change his plans in reliance on the statement. The reliance is likely to take such negative forms as failure to prepare or failure to send a notice of revocation, and hence is likely to be difficult or impossible to prove. To protect the offeror in such reliance, the power is terminated without proof of reliance." *See also* Farnsworth on Contracts §3.20, where the rationale is said to be that, in the case of a sale of goods, the "offeror may rely on the rejection, by action (such as selling the goods elsewhere) or by inaction (such as failing to prepare to deliver them) or by merely failing to revoke the offer."

3. *See* Restatement (Second) of Contracts §38 cmt. *a* (1981).

4. Similar reasoning would suggest that a purported principal that has indicated to the third party an intention to disaffirm should be precluded by a bright-line rule from later affirming. As is pointed out in note 15 to Chapter 6, the Restatement (Second) of Agency regards the relation of third party to purported principal as similar to that of offeror to offeree.

5. Restatement (Second) of Contracts §37 (1981). The same may not be true for an option contract that is not purchased.

6. *See* note 19 to Chapter 6.

7. *See* A. Bartlett Giamatti, Take Time for Paradise: Americans and Their Games 60 (1989) ("By imposing identical conditions and norms upon play, the essential assumption of all the rules is that skill or merit, not chance, will win out.").

8. Since 1954 the batter has had the option to ignore the balk call, on condition that all the runners advanced one base. A rare application of this condition occurred in 1977, when with a runner on third base, a balk was called on a Blue Jays pitcher, but Lou Piniella, the Yankee batter, hit the pitch to the centerfielder, who dropped it, enabling Piniella to get to second. The runner, having tagged up at third, stayed there, and, because he did not advance one base, the balk call

had to be honored. Piniella, back at bat, struck out and the Yankees lost. Glen Waggoner, Kathleen Moloney, & Hugh Howard, Baseball by the Rules 191 (1987).

9. *See* 68 Sports Illustrated 98 (May 2, 1988), noting that under Commissioner Giamatti's edict of strict enforcement, balks were "called with the bases loaded, or with slowpokes like Ron Hassey on first, situations in which pitchers clearly are not trying to deceive base runners, which is what the balk rules were designed to prevent").

10. Collins v. Thompson, 679 F.2d 168 (9th Cir. 1982).

11. Pepsi-Cola Bottling Co. v. NLRB, 659 F.2d 87, 89 (8th Cir. 1981).

12. NLRB v. Burkart Foam, 848 F.2d 825, 830 (7th Cir. 1988).

Chapter 19. Preclusion by Election

1. 3 Comyn's Digest Tit. Election, c. 2.

2. Henry W. Longfellow, Masque of Pandora, Tower of Prometheus on Mount Caucasus (1875) (Hermes to Prometheus).

3. The discussion here assumes that the election is made with knowledge of the material facts. *See* Restatement (Second) of Contracts §378 cmt. *b* (1981), stating that a party that "made his original choice while ignorant of facts that give him a remedy based on, for example, misrepresentation or mistake and later discovers those facts . . . is not bound by his original choice because he made it when mistaken." However, action that may not amount to an election may, if relied on, result in estoppel.

4. The holder of an option contract does not have a power of election under this definition because the consequence of the holder doing nothing is that the option expires and no relationship exists.

5. According to the Restatement (Second) of Judgments §49 (1982), a "judgment against one person liable for a loss does not terminate a claim that the injured party may have against another person who may be liable therefor." Comment *c,* however, concedes that a different rule has been applied to discharge an undisclosed principal if the other party, with knowledge of the principal's identity, recovers judgment against the agent for breach of contract.

6. Miner v. Brady, 39 Mass. (22 Pick.) 457, 458 (1839). *See* Restatement (Second) of Contracts §383 (1981). It is said that if an obligation incurred during minority is unilateral, it is possible to "ratify" it in part. *See* 1 Samuel Williston, The Law of Contracts §154 at 337 (1920). But "ratification" in such a situation is better considered as a promise to perform a moral obligation (Chapter 8).

7. Merchants Indemnity Corp. v. Eggleston, 179 A.2d 505, 513 (N.J. 1962); Link Associates v. Jefferson Standard Life Insurance Co., 291 S.E.2d 212 (Va. 1982); Restatement (Second) of Contracts §380 (1981). Corbin attributed this to "the reason that the purpose of the law is merely to protect the party from obligations that are not the result of his own mature and untrammeled expression of will. For this purpose, it is enough to make sure that the facts that made the original transaction voidable no longer exist, and that the newly occurring facts of ratification or avoidance are sufficient to be legally operative if the transaction were an entirely new one." 5A Corbin on Contracts §1215 (1964). But if there is no consideration or reliance, how are the "newly occurring facts . . . legally operative"?

8. In addition, where the contract is voidable, as for example for fraud, the other party may rely on affirmance in such a way as to make it more difficult to make restoration in the event of subsequent avoidance.

9. *See* Dan B. Dobbs, Pressing Problems for the Plaintiff's Lawyer in Rescission: Election of Remedies and Restoration of Consideration, 26 Ark. L. Rev. 322, 340 (1972), characterizing this as a contract approach as distinguished from an estoppel approach because it "treats the election to affirm a contract much as one might expect an intentionally bargained-for agreement to be treated—that is, it is enforceable, even though the other party has not changed his position in reliance upon it."

10. *See* Restatement (Second) of Contracts §382 & cmt. *a* (1981). Under §382(2), however, a "party has not exercised his power of avoidance" until "he has regained all or a substantial part of what he would be entitled to by way of restitution" or "obtained a final judgment," or "the other party has materially relied on or manifested his assent to a statement of disaffirmance."

11. 1 George E. Palmer, Law of Restitution §3.10(c) (1978). An example is Schlotthauer v. Krenzelok, 79 N.W.2d 76 (Wis. 1956), in which the court explained that "a suit at law to recover damages for fraud bars a subsequent suit for rescission . . . because . . . the act of instituting an action at law for damages recognizes the existence of the contract and affirms it"—and once the contract has "been so affirmed, the right to rescind is forever lost"—but declined to apply this rule where the plaintiff first instituted a suit for rescission for fraud and subsequently brought an action for damages.

12. A possible explanation is that affirmance after avoidance, in contrast to avoidance after affirmance, does not raise the possibility that it has become more difficult for the other party to make restoration. According to one court, "The notice of rescission should not be held to

be an 'irrevocable' election until it is made 'effectual' by the innocent party receiving back the consideration with which he has parted." Karapetian v. Carolan, 188 P.2d 809, 815 (Cal. Ct. App. 1948). But this rationale applies only if the fraudulent party refuses to make restoration.

13. *See* Grymes v. Sanders, 93 U.S. 55, 62 (1876).

14. Walker v. Stokes Bros. & Co., 262 S.W. 158, 160 (Tex. Civ. App. 1924).

15. Harrison v. Cage, 87 Eng. Rep. 736 (K.B. 1698).

16. *See* Restatement (Second) of Contracts §379, requiring that the injured party "manifest to the other party his intention to [treat self as discharged] before any adverse change in the situation of the injured party resulting from the occurrence of [the fortuitous] event or a material change in the probability of its occurrence." That there is an exception to the promptness requirement if the party seeking to rescind the contract does not possess property that must be returned in the event of rescission, *see* Allen v. West Point-Pepperell, Inc., 908 F. Supp. 1209 (S.D.N.Y. 1995).

17. *See* Restatement (Second) of Contracts §381.

18. *Walker,* 262 S.W. at 160.

19. Uniform Commercial Code §2–601.

20. Uniform Commercial Code §2–606(1)(b).

21. The buyer can, in limited circumstances, reverse acceptance of goods by revocation of acceptance. Uniform Commercial Code §2–608.

22. Beverly Way Assocs. v. Barham, 276 Cal. Rptr. 240 (Ct. App. 1990), where the court saw an analogy to the rule under which a rejection terminates an offer, thinking that "the party having the power to approve or reject is in the same position as a contract offeree." But the analogy is not apt: first, because the offeror, having a power of revocation, is not at the mercy of the offeree, and, second, because if the offeree says nothing the offer expires and the offeree is not bound.

23. The report of the case describes the parties only as "K. B." and "N. B."

24. K. B. v. N. B., 811 S.W.2d 634, 639 (Tex. Ct. App. 1991). In the actual case, some of K. B.'s conduct preceded the artificial insemination. He had "willingly participated" in the artificial insemination and had, together with N. B., "visited for an hour and a half with the infertility specialist and reviewed the procedure with her." But the finding of ratification did not rest on this conduct alone or—so it appears—even in large part.

25. *See* Dan D. Dobbs, Pressing Problems for the Plaintiff's Lawyer

in Rescission: Election of Remedies and Restoration of Consideration, 26 Ark. L. Rev. 322, 326–327 (1972), where three of the aspects of the election doctrine are described as follows: (1) "it requires the plaintiff to choose the remedy he will follow at a fairly early stage"; (2) it "holds that the choice . . . may be made by a variety of conduct and without any intent on the plaintiff's part to make any election"; (3) "once the election is made, it is final and irrevocable, even though no prejudice would result if the plaintiff were allowed to change his mind."

26. *See* Schenck v. State Line Telephone Co., 144 N.E. 592, 593 (N.Y. 1924), in which Cardozo stated that ratification "is not in itself the choice of a remedy, though the choice of a remedy may be evidence of ratification," and explained that even under the doctrine of election of remedies, a party that pursues a remedy that is not available has not made an election because that party had no choice.

27. Bigger v. Glass, 290 S.W.2d 641, 643 (Ark. 1956).

28. Belding v. Whittington, 243 S.W. 808 (Ark. 1922).

29. Under Restatement (Second) of Contracts §378, making a choice between inconsistent remedies by bringing suit is not irreversible unless "the other party materially changes his position in reliance." *See* Uniform Commercial Code §2–703 cmt. 1 (rejecting "any doctrine of election of remedy as a fundamental policy"). California has been a leader in applying such a rule. *See* Pacific Coast Cheese v. Security First National Bank, 286 P.2d 353, 356 (Cal. 1955) (doctrine of election of remedies "is based on estoppel and . . . operates only if the party asserting it has been injured").

30. That bringing suit on the contract is a manifestation of the "intention to affirm the contract only if damages are paid" *see* Restatement (Second) of Contracts §380 ill. 3.

31. Under Restatement (Second) of Contracts §382(2), a party has not exercised a power of avoidance until "he has regained all or a substantial part of what he would be entitled to by way of restitution" or until final judgment or the other party's material reliance or assent. Restatement (Second) of Agency §210(1) (1958) states an anomalous rule under which an undisclosed principal is discharged only if the other party, with knowledge of the principal's identity, recovers judgment against the agent.

32. This principle is not always paramount, however. Thus the Supreme Court has held that despite the desirability of conserving judicial resources, the doctrine of collateral estoppel does not apply against the United States because it would "thwart the development of important questions of law by freezing the first final decision rendered

on a particular legal issue." United States v. Mendoza, 464 U.S. 154, 160 (1984).

33. *See* Farnsworth on Contracts §8.3. For an exception that proves the rule, *see* McKennon v. Nashville Banner Publishing Co., 115 S. Ct. 879 (1995), in which the Supreme Court held that an employer cannot use evidence discovered after discharge to justify discharge in violation of the federal age discrimination law.

34. *See, e.g.,* Fed. R. Civ. P. 12, 15.

35. Railway Co. v. McCarthy, 96 U.S. 258, 267 (1877).

36. That the rule is different before litigation has begun, *see* First Commodity Traders, Inc. v. Heinhold Commodities, Inc., 766 F.2d 1007, 1013 (7th Cir. 1985). This usually means that the pleadings must be complete. *But see* Horwitz-Matthews, Inc. v. City of Chicago, 78 F.3d 1248, 1252 (7th Cir, 1996) (Posner, C. J.: also applies when the case is on appeal before the defendant's answer "and the defendant is emphatically asserting its positions concerning its rights under the contract").

37. *See* Harbor Insurance Co. v. Continental Bank Corp., 922 F.2d 357, 363 (7th Cir. 1990). Judge Posner added, at 364: "[T]he doctrine only bars a party from changing his position *in litigation.* So interpreted, the doctrine is a cousin to judicial estoppel, which forbids a party that has won an earlier suit to take an inconsistent position in a subsequent one. . . . The present case is indeed one in which a party does his *volte-face* in litigation." It is not easy to see why defendants should be suspected of hoking up defenses any more than plaintiffs are suspected of hoking up claims, and, if the notion of election of remedies is rejected, why a defendant should not be allowed latitude similar to that allowed a plaintiff.

38. Trapkus v. Edstrom's, Inc., 489 N.E.2d 340 (Ill. Ct. App. 1986). *See* Gevinson v. Manhattan Construction Co., 449 S.W.2d 458, 466 (Tex. 1969) (explaining that this is "on the theory that it would be absurd and manifestly unjust to allow a party to recover after he has clearly and unequivocally sworn himself out of court").

39. *See* Restatement of Judgments §1 & cmt. *a* (1942) (doctrine serves "the interests of the State and of the parties" and "is based on the public policy of putting an end to litigation"); Fleming James, Jr., Geoffrey C. Hazard, Jr., & John Leubsdorf, Civil Procedure 581 (4th ed. 1992) (doctrine recognizes "that the purpose of a lawsuit is not only to do substantial justice but to bring an end to controversy" and give judgments "stability and certainty"). Nevertheless, the defense must be raised by a party and will not be raised by the court on its own motion.

40. The doctrine that bars a plaintiff who has won is called merger;

the one that bars of plaintiff who has lost is called bar. *See* Restatement (Second) of Judgments §§17–19 (1982).

41. Parklane Hosiery Co. v. Shore, 439 U.S. 322, 326 (1978) (Stewart, J., analogizing collateral estoppel to res judicata).

42. Klein v. Arkoma Production Co., 73 F.3d 779, 784 (8th Cir. 1996).

43. Allen v. Zurich Insurance Co., 667 F.2d 1162, 1166 (4th Cir. 1982). On the acceptance of the doctrine and its limits, *see* Douglas W. Henkin, Judicial Estoppel—Beating Shields into Swords and Back Again, 139 U. Pa. L. Rev. 1711 (1991); Rand G. Boyers, Comment, Precluding Inconsistent Statements: The Doctrine of Judicial Estoppel, 80 Nw. U. L. Rev. 1244 (1986).

44. Teledyne Industries, Inc. v. NLRB, 911 F.2d 1214, 1218 (6th Cir. 1990).

45. Hampton Tree Farms v. Jewett, 892 P.2d 683, 691 (Or. 1995). It has, however, been held that the purpose of "safeguarding the integrity of the judicial process" is not served where there is no knowing misrepresentation, and "the party seeking to invoke judicial estoppel had equal or better access to the relevant facts." Salt Lake City v. Silver Fork Pipeline Corp., 913 P.2d 731, 734 (Utah 1995).

46. Kyker v. Kyker, 453 N.E.2d 108, 112–113 (Ill. Ct. App. 1983); *see* Thomas E. Atkinson, Handbook of the Law of Wills §§33, 138 (2d ed. 1953). For a minority view, *see* In re Estate of Burrough, 475 F.2d 370, 371 (D.C. Cir. 1973), concluding that there was no problem of election when the claimant received less under the will than she would otherwise have received since there must be "a change in position on the part of others"). Even under the majority rule, the election may be avoided on the ground that it was the result of a misapprehension.

47. 5 Bowe-Parker: Page on Wills §47.1 at 596 (1962). The analogy to an offer has been often repeated in Illinois since Blatchford v. Newberry, 99 Ill. 11, 62 (1880), where the court said that a "provision by will in lieu of dower is, in fact and in legal effect, a mere offer by the testator to purchase out the dower interest for the benefit of his estate" that in that case was "never accepted."

48. *See* note 15 to Chapter 6, *supra*.

Chapter 20. Preclusion by Prescription

1. Thirty-Four Corp. v. Sixty-Seven Corp., 474 N.E.2d 295 (Ohio 1984).

2. Under Uniform Commercial Code §2–607(3)(a), a buyer is pre-

cluded from any relief by failing to notify the seller of breach within a reasonable time, and notice will alert the seller to the need to gather evidence but will not keep evidence from becoming stale.

3. Max Lerner, The Mind and Faith of Justice Holmes 417 (1943).

4. United States v. Kubrick, 444 U.S. 111, 117 (1979).

5. 46 Luther's Works: The Christian in Society III (On Marriage Matters) 288 (Robert C. Schultz & Helmut T. Lehmann eds. 1967).

6. Warsaw v. Chicago Metallic Ceilings, Inc., 676 P.2d 584 (Cal. 1984).

7. Restatement (Third) of Property (Servitudes) §2.10(1) (tent. draft no. 1, April 5, 1989). *See* Stoner v. Zucker, 83 P. 808, 810 (Cal. 1906), holding that an oral license became irrevocable when the defendant relied on it by spending over $7,000 to build an irrigation ditch.

8. Restatement (Third) of Property (Servitudes) Foreword (tent. draft no. 3, April 5, 1993).

9. Cal. Civ. Code §1007.

10. *See* William B. Stoebuck, The Fiction of Presumed Grant, 15 Kan. L. Rev. 17, 19 (1966).

11. *See* Restatement (Third) of Property §2.16 cmt. b (tent. draft no. 3, April 5, 1993).

12. For a discussion of the prevailing view along with a dissent, *see* John G. Sprankling, An Environmental Critique of Adverse Possession, 79 Cornell L. Rev. 816 (1994).

13. Cal. Code Civ. Pro. §321. The Restatement Third admits that the statute of limitations rationale will not explain why use for the prescriptive period not only bars the owner's right to legal relief against the user but also creates property rights—an easement—in the user and attributes this consequence to "acquisitive prescription theory." Restatement (Third) of Property §2.16 cmt. *b* (tent. draft no. 3, April 5, 1993).

14. Restatement (Third) of Property (Servitudes) §2.16 (tent. draft no. 3, April 5, 1993).

15. Roger A. Cunningham, William B. Stoebuck, & Dale A. Whitman, The Law of Property §8.7 at 453 (2d ed. 1993).

16. Restatement (Third) of Property (Servitudes) §2.17(1) (tent. draft no. 3, April 5, 1993). A second type of prescription, used to cure defects in an imperfect conveyance, is dealt with in §2.17(2) but is ignored here.

17. Restatement (Third) of Property (Servitudes) §2.16 cmt. *g* (tent. draft no. 3, April 5, 1993). The fiction of a lost grant requires that the claimant have acted in a manner consistent with the supposition of a

grant. *See* Ricard v. Williams, 20 U.S. (7 Wheat.) 59, 110 (1822) (Story, J.: claim under a lost grant "cannot arise where the claim is of such a nature as is at variance with the supposition of a grant").

18. For a study concluding that "where courts allow adverse possession to ripen into title, bad faith on the part of the possessor seldom exists," *see* Richard H. Helmholz, Adverse Possession and Subjective Intent, 61 Wash. U.L.Q. 331 (1983). *But see* Roger A. Cunningham, Adverse Possession and Subjective Intent: A Reply to Professor Helmholz, 64 Wash. U.L.Q. 1, 7 (1986); Introduction to Restatement (Third) of Property (Servitudes) xvii (tent. draft no. 3, April 5, 1989),

19. Restatement (Third) of Property (Servitudes) §2.17 cmt. *f* (tent. draft no. 3, April 5, 1993). That in most jurisdictions hostility is not negated by the adverse possessor's "so-called 'mistake,' i.e., an absence of knowledge that he does not own," *see* Cunningham, Stoebuck, & Whitman, note 15 *supra* §11.7 at 812. *See also* Margaret J. Radin, Time, Possession, and Alienation, 64 Wash. U. L.Q. 739, 746–747 (1986), explaining: "There are three positions that have existed in legal doctrine [on adverse claim]: (1) state of mind is irrelevant; (2) the required state of mind is, 'I thought I owned it'; (3) the required state of mind is, 'I thought I did *not* own it [and intended to take it].' These can roughly be thought of as the objective standard, the good faith standard, and the aggressive trespass standard."

20. It has been suggested that a "letter of protest, forbidding the use to continue, written while the easement was still inchoate, would thus seem to be fatal to a prescriptive right since it negatives acquiescence," but "if the true basis is the adverseness of the use, the protest would seem to strengthen the case for the claimant and would not prevent the acquisition of the easement." Some courts "have wisely jettisoned the acquiescence requirement." John E. Cribbet & Corwin W. Johnson, Principles of the Law of Property 374 (3d ed. 1989).

21. *See* Cunningham, Stoebuck, & Whitman, note 15 *supra* §8.7 at 453–454, arguing that prescriptive rights are not founded in the owner's "acquiescence" but rather "in wrongful, hostile, trespassory acts that ripen into title when the statute of limitations bars the owner's action of trespass or ejectment," and suggesting that since "the notion that unsolicited consent is not permission seems to rest on a weak theoretical basis, . . . an owner who discovers adverse use . . . should be able to 'thrust' permission on the wrongdoer, perhaps by giving and recording a notice."

22. *See* Richard A. Posner, Economic Analysis of Law 79 (4th ed. 1992).

23. Chicago Metallic argued unsuccessfully that it should be com-

pensated for the easement that resulted from the doctrine of prescription. 676 P.2d at 590.

24. For a reliance-based justification, *see* Joseph W. Singer, The Reliance Interest in Property, 40 Stan. L. Rev. 611, 666, 667 (1988), explaining that the owner has "allowed the possessor to take control of . . . the owner's property" and has "generated" the possessor's "expectations that the true owner will continue to allow her to control the property." But what is relied upon is neither a representation, as in the case of equitable estoppel, nor a promise, as in the case of promissory estoppel. Singer describes what is relied on as "the *fact* that the true owner will not interfere," and as "continued *access,* both in the sense of relying on use of the land itself and relying on the relationship that makes such access possible" (emphasis added). *See also* Joseph W. Singer, Property Law: Rules, Policies and Practices 169 (1993), conceding that this does not explain why the use must be nonpermissive. For another reliance-based explanation that fails to specify what is relied on, *see* Thomas W. Merrill, Property Rules, Liability Rules, and Adverse Possession, 79 Nw. U. L. Rev. 1122, 1131 (1985). *See also* Restatement (Third) of Property (Servitudes) §2.16 cmt. *c* (tent. draft no. 3, April 5, 1993).

Arguments based on the adverse possessor's reliance should not be confused with arguments based on reliance by purchasers and creditors who act on the basis of the adverse possessor's apparent ownership. Such third persons could be protected without protecting the adverse possessor.

25. Max Lerner, The Mind and Faith of Justice Holmes 417 (1943). *See also* Oliver Wendell Holmes, The Path of the Law 10 Harv. L. Rev. 457, 477 (1897) ("A thing which you have enjoyed and used as your own for a long time . . . takes root in your being and cannot be torn away without your resenting the act and trying to defend yourself, however you came by it.").

26. *See* Restatement (Third) of Property (Servitudes) §2.16 cmt. *b* (Tent. Draft. No. 3, April 5, 1993). For reasons, *see* id. cmt. *e* ("Among the reasons for the rule are that government lands are extensive and difficult to monitor for intruders. Monitoring efforts may not be effective because of overlapping or non-existent bureaucratic responsibility, or because the people in charge lack strong incentives to act diligently, or because of corruption. The public interest in preserving government-owned lands and lands devoted to public uses outweighs the claims of prescriptive users.")

27. 16 Richard R. Powell, Powell on Real Property §1015 (Patrick J. Rohan ed. 1990) ("rigor of the common-law barrier has been relaxed by statute" in about a third of the states).

28. Cases are collected in William B. Stoebuck, The Fiction of Presumed Grant, 15 Kan. L. Rev. 17, 29 (1966), where the author states that the "Supreme Court and approximately one-third of the states have asserted the doctrine."

29. United States v. Fullard-Leo, 331 U.S. 256, 271 (1947). To this Justice Rutledge protested in dissent, "I do not think this Court should expand the established bases for acquiring title to government lands so as to include acquisition by adverse possession, as in effect the Court's opinion does." Id. at 282–283. This protest overlooks the fact that, in contrast to the doctrine of adverse possession, the fiction of the lost grant is rooted in acquiescence.

Epilogue

1. People v. Navarroli, 521 N.E.2d 891 (Ill. 1988).

2. The due process clause would have protected Enricho if he had gone so far as to plead guilty, but he had not done so and was still at liberty to proceed to trial. Santobello v. New York, 404 U.S. 257 (1971).

3. It would be otherwise, however, if the grounds for review are purely constitutional. *See* Mabry v. Johnson, 467 U.S. 504, 507 (1984) (habeas corpus).

Index